# THE BOOK:
# THE STORY OF RED TAIL HAWK

## ONE FAMILY'S JOURNEY THROUGH ADDICTION

# K.A. MORINI AND AMANDA BETH RANDALL

BALBOA.
PRESS

A DIVISION OF HAY HOUSE

Balboa Press books may be ordered through booksellers or by contacting:

Balboa Press
A Division of Hay House
1663 Liberty Drive
Bloomington, IN 47403
www.balboapress.com
1 (877) 407-4847

Because of the dynamic nature of the Internet, any web addresses or links contained in this book may have changed since publication and may no longer be valid. The views expressed in this work are solely those of the author and do not necessarily reflect the views of the publisher, and the publisher hereby disclaims any responsibility for them.

The author of this book does not dispense medical advice or prescribe the use of any technique as a form of treatment for physical, emotional, or medical problems without the advice of a physician, either directly or indirectly. The intent of the author is only to offer information of a general nature to help you in your quest for emotional and spiritual well-being. In the event you use any of the information in this book for yourself, which is your constitutional right, the author and the publisher assume no responsibility for your actions.

Any people depicted in stock imagery provided by Thinkstock are models, and such images are being used for illustrative purposes only.
Certain stock imagery © Thinkstock.

Print information available on the last page.

ISBN: 978-1-5043-5532-2 (sc)
ISBN: 978-1-5043-5533-9 (hc)
ISBN: 978-1-5043-5534-6 (e)

Library of Congress Control Number: 2016909225

Balboa Press rev. date: 07/14/2016

In my dream, I'm a red tail hawk, soaring high above the sky……

## Dedication

This story was written in loving memory of Amanda Randall for all of us who have suffered a loss from the epidemic of addiction; may we never forget those that we have lost and the love they brought to our lives.

Thank you to my family for the endless loyalty and love, my friends for always knowing exactly what to say and J.P. for the Wednesday night writing sessions.

And as she turned to walk away,
I heard a voice softly say
"Everything will be OK,
The Lord has called her home today.
To the place where she
can finally lay
in tall soft grass that
leans and sways.
Where she'll be bathed
in Heaven's rays,
growing stronger in every way.
And she'll be there for
you some day,
as you finally make your way;
an embrace to make it all ok;
a love that never goes away."-Katie Morini

"The struggle of life is one of our greatest blessings.
It makes us patient, sensitive and Godlike. It teaches
us that although the world is full of suffering, it is
also full of the overcoming of it."-Helen Keller

# PREFACE

I T WAS A GOOD life; a simple, yet complicated life all in one. People seemed tougher back then, as every generation claims. When we weren't strong enough to handle something on our own, we leaned on those around us for support and strength. Communities stood together, parents and coaches helped each other. It was ok to give a kid a ride home or to let them sit in your car at the bus stop on a rainy morning. Parents ruled their homes with discipline and an expectation of respect. It was during this time that we grew up; when things seemed so much simpler. It was back when people weren't always trying so hard to be happy, they just simply were. I wonder where it all went wrong. I wonder when we became ashamed to show our real beings and started hiding behind the artificial lives we portray on our computer screens. I wonder when we decided it was better to be numb than to feel, and when we decided that pain should never be tolerated. I wonder if future generations will ever know the wonder of seeing the President of the United States on television and thinking 'that's my hero' or if they will ever know the peace that comes from being lucky enough to live in the greatest country in the world. I wonder if we all messed it up, or if it was just part of some master plan devised by the insurance and pharmaceutical companies that's spiraled horribly out of control. I wonder about all the people like us, who look back and think 'what-if'. But, this isn't a story about all of those people and this isn't a sorrowful tale of regret, either. This is the story of addiction, and what it will do if you let it. This is the story about family, my family, and what it means to never give up on each other. This is the story about hope, struggle, triumph, defeat, forgiveness and letting go. This is the story of a love and bond so deep, that it will never be destroyed or forgotten, because true love never dies.

# LITTLE HOUSE ON THE POND ————————

I T ALL STARTED OUT innocent enough,-3 young girls and one second marriage. Three babies in four years is tough on any parents. Mix in a child from each prior marriage gone wrong, two beautiful, young parents with baggage of lives lived wild till now, family dysfunction and a struggling economy that decimated the middle class and you've got a pretty easy recipe for disaster. Throw in some laughter, lots of love and the occasional unexpected surprise and you've got the life most of us lived back when things were real; when emotions were expressed through smiles or tears, not emoji symbols and it was ok if life wasn't always perfect. That was the only life we knew and a fairly common setting back then. It was built on good intentions, strong love, and a new solid faith which added a dusting of hope to less than perfect circumstances. We had our share of hard times, but through it all we had each other, all together, under one roof in our new little home by the pond. We were close. We laughed together, cried together, prayed together, and dreamed together. A bond of sisterhood was built that would be the tracks of the up and downs of life's rollercoaster ride. Yes, it all started out innocent enough in the crazy life of 3 little girls. Little girls who grew up when there was still a shred of innocence left for the children to stake claim to; when My Little Pony was on every birthday wish list, and Brownie patches sparked inspiration.

I remember the first time I saw the tiny house thinking it was a little piece of heaven, put here just for us. After years in small apartments in less than desirable neighborhoods, the small cottage on a pond was like a vacation that never ended. We had a large yard and a tire swing and a driveway to ride our bikes and roller skate. The home itself was small and crowded, but we all managed to fit in the three small bedrooms.

There was only one bathroom and it was terribly ugly. The blue tiles were old as the house and the toilet matched the sky blue walls as well. The kitchen was equally unimpressive. The counters were mustard yellow and the room was dark and dreary, but it had a dishwasher and that was enough to excite Mom. We also had our own washer and dryer which we never had before. The best part of the house though was by far the pond. There were 2 ponds actually, a frogging and fishing pond was the edge of our back yard and the big beautiful swimming pond was just under 100 yards from the front door and through a short pathway. The dining room, which was attached to the kitchen, received the first fixer upper project. As soon as we moved in, Dad put in a large picture window so we could see the daily happenings of the pond. That was our morning excitement; who was fishing or who had their boat out, who was swimming and who was skating or playing ice hockey. 'Nature's entertainment' Mom called it. In the back of the house was a smaller pond. The mucky, murky waters were full of frogs and fish. The sound of the crickets in the fall was the backdrop for many nights spent together doing our hair and our homework inside the walls of the little house. Our older brother Daniel, Danny as we called him, would visit frequently and lived there for a short time. Jamie, Mom's daughter from her first marriage, lived with us full time and we looked up to her as the coolest person in the world. When the house was purchased Beth hadn't been born yet. When she came home shortly after we moved in, the seams of the little house were bursting.

Mom and Dad would spend the next 20 years trying to make the house big enough for the ever growing demands of the family. Eventually the process became stressful and a source of fighting. The house sucked any extra energy out of my parents especially Mom, who worked tirelessly to beautify the house. It became an expensive frustration as the family grew and we stumbled over each other daily. Time that could've been spent playing and teaching us kids was spent on projects regarding the home and working to pay for the projects, all with the intentions of providing a better life. My sisters and I fought constantly, especially in the colder months when our high energy spirits were confined to staying indoors instead of running wild outside. There was nowhere to go for quiet time or time outs without one or the other of us there to poke fun. It was hard to manage, even for the greatest of parents. Mom and Dad did their best, but often times, tempers were lost. Despite the frustrations that came with the lack of space and privacy, the size of the little house was actually the best part about it. It forced us to be close. It took away the option of privacy. Sometimes we don't understand our circumstances while we are lost in the midst of them, but looking back it makes sense. If we had more wide open space in that little house, the tornado that ripped through there years later would have only picked up speed and caused more destruction. Instead, we all stood in the way, crowded together like a mountain range in the middle of a huge plain, trying to stop a deadly storm, and we didn't even know it.

'And we know that in all things God works for the good of those who love him, who have been called according to his purpose' Romans 8:28 (NIV)

For many years, we kids believed the house itself was evil. Doors would open on their own, and floor boards would creak where no one was walking. As kids we spent hours searching for a "body" in the large pile of dirt that remained in our basement where the foundation was dug. Every creak of a floor board or rustling of leaves outside was proof to us that there were spirits coming to claim stake to the house that they still held as their own. We were scared and dramatic little creatures. We were terrified of that house in the dark hours. We were completely convinced it was haunted. Never-the-less, it was OUR haunted house and it boasted the most beautiful sunsets you'd ever see every night as the sun went to sleep over the pond. It was a symbol that another day was done and it was time to make new dreams for tomorrow.

I was the older of the 'second batch', the first child of my parent's marriage together. I was easy by most accounts except for one crying fit which caused my parents to cut their bowling date early when I was about a year old. Molly came next. Moms pregnancy was tough and she was sick with stomach aches most of the time. I adored my new sister. She came home from the hospital one Christmas Eve. Mom said she was our Christmas angel. My Grammy put her under the tree in a wicker basket.

Grammy came over to me and said "Jenny, want to see your new sister?"

She picked me up and I wrapped my arms around her neck, nestling my head against her shoulder and breathing in her freshly set, sweet smelling silver hair. She placed me down by the glistening tree and I peered cautiously over the edge of the basket.

"She's in a basket just like baby Jesus," Grammy said.

That's when I saw my sister Molly for the first time. She had a full head of dark hair and chubby perfect cheeks. I wanted her for my own;-one of my earliest memories. In the middle of everyone strumming on their guitars and singing Christmas music and eating Chinese food and laughing, our eyes somehow met each other's and our souls connected. It was as if for a moment in time we were all alone. Our bond was formed right there. From then on, I wasn't the little one in the family anymore. I had a little sister, and I was so proud. That was the most magical Christmas ever.

A few years later when Beth was born, Mom was already tired and her post-delivery illness put the stress level of the family over the top. She was in the hospital for months battling infection and blood clots after Beth was born. It's ironic that Mom fought the same things when Beth was born, that Beth herself fought during later years. While Mom was sick though, we were all separated in different homes of my parent's friends and church members who signed up to help with us. Dad tried to work and pay as many bills as possible. It was a difficult time, but with the support of family and friends, especially my Aunty Rose and Uncle Rob, we got through it.

Grammy, my Dad's mother, took us as much as she could and helped Dad with the house work and bringing us to the hospital to visit mom. She was a bright light of warmth and comfort during this confusing time. She would always be there to put our clean clothes on and help us with baths. She helped me to get on to toilet when I couldn't get up alone and tried desperately to get Molly sleep through the night. She would let us eat cocoa puffs for dinner on a tray in front of the TV. Her apartment was fun. We forgot about being away from Mom while we were there. We focused on the stories Gram would tell us of when our dad was little. I would try to help with Molly as she was still a baby herself. We went to church on Sundays and prayed for mom. We went to Aunty Rose's to visit Beth so we got to see her time to time. We stayed busy.

One Sunday Gram took extra time to get us ready. Molly and I had on new purple dresses and I remember feeling proud. Gram was getting Molly out of the back seat behind me and I started toward the church door. I was hoping Dad would be there this morning. I missed him. Then, I remembered that I left my little Bible in the car and ran back to get it. Gram saw me out of the corner of her eye.

"Jenny don't dilly dally. We are late already," Gram said.

She went to close the car door thinking I was already out. Only, I wasn't all the way out. My leg was still inside and she accidentally closed the door on it. I let out a scream. Gram frantically fought with her keys to unlock the door and free my leg from the car. I remember sobbing inconsolably. I wanted my mom. I wanted her now! Out of nowhere my dad appeared and engulfed me in his arms.

"Sshhh, its ok Jenny, don't cry, it's ok," he said rubbing my hair.

Gram was so upset she was crying too.

"I'm so sorry," she kept repeating.

My pain was relieved by the comfort of Dad. I was so happy to see him that for a moment I forgot about the injury my leg had just sustained. I learned to move past physical pain. Physical pain would eventually pass. Emotional connections were what was the most important. In just a few short moments, I was sitting inside church on Grammy's lap. Dad was beside me holding Molly. We were singing Amazing Grace and the sound of the choir music gave comfort to my burdened heart. My cousin turned around from the front pew and smiled at me. All was well again.

Eventually, Mom got better. Dad said it was a miracle. We returned home and awaited Mom to join us. Beth shortly followed and soon there were 3 kids under the age of 4 in the little house. But times weren't as they should've been. We celebrated Mom and Beth coming home, but the atmosphere was tense. There hadn't been an immediate family connection with Beth. No family bonding. We had all been apart for so long that it was awkward in the beginning. Mom had to learn all of Beth's routines and particular habits; a frustrating scenario for any mother to encounter. But, eventually, life picked up and went on with all the new routines a baby brings. Sleepless nights of diaper changing and feedings led Mom and Dad to be exhausted and grouchy. Money was tight with paying for a new house and new babies and tensions ran high. Molly and I tried to be good, but Molly was still so little and I was fresh out of diapers myself. Still, I remember these days. I remember sharing a tub with my sisters, all 3 of us crammed in together, pretending to be mermaids. I remember sharing a toilet seat with Molly when we both suddenly had to go at the very same time. I remember Bethy sitting in her high chair at the kitchen table and Mom saying 'before you know it Beth will be at the table just like you girls'. I remember dancing in the summer rain together and splashing in the mud. I remember the cherry blossom tree in the front yard. It was in the spring time when the silky flower petals floated to the grass below to make a blanket of pink over the ground, that's when we would picnic there. I remember the smell of Dad's grill with the huge deli dogs he loved to make us in the summer to eat while we watched the Red Sox. I remember so many things that made our life rich in every way, with things that money can't buy. I remember the love and the dedication through the good times and the bad. My sisters and I clung to each other and wove a net between us of trust, loyalty and hope.

'Fireflies gather above the sweet cool grass
The moon glows a bright yellow brass
Dew on my feet
Oh what a treat
To experience one spring night
And hold forever this delight
In my heart
Never to part
The girlish giggles
And banana curl squiggles
Light cotton dresses
Make believe messes
Beauty of youth
And innocent truth
Sisters are blessings
Of ribbons and tressings—Katie Morini

Before we all were school age, the days ran into each other in seamless afternoons of Barbie dolls and roller skating in the driveway. One afternoon Molly and I were playing with some rocks we found by the shore of the pond.

"Molly, I bet if we open this there are gems inside," I said.

"Really?" Molly said eyes wide.

"Yeah," I said, "and if we get enough we can give them all to Mom and Dad and they can buy a new car."

"Ok" Molly said. "I'll collect more."

We gathered up some stones and arranged them in a row.

"How are we going to open them?" Molly asked.

"With a hammer" I said matter-of-factly.

I ran inside and got a hammer.

"What are you doing?" Mom asked as I ran by her in the garden.

"Nothing," I said hurrying past her with the hammer toward the pond.

Beth caught wind that we were up to something and ran along behind me.

"Watch your sister," Mom instructed me as she worked on her flower pot.

"K," I answered back as I ran through the path heading to the pond.

Beth's little feet tried to keep up, but she was slow. I bent over and carried her with one arm, her body half the length of mine. I set her down beside the rock line.

"Put one on top of the other and I'll hit it with the hammer," I told Molly.

She did and I lifted the hammer up the strike the rock. As I did Beth pointed to the rock with her finger just as I was about to hit it. I tried to stop but the momentum was just too much. I hit her pointer finger. She screamed. I threw the hammer into the woods behind me and picked up my wailing sister. Mom came running over and took Beth in her arms.

"What happened?" she turned to me.

"I don't know," I lied.

"I think she hit it on a rock," Molly covered.

Mom kissed Beth's booboo and examined the injury.

"Looks like just a little cut," Mom said.

"Band aid." Beth said.

Mom carried her home and set her in the garden.

"Girls come home now. I want you where I can see you," Mom hollered over to us.

"I feel so bad," I said as I turned to Molly.

"It was an accident, let's go play with her," Molly suggested.

We got back to see that Beth was better but still repeating "band aid" over and over.

We started playing a new game but each time we got to Beth's turn, she would just look at us and say "band aid!"

She never did get the band aid and our secret disappeared as the cut on her finger scarred over. It was one of the many battle scars we accrued during our time spent playing as the golden sun rays danced off the shimmering pond. Our only witness to the secrets and bonds we formed.

As we grew older, things seemed to get easier for a time. We were able to play with less observation and less injury. The evenings were marked by dinner and bedtime arguments. At night we would huddle in to one bed as the chilling voice of the Unsolved Mysteries host ran through the house despite our pleas with Mom and Dad to turn it down. "Well, you're just going to have to conquer your fears I guess" Mom would say when we told her how scared we got from the eerie stories. I would shudder at the thought of the fear I knew was sure to come. A poor night sleep would certainly follow. I personally would hold off as long as I could before contemplating my options: lay here awake all night and try to focus on the dull hum of Molly's nightly rocking herself to sleep (a habit that would continue into her thirties), sneak out of bed and hide at the end of the couch where Mom and Dad sat- at least safe with them close by, or climb into bed with Beth who would welcome a snuggle. When my older sister Jamie was home I could sometimes get her to let me sleep in her room. But usually it smelled like cigarettes and she talked on the phone until late into the night. The most frequent option was climbing into bed with Beth. As we both got older, this habit continued; a sort of safety zone. I would lay in bed with her, talking until we fell asleep. As children, we would make plans for the next day- where to go exploring and which neighbor to spy on. Our imaginations ran wild and we were convinced that at least someone in our neighborhood was a murderer or a witch at any given time. Delusions no doubt fueled by the scary stories sounding from the living room television. We would feed each other's desire for fantasy with "oh guess what, I heard the ghost train today it sounded louder than usual. It was around lunch time. We have to remember to listen for it tomorrow". We would fall asleep holding hands most nights, safe in each other's presence. It is these times that I look back on with a peace in my heart, grateful for the fear that drove me into my little sister's room to find a comfort. A comfort I'm missing so deeply now.

Some of our happiest memories were spent with our extended family. Before the days of Facetime and Facebook and i-Phones, if you wanted to visit with someone you had to physically go and see them. My grandmother was Syrian and first in her family born in this country. Her parents were successful business owners and my great aunt and uncle still lived in the triple decker they grew up in as children in the city. My great aunt Jeanette never had children of her own and when we visited her we knew we were in for a special treat. We loved to drive into the city and stare in awe at the tall buildings grazing the sky line. Molly and Aunt Jeanette shared a birthday two days before Christmas on December 23. It was a great excuse to celebrate. The triple decker seemed so grand to us as children but held some elements of mystery that enticed our imaginations. The main dining room still had my great grandmother Alexandria's large dining table where she entertained the wealthy members of society in her time as a young woman. Grandma and Aunty would tell us stories of visitors they had and tales they overheard as they too spied as children during their parents parties. There was a cabinet of fine china sets and silver serving sets that looked like belongings of royalty to us.

But there was the spooky side of this house too. If you walked past the dining room you would be in great grandma's old room. It was left exactly how she left it before she passed away. Her clothes for the day still lay out on the bed. Her photos and perfume bottles arranged just so on the bureau. Her fur thrown over the chair in case she had to go out in the cold quickly. We couldn't stop ourselves from going in this room as children. Her life piqued our interest. Who was this beautiful, brave woman who traveled here from a foreign land and built such a beautiful life? We would use this time to scare each other as well. As sisters we shared the deepest fear of ghosts. If one of us dared to let the other two trick her into going into that room alone, we were sure to find ourselves locked in the closet. We would be crying and banging on the door until Mom or Aunty heard our cries and let us out. Molly and I often did this to Beth. She was an easy target as the youngest. We would shut the door behind her as we mischievously got her to peer in the closet doorway to help us find the earing or button from our shirt that we were certain fell and rolled into the corner. We would shut the door and scurry down the narrow hallway into the spare room with pictures of Jesus and Virgin Mary hanging on every wall, condemning us for our behavior. We would collapse in a fit of laughter on to the bed until Mom would come in holding our crying sister. She would give us a taste of our own medicine and leave us alone with the door shut in that room of religious condemnation. We weren't as brave as we thought. The spare teeth soaking in the jar on the bedside table and brassieres hanging from the drying rack was enough to creep us out after a short time and we would emerge as pitiful sights begging forgiveness from poor little Beth.

For the most parts visits to auntie's meant the best food you'd ever have. On some visits we would have subs that grandma would pick up from famous Maria's sub shop on her way or a bucket of K.F.C. but the highlight was certainly aunties famous mashed potatoes which boasted cream, not milk, and 2 whole sticks of butter. After dinner there was no doubt dessert, pies from Lyndelle's bakery, and no one escaped Aunty's table without pie. One birthday celebration, Aunty got a large rum cake which Molly took a special liking to. She got herself a rather large piece and sat under the table eating it until she was stuffed as a turkey. The rum kicked in short time later and our visit was ended with Molly's vomiting up the drunken cake mix.

On some occasions, Aunty would let us stay overnight. We would wake up and jump into bed with her where she would let us eat left over dessert for breakfast while watching cartoons. These occasions were just for me and Molly as Beth was still a toddler and too little for overnight trips. One morning Molly kept laughing and laughing and I couldn't figure out why. We were each on a side of Aunty propped up with pillows watching the morning show.

Finally I sat up. "What's so funny?' I asked.

Molly's face was red as a cherry and her eyebrows were high as she pointed to auntie's large breast which had fallen out of her robe.

"Auntie's boobie is out!" Molly exclaimed.

Aunty just about died and then began laughing hysterically. She tucked her breast away and wiped up the coffee she had spilled in bed. We were off on our adventure in the city for the day.

Our last sleep over was cut short when Molly awoke in the night with a bad tummy ache. She was crying so bad and just wanted Mom. Aunty tried to console her to avoid waking Mom for the hour trek in the city in the middle of the night but it was no use. Molly needed Mom. Aunty called Mom and told us she was on her way.

Aunty looked at me right in front of Molly and said, "Next time come alone."

I turned and saw the hurt on Molly's face. I never slept at Auntie's again. Where my sister weren't welcome, neither was I; we were a team. Our visits consisted of day visits from then on.

Our dedication to each other grew as we did. We were loyal to each other and defended each other's actions regularly. There were 3 of us and usually only one parent, if any, home at any given time. We all had our strengths and weaknesses. We usually knew how to get what we wanted.

Mom was a hairdresser and beautiful as they come. She made her living each day by going to other people's home and making them feel beautiful, too. She took us with her most days while we were tots and we grew up in an environment of beauty talk. "Beauty is pain" the ladies would tell us as we sat at their tables cleaning the curlers Mom just took out of their hair. "Keep your hair long and shiny girls. That's what the boys like. Long, pretty hair," they would say. It's no wonder we all grew to have long luscious heads of hair, mine bleached blonde and Molly and Beth's dark to match their chocolate eyes. We could do manicures, haircuts and French braids better than any adult we knew by age 8. We could recognize a woman with a fresh permanent by standing behind her odiferous hair in the checkout line at the supermarket. We loved when the customer would have a pool and let us swim while Mom worked her magic on them. It was a huge luxury in our simple life. As we played in the pool the quiet chatter of women talking about their shows, husbands and holiday plans would drift through the open windows with the scent of fresh coffee, setting our expectations of what was to come in the following months. After a long day we would eat sandwiches and apples in the old car. No fancy cars either, but they were clean and got us place to place. Mom would travel with a toothbrush for each of us, engraining mouth care in our brains. McDonalds was another luxury and we couldn't afford it. We were happy with our sandwiches and for a special treat maybe a couple cookies.

Mom also traveled with a shovel in her car. She was creating a magnificent garden in our yard and was always bartering for deals. She would happily trade a wash and set for a burning bush or a manicure for some dark purple iris.

"Just because we don't have a lot of money doesn't mean we can't fill our life with God's beauty," she would tell us.

On some trips home she would pass by a home with a beautiful garden and pull into the driveway. If there was another woman in the garden, and Mom had plants in her trunk, she would offer a trade. More often than not the woman would accept the trade and we would head home with a trunk full of beauty ready to be planted.

"Never be afraid to ask for what you want girls. It's not what you say, but how you say it that makes an impression. Talk with manners, confidence and a smile and you'll get what you want," she would say.

We listened intently. This life was all we knew and we accepted what Mom taught us as truth. We would sing songs together about the sinking of the Titanic on the way home, happy as clams. We were together and we were happy.

We were even happier to return home each afternoon; home- to our familiar surroundings and routines. Happiness meant our toys and whatever pet we had taken in for the time. A kitten or puppy was a frequent arrival to the home, but they never lasted long before they ran off or we gave it to another home. The first heartbreaks for each of us were the loss of one beloved pet or another.

I remember returning home one day and joyously running to the room we all shared. Molly and I shared bunk beds and Beth was still in her crib. It was summer and very hot and dry. I put on my bathing suit and started playing while Mom took Beth to eat. Molly stripped down to just her t-shirt and a diaper and we started to play and make our 'fort'. I was carelessly running and tripped over the cord to the humidifier. The tub of water spilled all over the floor and terror ran through my body. I panicked in fear of what my exhausted mother was going to do upon finding such a mess to clean up.

In my panic I ran to the kitchen and said "Mom, Molly spilled the humidifier and the water came out."

I scurried back down to my room and hid under the bed with my eyes peering under the dust ruffle. I heard her heavy footsteps running down the hall, a sure sign of an impending whooping. I could see Molly, innocently standing at the toy box playing with her favorite Hug-A-Bunch, turn at the sound of the footsteps coming toward our room. In one smooth swoop she was airborne, hanging from one arm as Mom spanked her diapered bottom over and over again. Once again, we locked eyes. Mine were full of tears watching the pain my sister endured because of what I'd done. Molly's eyes were dry as a bone and full of anger, kindling the fire that would burn between her and Mom for decades to come. Yet, she was loyal and never ratted me out as I deserved. She took it for me, as I would later do for her throughout the years, but never so painfully. At such a tender age she began to understand what it was to fiercely love someone despite the pain they cause. She was loyal to me, and I vowed that I would never again make her suffer for anything I had done.

For the most part summer was the happiest of times. The long days meant hours of play time outside where we didn't have to worry about the mess we were making. There was a freedom with being outside. Our little house sat between 2 ponds one for swimming and one for frogging and fishing. The surrounding swamp land and woods were mysterious and deep. There were new adventures to be had each day and wildlife to be caught. We would fill buckets with tadpole and frogs. Snakes were a trophy and catching one got us guaranteed celebrity status with the neighborhood kids for a couple hours. On any given afternoon someone's dad could be at the pond letting us jump of his shoulders in to the cool refreshing water of the 'big' pond. A line would quickly develop as kids came running for their chance to jump the highest. These were the days before electronics. When kids played and interacted all day long. Warm weather meant riding in the back of Dad's truck with the warm breeze blowing our hair around like crazy;-the perfect setting for a game of being pirates in a hurricane at sea. Everything was make believe or a fantasy. We could turn any situation into a game. We were good at this-the best. It was a well-developed defense mechanism that got us through the more unpleasant times; denial at a child's level.

Summer also meant cookouts. There's one cookout particular that I will never forget. We were visiting my mom's parents and Dad was cooking on the grill. We were all sitting around a wooden picnic table breathing in the sweet smell of Dad's barbeque and singing along to aunt Janice strumming 'how much is that doggie in the window' on her guitar. Beth was sitting in her stroller, content with the oversized lollipop all over her face. Molly and I had our bathing suits on and had just finished eating watermelon and running through the hydrangeas as Grandpa sprayed us with the hose; the aroma from his pipe floated on the breeze like a sweet perfume. Mom and Grandma spent the last couple hours putting color on grandmas graying hair and she looked beautiful and proud as she set the table with Mom. It was a great day so far. Grandpa even had sparklers for the evening and we couldn't wait to use them. The excitement hung heavily in the air. Mom came out with a large red Tupperware pitcher of apple juice she had just mixed up.

"Jenny you need more juice babe?" she asked walking toward the table.

Just then a bang of thunder and flash of light caught the corner of my eye. I saw Mom's face turn ghostly white. I turned toward the sound. The grill had exploded! Dad was hopping on one leg, his other leg completely engulfed in flames. He moved away from the table and let out a cry of pain.

"Roy!" my mother exclaimed.

She leapt into action and removed the cover from the juice container and ran to his aid, throwing the juice in the air to smother the flame. He dropped to the ground and rolled. It was too late. His entire leg had suffered tremendous burns. He was whimpering in pain. Until this very moment I didn't know my dad ever felt pain. To me, he was a super hero. I remember watching helplessly. Having nothing else to do, I ran to my sisters and held them as my mom helped Dad up onto his one good leg. She put one arm over her shoulder and helped him inside, trying to calm him with gentle words. My sisters and I sat there stunned. I wished there was something I could do to help my dad, but I knew there was nothing for me to do but wait and be a good girl for my mom.

The next couple hours were stressful as I tried to keep Beth quiet. She was hungry and needed her diaper changed. The grown-ups were busy tending to Dad and talking to the doctor on the phone. Grandma bleached and scrubbed the tub. Dad needed to soak his leg in water right away so Mom could scrub the burnt skin off. I tried to replace Beth's diaper and clean her bum but my fingers fumbled the safety pins. I had suffered multiple skin pricks before aunt Janice finally came over to assist. Finally, after Mom's prompting she took us for a walk to escape the wailing of Dad's pain coming from the bathroom.

Later Grandma drove us home. We were greeted by Jamie in the driveway who helped us out of the car. She hugged and kissed us and carried Beth on her hip. She told us to be good for Mom and Dad and not bicker. She brought us in and helped us into our p.j.'s. She brushed our hair and put the toothpaste onto each of our toothbrushes.

She asked "do you want to go see Dad before bed?"

Molly and I said "yes" and we went down the hall to Mom and Dad's room.

Jamie quietly knocked on the door and said in a hushed voice "Mom, it's me. They want to see Dad before bed."

Mom opened the door. She looked like she had been crying. Lying in the bed was Dad. A white bandage soaked with red and yellow fluid covered his entire right leg. He was hardly awake. I later learned the doctor had given him large doses of pain killers to numb the pain. Not only had he suffered a bad burn, but he dislocated his knee when he fell to the ground to roll. There he was; my hero, my dad; beaten and broken. My parents weren't super heroes after all. I lay awake in bed that night and couldn't sleep. I knocked on Jamie's door and she kindly let me in.

She brushed my hair and asked "Are your sisters asleep?"

I nodded yes and tears welled up in my eyes.

"Are you sure they're asleep?" she asked suspiciously.

I stared at her "Why do you keep asking me that?"

She whispered in my ear "Want me to sneak in the kitchen and get you ice cream?"

It was the best thing I'd heard all day. I drifted off to sleep with a belly full of sugar.

The sun rose and set many times over the pond with the hours spanning longer in between. Dad started to feel better and slowly began walking again. Mom worked more than usual to make up the difference and Dad did his best to keep us entertained. He would turn his bandage changes into a game. He would have us count to three and he would rip off his bandage, often heaving from the pain the removal caused. He would quickly recover though, and go back into his entertaining and fun loving self. He would look for shapes in the blood stains on the bandages like most people look for shapes in clouds.

"Look girls, this one looks like Elvis" he would exclaim.

We would run around the house holding it in the air like a victory flag of the enemy army we just defeated.

Jamie would roll her eyes and say "That's so gross" before she went to brush her hair or talk on the phone.

Things were returning to normal and started getting good again. Mom was planting more and more flowers in her garden and soon we were playing 'The Secret Garden' regularly. We ran from the garden to the pond looking for the hidden key to open the gate so we could welcome ducklings and frogs in to the garden. Mom would sing hymns to us. It was her happy place and it made us happy too. We imagined all the hawks that circled above were our guardians from whatever lurked outside our imaginative garden walls that protected us from the outside world. We incorporated everything and neglected no detail.

We would play the bus game.

Mom would say to Beth "I think I hear your sister's bus bringing them home from school".

She would shriek excitedly and run to the end of the driveway and wait at the big red gate Dad put there to protect us from traffic during the pond's busy summer months. As we grew summer served as a constant happy time when we were all together to be as playful or silly as we wanted.

One summer afternoon we were taking a break from swimming at the pond and we met someone new. Molly, Beth and I were sitting on our towel digging our toes in the sand and eating our tuna sandwiches when we heard the voices of two little girls approaching. They were little like us, one Beth's age and one still an infant, squealing and drooling in the carry pouch on her mom. Beth's eyes lit up. Finally, there was someone her size. She looked quickly at Mom, then back at the new kids. I can still see her brown hair shining in the sun. Mom got up and went over to help the other mother carry her chair and cooler. This mom was spectacular and Molly and I stared at her in awe. She was wearing a large straw hat and dark sunglasses. Her bright red lipstick was stunning against her bronzed perfect skin. She was slim and toned. Her toenails matched her fingernails. Yes, she was something alright. Beth got up and ran behind Mom, staying close to her legs, curiously peering around them at these new girls. Mom helped the woman set her things down in a shady spot close to ours. She introduced herself and all of us. The woman did the same

"So lovely to meet you! I'm Delia. This is Amy and baby Susie. We just moved in last week up the street. Oh you have no idea how excited I am to meet you girls!" she said to us. "I hate being home alone all day! We are from New Jersey and have no family around here. Promise me you'll visit! Promise!"

I think Mom was a little bit taken back by this glamorous woman who just blew into her life like a whirlwind. She laughed politely and promised Delia they would do coffee in the morning before Mom headed off to work.

"Perfect," said Delia. "Then this little one can stay and play with us while you go to work" she said scooping up Beth, her golden brown hair shining in the sunlight from the hot oil treatment Mom had given her last night.

Beth squealed with excitement at the thought of a new friend. Delia put her down, reached into the cooler, threw us each a juice box and we were sold! She plopped in her chair and lit up a cigarette.

"Seriously, I need her. She's sooo cute and Amy is bored all day with just her baby sister to play with. It's really for me. I need the entertainment for her so I can get a workout in and paint my nails.

Pleeeaaase," she pulled down her sunglasses and batted her eyelashes at Mom. "I'll take good care of her I promise. I'll even give her dinner"

Mom gave in and just like that, Beth had a best friend of her own.

That day we built the biggest sand castle any of us had ever made in the sand at the pond. We spent the rest of the summer and many summers to come inseparable from Delia and her girls. When Molly and I went to school, Beth and Amy played. When they were old enough for school, they went off together, confident with each other's company and support. We all loved them and they loved us. Beth loved them the most, they were her second family. She wove them into her life and they stayed there forever.

Summer time also meant music- music at the cookouts and campsites and at home while Dad barbequed. Beth had an especially strong love for music. She and Dad bonded through this. We all had piano lessons and loved the poetic lyrics that Dad played for us on his record player, but Beth was different. Her soul was deep and had a void that the beautiful words flowed into like a waterfall and filled. Even her voice was sweet and she sang all the time. Her showers served as a daily concert and before long she was the "star" in Mom's eyes. She dressed up in costumes and performed skits. She often sucked Amy into doing performances for her in Delia's large dining room while Delia taped their acts on a VHS camera. She could perform the song from any musical on cue. She gained beauty as she grew and she,too, was loyal. She never made us feel left out, being sure to assign us parts in her plays or giving us her newest Barbie to play with. She would plead with us to go with her even when she went to Amy's to play. She liked it most when we were all together. She hugged us all the time and insisted on being carried even though she wasn't a toddler anymore. She often refused to brush her teeth or her hair, knowing that Molly or I would do it for her if she put up a fight. She always got herself attention. We weren't always happy to give it, but we did. We cared about her. We loved her fiercely. She was our baby sister and no one could mess with her without going through us. We just did it naturally. We protected each other from life's unnecessary cruelties. But there's only so much protecting we can do and it only lasts so long. As we got older we weren't always there to protect each other. We weren't there with our watchful eyes.

I missed my first day of kindergarten. I didn't mind I was glad to spend another morning at home with the girls. It wasn't until I went to school the next day that I realized what I'd missed. The other kids got to ride the bus with their parents on the first day-a memory I would never have. They all had learned each other's names already and I immediately felt left out. There was one boy at my table who shared his purple crayon with me when mine broke, but that was it. I longed to return home to my safe place. The clock ticked slowly by. I rode the bus home uneasy in a sea of unfamiliar faces. I got home and cried. I didn't want to return the next day to that lonely place. The other kids had nice lunch boxes and new shoes. I felt shame for my paper bag and old clothes. I didn't know play clothes weren't to be worn to school. My hair was wild and I brought in the grocery list instead of a note from my mom stating why I missed the first day. The teacher read it aloud and the kids laughed at me before she realized what she was doing. It was an epic fail.

Jamie argued with Mom "How could you do that to her? You let her down", she said.

Mom's reply was: "Life's hard sometimes, she'll get through it stop making such a big deal".

Mom wanted us to be strong and tough. She had experienced life's let downs and wasn't one for babying us. Her favorite line was "Now, what can we learn from this? You can always learn from your mistakes." So, I learned from it and I felt a strength rise inside of me. I wouldn't let them get the best of me. I took inventory of what I had and made the most of it. I would make tomorrow better. I would get up early and get Mom up to help me get ready. I would not spend the whole school year like this. The next morning I got up early and did just that. The day was better and I returned home excited to share stories about my day. I kept my homework neat and worked on my letters. Soon I made friends and was often trusted to bring home the class guinea pig for weekends and school vacations. I made friends on my bus and played with them after school. I would conquer this. When the time came, I would make sure that my sister's first day was better, too. I would be self-sufficient. I would fix this. I would be a fixer.

School work was easy but the social aspect was anything but. We never had money for nice clothes or extras and that complicated my plans for success. It was hard to fit in and took effort. My lunches of sardines and hard boiled eggs were less than popular at the lunch table. When my sisters started coming to school things got a little easier. Once again we were together with our watchful eyes. Protecting each other and gaining strength in our numbers.

Eventually I made more friends in the neighborhood and we would all play together in the afternoons and weekends. Riding our bikes to the highest point in the neighborhood and going down the hill screaming in fits of adrenaline was the preferred activity most days before the winter months came and the afternoons were too dark and cold for outdoor activities.

One afternoon in particular, I was supposed to stay home with Molly and Beth and wait for Jamie to come home from work. I was restless and resented having to stay inside while the sun was still out. I was giving them both a peanut butter sandwich when I saw my friend Sarah go by with her bike. She circled around and knocked on the door.

Sarah was sweet and had no siblings of her own. When she was home she spent most of her time playing the violin. She moved the bow as smooth as silk over the strings. I felt awe when she played. It was as if her soul had lived a thousand years. I could listen to her for hours, but she preferred to play at our little house. She loved to run around with all my sisters and whichever animal we had presently taken in. She kept her hair in two long braids most days all the way down her back, much neater than my shaggy mane. She always made me feel good, even on bad days. We were buddies.

"Hello?" she asked while knocking. "I know your home; you just got off the bus with me."

I answered the door.

"Hey," I said my warm breath steaming up the cool autumn air. "I can't play, I have to stay with my sisters until Jamie comes home from work."

"Come on, don't be such a goody goody," she said. "Just one ride down the hill to see who goes the fastest. I got a new bike and I bet it's faster than yours."

She knew just how to get to me. I couldn't bear the thought of not proving her wrong. My mother took great pride in buying us all new bicycles last summer and I felt I owed it to her to prove mine was best. Besides I needed to take our puppy, Mikey, out anyways so he didn't mess on the floor. It was the perfect excuse.

I looked back at my sisters sitting cross legged on the floor in front of the TV eating their peanut butter sandwiches. They looked content enough. What was the worst that could happen?

I grabbed Mikey's leash and told the girls I'd be right back.

"Don't touch the oven," I said to Molly. "I'll be right back I'm taking Mikey out."

"No," she whined. "I don't want to be alone I'll get scared."

"When I get back we'll watch 'Annie' and I promise we can do some skits after, O.K.?" I promised.

"O.K." she said taking the bait.

I ran outside and tied Mikey to the tree by the shed. I patted his head and he nipped at me. He wasn't a very nice puppy, but I got a feeling for a split second that he was trying to warn me. I ignored my gut and grabbed my new shiny purple bike. I kicked up the kickstand and off I went. Sarah was waiting at the end of the driveway and we raced to the top of the hill.

When we got to the top she made me promise not to take off on her while she was on her way down. She always did that and I never did know why. She handed me her watch to time her and off she went. I watched as she went flying down the hill. She hollered at the bottom and I stopped the watch. 3.5 seconds of pure adrenaline.

"I can do better than that," I whispered to myself, "if I take a running start."

I was nervous but didn't want it to show. I could hear Mikey barking down the hill and knew I needed to hurry.

"Come on hurry up I got to go," I said.

"O.K., O.K." she panted coming back up to the top of the hill.

I handed her the watch and took a few steps back for my running start. She rolled her eyes and said "Go!"

Off I flew. The crisp air whipped in my face. I let go of the handle bars and put my arms out. It was bliss. It was freedom. It was childhood.

The moment was short lived. Panic set in as I realized my shoe laces were caught in the chain of my pedals. I couldn't free them. I yanked and pulled on them with my leg. A car was coming and I swerved out of its way. My little bike couldn't handle the turn and before I knew it I was tumbled down into the drainage ditch with my leg still tangle in the chain.

"Jenny! Jenny! Are you O.K.?" I could hear Sarah screaming as she ran to my side. "Are you ok? Is anything broken? Oh no, what do I do?"

She began to sob. "Don't do that! Stop crying" I snapped at her.

She stopped immediately.

I let out a whimper. In the distance I could still hear Mikey barking at the bottom of the hill. Good, my parents still weren't home. I knew I couldn't walk. I couldn't even move. Everything hurt. I lifted my head and looked at my hand. It was all scraped up with road burn.

"Jenny, you're bleeding really badly. I don't know what to do" Sarah said. She was starting to cry again.

Just then I heard Jamie's familiar voice calling for me. Sarah heard it too. She looked at me for approval.

"Go get her" I said.

Sarah ran off. I could hardly make out the muffled voices coming toward me as the ringing in my ears got louder and louder.

Then, I heard Jamie saying "Jennifer Ann you are so dead....Oh my gosh! Are you ok?"

She ran to my side and picked me up. She looked to Sarah for an explanation of what happened. She held me like a baby under my shoulders and legs. I hadn't been held like this in years.

"Oh I got to get you home right away," she said.

She brought me inside and put me in the tub. She changed my clothes which were all ripped up.

"Don't worry. Sarah brought your bike back. It's safe in the shed" she told me.

I started to cry.

"What were you thinking? You could've been killed!" she exclaimed. "You know I'm not lying for you. You have to learn your lesson."

I didn't argue I knew she was right. I was sneaking and this was my own fault. If she were Molly or Beth she would've made up a tale to cover for me, but Jamie was different. Not wrong, just different. She held her standards higher than I was ready to fill. I felt bad. I knew

Mom and Dad would be disappointed. They left me instructions and I disobeyed them. I hoped I didn't have a spanking coming to me, but I braced myself for the worst. Jamie carried me to my bed and brought me a drink. That night when Mom and Dad came home from work, she had dinner prepared already to soften their mood. Molly and Beth got themselves ready for bed early and when Mom and Dad entered my room that night, they found me sleeping between my two little sisters. Each of them was holding a cool cloth on my body to ease the pain of my injuries. We never let each other suffer alone.

When I was old enough Dad signed me up for town softball. He thought it was a good idea to get us involved in something with structure to fill our time. He coached my team and I thrived with the attention. We would drive to the field in his beat up old truck and spent time before everyone else arrived setting up the bases and lugging the heavy equipment bags around the field. We loved these warm evenings. Dad was always in a good mood and brought Molly and Beth to serve as the water girl and spirit leader for the team before they were old enough to play. Before long, we were all competing for the title of the "best" in Dad's eyes. He supported our efforts, sacrificing his own time to practice with us and showing us plays to put us ahead of the rest. We made more friends on these teams and enjoyed team parties at a player's pool or in our beloved pond. I took a special liking to the feeling of being part of a team. I loved the competitive nature and the outlet for frustration the game provided. I loved the sense of control it gave me. I loved everything about it. Jamie would come and cheer for us on the side lines. It made us feel special that our beloved older sister took time away from her social calendar to watch us. When Danny came too it was even better. We loved to have our older siblings watching us and giving us instruction. It made us feel important.

On the weekends when Danny visited we would give him our schedule for the week. He would play with us and Dad in the yard, teaching us how to throw and how to talk trash to other players. We were fresh when he was there and it drove Jamie mad.

"Stop," she would say. "Don't teach them those words."

"Quit nagging," he would say. "We are just having fun."

He would grab us and throw us up in the air. We were just little scrawny things still and loved to go high in the sky. We would wrestle and run around in the yard until we were dirty and sweaty. Childhood.

Dad had just put a new shower in the back of the house surrounded by four short walls. Mom loved it. We could rinse off after playing or swimming and not bring any of our adventure's dirt into the house. We loved it too. The air was fresh and clean outside. It fed our wild nature and you never felt cleaner then after a good rinse in the outdoor shower

"Go rinse off" Danny would say after we played. "I don't want Lily blaming me for the mess you make."

Off we scurried. We were oblivious to the tension between Danny and the rest of the family. We never noticed the troubles that came after his visits. We loved him.

The innocent oblivion didn't last forever though. One afternoon in late Spring I dashed off the bus and up the driveway. It was a Friday. I had a game that night. Danny was supposed to be coming over and he promised me we could practice together before my game. I ran inside letting the screen door slam behind me. I ran to the back room where he slept on the pull out couch, but he wasn't there. I saw Mom ironing clothes in the bathroom.

"Mom, where's Danny?" I asked panting from my haste.

"Not sure" she said abruptly as she lifted the laundry basket and headed toward the linen closet to put away the clean sheets she just collected from the clothesline.

I followed her "Well is he coming? We were supposed to play and..." she cut me off.

"Jenny I'm really tired and I'm not having a good day so just drop it ok? I don't know where he is" she snapped.

I turned and walked away with anger stinging in my eyes. I went outside to play with my new pitch back and wait for him, but he never came. During my game I kept looking out into the crowd, but he never came there either.

At dinner Molly started whining and asking where Danny was, but no one had an answer for her. We felt lost together. What had happened? Danny was suddenly just gone. It was as if he died. Jamie wasn't home so we couldn't ask her. There were no cell phones to call him on. No letter explaining why he never showed up. He was just gone.

Mom and Dad were tense and they put Beth to bed extra early. She was whiney and restless, too. I made funny faces at her to try and calm her. She would laugh with her puffy face, her smile boasting little baby teeth proudly. I tickled her and read her a story. Her eyelids started to close. I felt like I was doing something to help. Molly came in the room with our book bags.

"Here" she handed me mine. "Want to color with me?"

I tried to concentrate on my coloring, but I was distracted by the commotion in the kitchen. The phone kept ringing and I was afraid it would wake Beth who had just drifted peacefully off to sleep. I could hear Dad answered the phone and hanging up abruptly.

"Hello?" he said. "No I don't know…look I told you."

He would hang up the receiver and the phone would ring again.

"Hello! I told you I don't…oh you think so do you? Don't you dare….."

Finally he answered and yelled into the phone so loud the house shook "Stop calling here!!" He slammed the receiver down.

He ripped the phone off the wall and threw it across the room. Mom ran to her room and slammed the door. Then the house went silent. My throat was dry from my own crying, but I didn't dare to leave my room. I looked over at Molly. She had gotten in to bed without me noticing and was rocking and humming herself to sleep, drowning on the commotion of the night. I looked out my window but Jamie's car still wasn't home. Where are you? I thought, directing it toward both Jamie and Danny in my mind. I climbed in bed with Beth and tried to swallow my saliva to moisten my dry throat. I fell asleep eventually, cloaked in the simple pleasure of the clean sun dried sheets on Beth's bed. Our sheets always smell so good, I told myself. 'Yes, focus on that. We are lucky to have that,' I thought. I said my prayers and went to sleep.

That was only the beginning of the hard road we were all about to go down together.

One morning shortly after, I was awoken by our current dog, Spinney, barking like mad. She was only a little hot dog but her bark was ferocious. I looked out my bedroom window and saw a man in a suit standing at the door way talking to Mom. I could hear her pleading with him in a hushed voice. I strained my ears to listen.

"Please just one more week and we will have more I promise" she said trying to pull something out of his hand.

"I'm sorry miss I've done all I can. I can't lose my job. Please you have to understand…"

"No, you understand! I have three little…." She was starting to cry and so was Beth in the other room.

I ran to Beth to comfort her and keep her quiet. Mom didn't see me go by. She followed the man outside in her nightgown to the end of the driveway. I left Beth's side and returned to the window. What was going on? I was so confused. Who was this man? Molly came out of our room and asked what was happening.

"Sshhhh," I said, "come here and see."

We watched as Mom tried to pull a little sign out of the man's hands and he finally raised his voice to her.

"Stop!" he hollered.

"Dad would be so mad" Molly whispered.

I just nodded and stared at this strange, brave man. I was astonished that anyone would dare speak to Mom that way.

Mom turned and stormed toward the house. She mumbled under her breath and let the screen door slam behind her. The man in the suit staked the sign in the soil of Mom's daisies at the end of the driveway. It said FOR SALE.

The following months, Mom and Dad's fighting was worse than ever. My sisters and I heard it often. They fought over who was at fault, what they should've done to stop this and whose fault it was that they didn't. We didn't care about any of that. We just wanted to keep our house. We loved that house. We were scared of what life would be like outside of our little nook in the world. We liked being tucked away into a place of nature and magical adventures. How would we ever play and laugh without our beloved pond? Who was going to live here is it wasn't us? Who would feed the ducks and tend to Mom's garden? This simply couldn't happen. So, one morning I devised a plan. I got up early and packed my bag.

"What are you doing" Molly sat up in bed, her hair its usual rats nest from the night of rocking and humming herself to sleep, "banging" we came to call it

"I'm running away" I answered "Want to come?"

We ran away many times as kids in to the canopy of the trees that surrounded the pond. This time was no different.

"If I can't live in this house, I'll just live in the woods" I explained

"Me too" Molly agreed

We set up camp in the usual place, making it easy to be found at dusk. It was Grammy who usually came to retrieve us with a promise of ice cream or a sleep over. She faithfully returned this night too. Her graceful smile pleading for our return to home

"Besides" she always said sweetly "Beth needs you"

She was right. We couldn't truly run away without Beth. We gathered our things and returned home. Grammy took all three of us to her place for the night. I remember finding it strange that Dad carried Beth to her car instead of Gram carrying her as usual. She told me to hold on to her as she went down the porch steps one leg at a time and slower than usual.

"What's wrong" I asked as we drove down the road.

"Nothing I just have a cold, honey" Gram said.

It was the only lie she ever told in her life. Gram was sick. And that was the last sleepover we ever had at her house. Soon she went to live with Aunty Rose so she could care for her around the clock. She wore oxygen and got frail and thin. Uncle Rob had to carry her room to room. I remember crying with my sisters, begging her to get better.

"Everyone dies, baby" she said one night breathlessly, "but I'll see you again in heaven. You know that. And I'll always be with you. Be a good girl. Take care of your sisters. Ok?"

She looked so different. She was thin and always had the oxygen on now. She never smelled sweet anymore. There were medicine cups everywhere instead of cocoa puffs. Everything was different and I hated it. I hated that she didn't live with us, too. I felt jealous of my cousin, Abby, that she got to be with her all day, every day, and my visits were always cut short. Abby always was nice to me about it, though. I think she knew it wasn't fair. None of it was fair for any of us.

"Ok, I promise," was all I could say.

I laid there with her in bed until Dad collected me to leave. When we got home Mom and Dad were making extra efforts to be nice. Beth went to bed and Molly and I got to stay up and watch TV and drink Pepsi. Mom and Dad stayed in their clothes and stayed up, too. After a couple hours the phone rang. Dad answered it and quickly hung up. I couldn't hear what he said. He went to Jamie's room and she came out teary. Mom put her coat on and they went out to the car and drove off. I didn't speak the whole time they were gone. Molly and I sat in silence while Jamie tried to joke with us. A short time later, Mom and Dad returned. Dad came over and knelt down in front of us.

"Grammy's gone, honey" was all he could manage to say before choking on his words.

Mom came and got him and brought him to their room. I stood there stunned. Jamie tucked me and Molly in on the couch and told us we could stay up with her if we wanted. We laid there watching TV until we fell asleep together. We were scared of our new world without Gram to rescue us from whatever troubles we may find ourselves in. What would come of us now?

I don't remember much about it after that. Mom and Dad left us with friends while they went off to the services. Beth went off to stay at Delia's, and Molly and I went to a new friend, Martha, mom had made. She was a seamstress and had a son the same age as Beth. Mom had known her back when Jamie was younger from soccer, and they had recently reconnected when they both moved to town. We loved to play in her back yard under the huge willow tree.

A few weeks after the services, Dad put us all in the car and we went to the bank. Dad had on a tie and a nice jacket. He usually only dressed that way for church, so we knew this must've been something serious.

"Behave girls, this is important. I'll be out in a minute" he instructed.

He walked past the nice lady at the desk. She smiled and nodded approvingly. He went through a door into what looked like an office and returned a short time later.

"O.k. let's get out of here" he said.

We waved goodbye to the nice lady. She had given us lollipops and crayons to play with while we waited. We liked her. She waved back and off we went

Dad turned the music up loud and was singing the whole ride home. When we pulled into the driveway he walked over to the FOR SALE sign, picked it up and broke it over his knee.

"Who wants a cheeseburger?" he asked. He threw the sign onto the ground and we left the whole mess behind us.

That night we had cheeseburgers and hot dogs on the porch. We listened to the bullfrogs in the shallow waters as we ate and laughed together. Mom came home with a new outfit for each of us. Things were going to be ok. We were going to stay in our little home.

As we all got more into our elementary school years, we played more often with kids outside of the family. Mom, Delia and Martha were good friends and there was always a large group of kids to play with on the weekends. During the week, Sarah and Amy were just a short walk away. Our personalities started to change into the young girls we would each become; each of us similar to each other as sisters are, but still unique enough to make us stand apart from each other.

I was more focused and task oriented. I wanted to keep the peace and please and protect everyone. I was determined to keep the house peaceful at any cost.

Molly was the fun one. She was a comic and could make us roll on the ground with laughter. She did impersonations and had alter egos of Corky and Squiggy. Molly was also the most mischievous. She could push every button Mom had and they would argue daily. "Negative attention" Mom would call it. Whatever it was, it worked and Dad tried to get us out of the house often as possible. We would play softball and audition for plays, Beth being the only one who ever got called back. Molly and I didn't mind, we just went along for the ride to support her.

We would all do skits and dances to the old movie classics that Mom showed us, but it was Beth who truly had an artist's soul. She would dress in elaborate costumes and even dress up the pets to be in her acts. Her voice was high and sounded like an angel. She loved to be an actress. She was poetic and deep. She could cry on cue and did, often. Even at such a young age, she seemed to long for more than what this world had to offer. I remember thinking she was going to be a star someday. She would spend hours alone in her room building her beloved Barbie dolls the most beautiful home out of Legos and folded up tissues.

Even her Barbie's life was bigger than what we had. She could spend an entire day in her room leaving only to use the toilet. When we finally would enter to see what she was doing we would be amazed at what she could create. She was a dreamer, and she dreamed big.

I still climbed in bed with my sisters at night, even as we grew. It was what I was used to and to be honest, I was afraid of the dark. I always felt like someone was watching me. It felt like someone was staring right at me as I closed my eyes and tried to drift off. Mom would ask me why I was always in their beds in the morning and I told her over and over I was scared all alone in the dark. She tried to understand, but it's not easy to explain that you feel like someone who isn't there is watching you.

"You're never really alone if you have Jesus with you," she would tell me.

"I know" I would say and that would be the end of it. I would agree and keep the peace even though I truly was deeply bothered by this

One night, I lay at the foot end of Beth's bed. I was reading 'The Diary of Anne Frank' for school and didn't want to stop when Beth went to bed. I figured if I lay at the foot of the bed I could use the lamp on the other side of the room and not disturb her. The light was very dim for reading and soon my eyes got heavy. I fell asleep and woke with a startle. I looked at the head of the bed where Beth was sleeping and standing there was a little boy. He was watching her as she slept. I'll never forget the paralyzing fear I felt. I couldn't move. I couldn't speak. I just stared at him. He was right over her head slightly bending over her. He was small. He had on overalls and had blonde hair. He turned to look at me and I saw his dazzling blue eyes. Then he faded out. That was it. He wasn't ugly or scary. He wasn't mean. He was just there watching her sleep, and then he was gone. She slept through the whole thing. When I could finally move I threw off the covers and ran directly to Mom. She was lying in bed reading. I told her about what had happened and what I had seen.

"Honey, honey calm down" she said holding my face in her hands. "There is no such thing as ghosts. You were probably dreaming."

"No, Mom I definitely wasn't dreaming. I'm telling you it was real" I insisted.

"Ok" she said. "Let's pray together."

That was Mom's answer for everything. Pray about it. So we did. We prayed for peace and protection. We prayed that God would send an angel to fight off our fears. We prayed for a good night's rest. She hugged me and sent me on my way.

I slowly entered my room and climbed in bed with Beth. I must've said the 'Our Father' about a hundred times before I finally fell asleep. I couldn't get that boy's face out of my mind. I was astonished at his blue eyes and angelic appearance. What was he doing? Why was he staring at my Beth? That question haunts me still to this day. That was the first of many times I saw that little boy. Every time I saw him, he was watching one of us as we slept.

Things continued to get a little easier for a while. Mom started a new job as the hairdresser for a few local nursing homes. We would all take turns over the years going to work with her and having our own experiences as little children in the old fashioned nursing homes. We would come home with tales of who peed in their diapers and who passed away last night. Mom would have her favorites that she felt sorry for, the ones with no families at the holidays or no one to pluck their eyebrows. Mom was good like that. We usually had a "guest" for Christmas or Thanksgiving, sharing what little we had.

"It's important to give, there's always someone with less than you" Dad would say when we whined about having the stinky old ladies over for dinner.

We got used to it quickly. One year we had all of our friends doing a Christmas skit for the nursing homes. We had songs that we sang and little dances that we did. It was our way of giving back and helping those who had no joy in their holidays. We enjoyed those times, innocent times. Things kids don't seem to do or even think about anymore. Experiences like this led my sisters and I to always talk about what would become of us when we got old.

"We will definitely all live together" Beth would say.

"Yeah, but only two of us can share a room at a time" Molly would say.

"Well by the time we are old," I would say, "they will make three people rooms and then we can share. And we will definitely have our own bathroom because three of us will be a lot of stockings and makeup."

"You're right" Beth would say grinning.

"Promise me we will all live together when we are old, just like now" I would demand and they always would promise. They both meant to keep that promise too. We all did. It was made so many times over the years, but one of us just couldn't make till old age. We would only need a two person room after all.

The summer before my second grade came to be a memorable one for all of us. Jamie had shocked all of us when she confessed to Mom and Dad that she was pregnant that previous winter. She was about to be a junior in high school.

"We have to make sacrifices to help her, that's all," Mom would say.

But, I could tell she was nervous. She argued with Jamie a lot. She and Jamie cried all the time, sometimes together. They moved our rooms around. Jamie and I had just started sharing the newly built bedroom in the back of the house.

"You're going to have to stay with your little sisters a bit longer," Mom said.

I was disappointed but more excited to have another baby in the family. I liked Jamie's boyfriend. He was nice. When there were big snapping turtles in the yard he would come over and get rid of them for us. I thought he was cool.

I remember the day Jamie finally had her baby. I had stayed after school that day for my Brownies meeting. At first, I wasn't very worried when the other kids were getting picked up and I was still there. Soon, though, there were only a couple kids left, and then it was just me. As usual, my imagination got the best of me. I started to imagine that there had been a fire at the house and everyone was dead, or they all decided to go on vacation and forgot that I wasn't in the car with them yet. How far would they get before they realized they forgot me? Georgia? Mississippi? I tried to play it cool with Mrs. Johnson as she waited with me.

"Honey, I've tried calling you're parents and no one's answering the phone. Do you have a key? Maybe I should drive home, or to your Aunty's?" she asked.

"No, I better wait. If my parents come and I'm not here they'll be mad" I answered.

She turned and reached in her purse for a granola bar.

"Oh, there's a car. Is that them, honey?" Mrs. Johnson asked.

Up the drive I saw Dad's green truck come flying. He pulled up beside us.

"Jenny, I'm so sorry. Mrs. Johnson I apologize" he said coming to get me and shaking her hand excitedly.

"Dad, where were you?" I asked

"Jamie had her baby! J.P. is here! I'm sorry honey. I guess in the excitement we forgot you stayed after for Brownies today. Come on we have to go" he said ushering me to the truck.

"Well, congratulations! Is Jamie your sister?" Mrs. Johnson asked Dad.

Without hesitation Dad said "No, she's my daughter. Bye now, thanks again."

Just like that we were on our way to the hospital. Of all the scenarios that ran through my head, I hadn't thought about Jamie having her baby that day.

When we got to the hospital, I ran all the way to Jamie's room. Dad let me hold the flowers he had stopped and bought for her at the store. I felt so proud of my family. That was a great day.

Beth's birthday and Amy's birthday fell in the same week in August. Every year we would go to Amy's exuberant party with face painters and magicians and stare in wild amazement at the exotic animals that were on display. The food was amazing and laid out in decorative displays. We would play games and go home with goodie bags full of treasures.

Then would come Beth's birthday party. Simple. Inexpensive. Translated to me as 'unimportant'. I wanted Beth to have a great party of her own this year. Jamie had her baby a couple years before this particular birthday, and I knew Beth missed being the 'baby' of the family. I so badly wanted to give my sister a memorable day that was all about her. I asked her what kind of party she wanted one day while she was playing Barbie's.

"I don't care" she said "as long as there is a cake its fine."

I cared. She deserved a big party too. I had been saving my money all year from walking the neighbor's dog after school. I was saving for a new bike but summer was coming to an end soon anyways. I could get away with the bike I had until next year. I opened my piggy bank and counted out $42.00. I opened the Yellow Pages and looked up 'parties'. I scrolled down until an ad caught my eye. 'Ponies for Parties' it said. I called the number and spoke to the nice woman on the phone.

'Ponies for Parties' she answered.

"Hi, how much do you charge for pony rides?" I asked trying to sound as grown up as possible.

"Where is the party to be located?" she asked.

"Plymouth" I answered.

"And what kind of horse were you looking for?" she asked.

"I don't know. A pretty one please," I answered.

She laughed "Ok how old is the child of the party?"

"She's turning 6" I answered proudly.

"What is the date?" she asked.

I ran to the calendar and came back to pick up the receiver "Saturday August 8."

"I have a white large pony I can get you for $40 for an hour" she answered.

I couldn't believe my luck! A white, large pony! How magnificent that sounded. Beth would love that for sure.

"Yes I'll take it" I said.

I gave the woman my phone number and hung up the phone. I couldn't contain my excitement over the next few days as I awaited the revealing of Beth's birthday surprise. When the trailer pulled up to her party and the beautiful white pony came walking out I felt overwhelmed with joy. Her face beamed with excitement. Mom picked her up and put her on the beautiful brown leather saddle.

"Hold on tight" Mom said.

I could tell what Beth was thinking as she rode around the pond, her eyes twinkling with delight. She was a princess riding through the meadow. She was a beautiful fair maiden looking for her prince. She was off in her make-believe land and she deserved to be. She deserved the best. She was the best little sister we could've asked for and she had the best party we could've given her.

That night as we fell asleep in our crowded room she rolled over and put her arm around me.

"Thanks Jenny" she said. "I loved my party."

"You're breath stinks" I laughed. "Did you brush?"

She laughed and said "Love you."

"Love you too" I said and we drifted off to sleep.

As much as Beth missed being the family 'baby', she completely adored J.P. They were so close in age that they were more like brother and sister than aunt and nephew. Beth brought him into her world of imagination and fantasy, often dressing him up in costume or incorporating him in her skits. They were inseparable.

Jamie was a great Mom. She took such good care of little J.P. It wasn't always easy for her, though. In fact, it usually was pretty hard. People weren't always kind to her. I remember one lady standing behind us in the checkout line as I helped Jamie unpack her diapers and formula onto the conveyer belt.

"Kids these days, babies having babies" she was saying to her girlfriend.

I was mad. How dare she talk about my sister that way? This was a new role for me. I had never had to defend my older sister, she was always defending us. Jamie was paying with her WIC checks. She either didn't hear or didn't pay attention to the women's rude remarks, I'm not sure which, but she didn't show that they bothered her.

"Ok, let's go" she said and I put down the magazine I was thumbing.

"You know there are places girls like you can go" they woman scoffed.

Jamie stopped for a second. She squared her shoulders and started walking again. She never even looked back at the woman, but I did. As my sister proudly walked on pushing the carriage with one hand and with the other hand holding mine, I turned around and stuck my tongue out at those nasty women. They saw me too and made a gesture of disapproval. I didn't care.

"Why did you let them say those things about you?" I asked.

"I don't care what they say. I'm going to prove them wrong. I'm going to go to college and give J.P. a great life. I need my energy for that, not arguing with the likes of those women" she explained "They aren't worth our time."

College? That was a new idea.

Jamie dropped me off at Sarah's and told me she'd be back to get me after she unpacked the car and gave the baby a bath. I ran up Sarah's driveway and straight to her room.

"You aren't going to believe what happened to us at the store" I told her the story of the rude woman and we cursed them with wishes of misfortune.

"Why are people so mean?" Sarah asked

"Beats me" I said. "Born that way I guess."

"How are babies born?" Sarah asked.

"I don't know but I think it's gross" I answered.

"Did you see J.P. get born?" she asked.

"No" I answered "but my mom did and she said she cried. So if mom's cry then it must be really yucky" I reasoned

"Jenny, your sister called. She said you should get ready. She's walking up to get you" Sarah's mom called up the stairs.

I got my things together and waited by the window for Jamie. Sarah's mother saw Jamie walking up the hill pushing J.P. in his carriage.

"Isn't your sister a little old to be playing with dolls?" she innocently asked.

"That's not a doll. That's her baby" I said and I turned and walked out the door.

I ran to the carriage and kissed J.P.'s little head and I kissed my sister.

"What's that for?" Jamie asked surprised by my display of affection

"I just love my family," I said.

We walked home singing to J.P. and watching the sun set over the pond. The sky was a brilliant pink that night.

"Pink sky at night," Jamie said.

"Sailor's delight," I finished.

I decided that night I didn't care what anyone ever said or thought about my family. I didn't need anyone except for the people that lived in that little house with me. I needed them and they needed me. We were each other's pink sky delight.

Soon after that day, I threw myself into softball. I burnt off any extra energy I had in my quest for perfecting my performance. I wanted to excel in something and bring pride to the family, I guess. I started jogging and doing crunches. Any extra time was spent practicing or watching the Red Sox with Dad. My sisters and I had seen our Dad play softball regularly on his summer men's team and now that we were getting older we enjoyed it more and more. Mom came when she could, but she had started taking nursing classes and mostly used the time to study while we were occupied. We didn't mind. We adapted easily to pretty much everything. We made the most of it and ended up finding ways to be useful. We sold sodas at the refreshment stands and help keep the coolers full of ice. Dad taught us to keep the score books. We were needed and we loved it. We loved to be part of the team.

Molly and I loved to play ball together too and we were getting better and better each season. She was a catcher and I was a pitcher. She loved to talk trash to the girls up at bat.

"You think you can hit my sister?" she's ask, her glove out in ready position "Ooh swing and a miss. You're going to have to do better than that," she'd tease.

We earned quite the reputation and by the end of fifth grade summer we had been the undefeated champs 2 years in a row. We walked triumphantly in the Fourth of July parade, sweating in the hot July sun in full uniform. Dad was proud and that made us over the moon excited. Beth earned the nickname Buzz from "buzzing" around in the outfield trying to catch fly balls during our batting practices. She was our little mascot, our Buzzy. The name and our memories stuck with us through the tumultuous years to come serving as a soft place to rest along life's difficult road.

One night, we were all in the living room listening to Mom reading us a story. Beth was sitting on the ground playing with her Barbie's as Mom spoke. Molly had just gotten out of the shower and I was French braiding her hair. We heard the front door open and J.P.'s squeals as Jamie walked in the front door with him. She had her work clothes on and looked tired. Her boyfriend and J.P.'s daddy, Jacob, was behind her carrying in the car seat and baby bag.

"You're late!" Mom hollered at Jamie, "I told you to call if you were going to be late!"

"Not now Mom, please, I'm too tired" Jamie said.

"You've got to follow the rules Jamie. Life has rules" Mom kept going.

My sisters and I sat there silent. We knew they had been fighting more than usual and we didn't want to say anything to make it worse.

Jamie ignored Mom and started making J.P. a bottle

"Jamie, do you hear me?" Mom asked

"Oh give it a rest, Lily" Jacob said with just enough attitude to send Mom into action.

She threw the book down and sprang out of her seat. I don't remember anything about the arguing match that blew up at that point. There were a lot of words being used that we didn't understand. We just sat there together. I remember looking at Beth and she was crying. I put my index finger up to my lips and made the 'sssshhhh' sound. I tried so hard to make sense of what was happening. I kept braiding Molly hair pretending not to be paying attention to what was happening just a few feet away, and then, just as quickly as it started, it was over. Jamie took J.P. and left with Jacob. Now we were all crying. Mom was crying too. She never came back to finish the story. She went into her room and shut the door. I brought Beth into her bed and tucked her in. Molly climbed in bed too.

"Where do you think she went?" Molly asked

"No idea," I said to Molly

"Where is she going to sleep" she pressed

"Molly, I don't know but she's really smart, she'll figure it out" I answered.

I kissed Beth and told her to save me some room in the bed

I went to kiss Molly goodnight but she held her hand up in my face.

"Do not kiss me" she said. "That's so gross."

"You're gross" I said flicking her forehead. "I'll be back I'm going to check on Mom."

I crept down the hall. Dad still wasn't home yet. I went around the kitchen and living room and turned off the lights. I moved quickly in fear of seeing my little blue eyed friend hanging around some dark corner. I still got shivers down my back from time and time and felt like he was close by this night. I especially hated walking by the large picture window at night. In the darkness, I could only see reflections and I was afraid to see his reflection staring back at me. I pranced down to Mom's room taking long quiet strides.

"Mom," I whispered as I creaked the door open and poked my head in, "are you still awake?"

She turned her bedside lamp on "What is it" she asked

I walked over to where she was lying in bed. Her pillow was wet with tears. I pretended not to notice. "Want me to make you some tea?" I asked.

"No I just want to sleep…." she replied. She let out a long sigh as if she'd been holding her breath for years.

"Ok," I said disappointed that I didn't get an invitation into her big bed for a hug or consolation.

I turned to walk away. I looked back a couple times to see if she would stop me, but she had already fallen asleep. I went to bed with a heavy heart that night. Jamie wouldn't desert us like Danny did, I tried to convince myself. I climbed under the blankets and snuggled up to a sleeping Beth. Molly turned over and startled me as I thought she had already fallen asleep, too.

"Jen?" she asked. "Will you sleep in my bed tonight? I don't want to be alone."

I was shocked. She never wanted anyone in her bed. Without question I hopped out of Beth's bed and into hers.

"If you push me out of bed with your rocking tonight I'll never forgive you" I said.

We both knew I was kidding of course, but neither of us laughed. We were too sad to laugh; sad and scared. Who was going to watch J.P when Jamie went to work and school? Who was going to help Jamie with him while she got her groceries? Who was going to make sure he had his hat on when it was cold outside? All these worries flooded my little mind. We lay there in silence until we heard Dad come home.

Soon as the front door shut, I heard Molly say goodnight and I fell asleep.

I was getting ready for bed one night when I heard sudden sobbing coming from the bathroom. I ran down the hall to see what was wrong.

Mom came out of the bathroom and told me to get my coat. "We need to bring your sister to the hospital her stomach hurts. Get ready" she told me.

I peeked in the cracked door to see my sister curled over on the toilet sobbing. She looked up at me and I recognized pain in her eyes. This was the beginning of many doctor's appointments and hospital visits for Molly. She missed weeks of school at a time and her perception of routine and schedules became distorted. No one knew much about lactose intolerance back then. We couldn't understand why she would go from being totally fine one moment to crying hysterically the next. We wondered if she was faking. It was Mom who insisted she wasn't. Mom demanded answers and stood by her side rubbing her head while she cried in the hospital room time after time. It was a glimpse of the tender mother she may have always been if not so overwhelmed each minute with life's unrealistic demands. I hated to see my sister in pain, but I liked when my mom was gentle like this. She made us feel safe and loved in the moment of pain and suffering. It was the pain that made us worthy of such affection. Without the suffering there wasn't the tender attention; a dangerous pattern to form. We longed for the tender affection.

Molly's "condition" seemed to drag on forever and it was a couple years before a solid diagnosis was made. She would spend many nights away from us all as an inpatient in the hospital enduring testing for her mysterious condition. She would tell us how frightening it was to be alone with all of the strange people and sounds of the wards.

Beth and I didn't like it when she was sick for our own reasons. We were shuffled around between friends and family to help with us while Mom and Dad attended multiple doctors meetings. Mom tried to be at the hospital as much as possible but still had work and she was a year into nursing school. Dad was working numerous jobs to try and keep up with the medical bills and added expenses of traveling to the city every day. Beth was mostly at Delia's and I spent a couple nights a week with Martha. Jamie was either working or with her boyfriend most nights, but did take Beth and I frequently for some time together. We wanted Molly to get well. We wanted everyone back home together again. We missed the repetition of our normal life. It was disruptive bouncing around all the time. We did our homework in the car or the waiting rooms most nights. I remember not having anything clean to wear to school for picture day and feeling like a misfit with the other kids in their new shirts and haircuts. We tried to make friends with the other families on the pediatric ward. We tried to make the most of it and put on a brave face for Molly, Mom and Dad, but the whole thing sucked for everyone involved.

Molly finally snapped one night and slapped a nurse who took away her Popsicle. She had been in this particular ward for 5 weeks. To an 8 year old, that's a very long time to be away from your family and home. The doctor came to see Molly and determined her to be 'unremorseful' of her actions. That was when they moved Molly to a psych ward.

The pediatric psych ward was awful. There were children there who committed unspeakable acts. One girl set fire to her home while her family slept. Another boy was bulimic and used to vomit all over the cafeteria after each meal. It was a disturbing wake-up call into life's harshest reality for all of us. We hated it there. Molly became miserable and distant even during our play time visits. Mom finally had enough after just a few days there. She confronted the doctor after a 'family session'.

"What exactly are you doing about my daughter's stomach pain?" she demanded to know.

She was standing outside of the 'family room' where we had all just met, but speaking loud enough for us all to hear without even trying.

"Her symptoms just aren't consistent enough" one doctor told Mom. "We don't see how this could be a physical affliction. We believe it may be mental and she's showing signs of aggression."

Mom just about lost it one the man in the white coat as Beth and I sat quietly, pretending we weren't listening.

"Don't tell me I don't know if my own daughter is really suffering!" she yelled at him, "and of course she's aggressive! She's upset she wants to go home and get away from all YOU people! So do I!"

Nurses and visitors slowed down and looked to see what all the commotion was about.

"Something is wrong with that girl and you better find out what it is fast before I sue the pants off you" Mom growled the words.

She was mama bear now and it worked. Molly was transferred off the unit of drooling, over medicated children in strait jackets and back on to a medical ward where she belonged. I wonder, though, if Molly hearing how she had 'something wrong with her' over and over set off something in her brain without her even knowing it. I wonder if she hadn't had to go to those hospitals and hear all that talk, if her life would've turned out very differently; if she would have smiled more and laughed easier. Maybe she wouldn't carry such a chip on her shoulder and insist on being so defiant all the time. Maybe she would've gotten along better with Mom and Dad in the years to come and not just enjoyed life more. Maybe a part of her stayed behind in that psych ward, the hopeful and pure part. Maybe, a part of all of us did.

"Now, isn't this better?" Mom said once we finally arrived to Molly's new room.

I remember Molly's bruised up arms from the IV's and her snarly greasy hair. She was sad. She was broken and on top of it she was sick. Christmas was coming and they were making decorations in the activity room.

"I'm too tired" Molly said. "Just go without me I want to sleep."

"You can't just sleep all the time! How will you get better if all you do is sleep?" Mom didn't understand this girl and her behavior.

Mom was never one to sleep unless it was nighttime. Even when she had been sick after Beth, I remember her always being wide awake for our visits.

"Just let her sleep" Dad said and we went to leave.

I ran back and kissed her on the cheek.

"I love you" I said.

She opened her eyes and said "I love you too Boo Bear."

It was only a few days after that and Molly was backing home with us. That first Christmas was hard for her. She couldn't eat anything with milk in it or she'd get awful sick. She was diagnosed as lactose intolerant with a highly irritable bowel. She could go from being 100% fine to wailing in pain in an instant. She was good on her diet though. She didn't like being sick and definitely didn't like the hospital. She got thin. She liked being thin. She liked the attention people gave her saying "oh look at how slim you are you look so good". She started doing gymnastics and soon she was flipping all over the yard. She bounced back and once again we were all together, but Molly was different. She was tougher and wiser than she used to be. She'd pick fights with us all and do the opposite of whatever she was asked. She learned that she was good at pushing people's buttons.

Middle school started. It was a whole new world of makeup and bras. No more playing like little kids. I didn't care for the new 'mature' attitude I was supposed to have. I didn't want to care about boys and being popular like the other girls in school. I wanted to still ride my bike and play ball.

My sisters and I even invented a game-'booby bunkers' we called it. We would put pillows down our shirts all folded up like a big set of boobs. We would run into each other as fast as we could yelling "boobie bunkers" and bounce off of each other over and over until we were rolling on the ground, our cheeks sore from laughter.

We were playing this very game one afternoon when Sarah came down with a couple girls from school. She came to the sliding door in my room and they saw us playing.

"What are you doing? They asked with-a look of shock on their faces

We were totally caught off guard. No one ever really saw us in our raw form playing together before. We sat there silent for a minute then I said matter of factly "We are playing a game what does it look like?"

"Can we play?" Sarah asked.

I couldn't believe it.

"If you want" I said.

They shoved the pillows down their shirts and picked up where we left off. Maybe we weren't so different after all.

My little sisters liked when the girls my age came around. They quickly made friends with them. They were much more into the boys and makeup and secret phone calls then I was. They fit in with my friends more than I did. I didn't care. I had other things to occupy my time. I was still practicing my softball all the time and liked to babysit to earn money. I enjoyed being independent and started dreaming about running away from all the social pressures I was feeling. I started saving.

One night me, Molly and some girls from our softball team devised a plan. It was a full moon that night and we were going to sneak out on our bikes and meet at the cemetery in town at midnight. Molly and I went out our bedroom window and out back to the shed.

My bike had two flat tires.

"I'll ride Beth's and you can ride mine," Molly said.

"Molly, Beth's bike is brand new. I don't think we should take it. Maybe I'll just jog beside you," I answered.

"Then you'll be all sweaty and beside it's too far for you to jog" Molly answered "It's not like she'll ever know anyways."

I was easily convinced. I really wanted to go meet our friends, and besides they were going to be waiting for us.

"O.k." I answered.

I should've listened to my gut that night because, sure enough, things didn't go as planned. While we were playing around in the cemetery, someone stole Beth's new bike. We were beside ourselves with guilt. We looked everywhere for it before starting the long trek home.

"You got to walk with me" I huffed. "I can't jog anymore I'm going to puke."

We were only about half way home with about 3 miles still to go.

"O.k." Molly said.

"I feel so bad. We shouldn't have taken her bike" I said.

"I know," said Molly.

"We have to replace it," I said, "you got any money?"

"Why would I have money?" Molly asked.

"I don't know don't you ever save any?" I replied sarcastically.

"No I don't" Molly scoffed. "I like to spend my money and enjoy it."

"Great" I sighed. "It looks like all my babysitting money is going to buy Beth a new bike."

"I'll pay you back for half" Molly said.

"Fine" I said.

We hurried home and put the one remaining bike back in the shed. The next day we told Beth what had happened and I paid her for her bike. She took it well and didn't tell on us for sneaking out. That was the last time Molly and I did anything like that together for a long time.

As middle school pushed on, I felt more and more like an outsider in my own world. Maybe it was hormones or silly adolescent pressures, but whatever it was, it wasn't a great time for me. I wasn't comfortable in my body with all the 'changes' going on. I remember getting my period and feeling lost and ill prepared. I didn't know how to handle what was happening to me and I was too embarrassed to ask for help. Jamie would think I was a little baby if I asked her. Gram was gone and I missed her terribly, especially at times like this. I felt very alone.

"Molly, come here," I said.

She came over to the bathroom with Beth close behind.

"Come in here," I said. "I got my period and I don't know what to do."

"Just ask Mom," she said.

"Does it hurt?" Beth asked.

"Kind of," I answered Beth.

"Is that why you stayed home from school today and yesterday?" Molly asked.

"Yes," I answered. "Can you go get Mom? Is she in a good mood?"

"I don't know, I think so," Molly said and she went off to find Mom. Beth stayed in the bathroom with me.

"What happened to your hair anyway?" I asked Beth.

"Mom gave me another 'new look'. Hope it grows out fast" she said.

"It's a mullet" I laughed.

"Shut up," she shoved me.

"I'm sorry. It looks cute on your little face" I said teasing her.

Mom was always trying new hairstyles on us, but this was taking it a little too far. I was just about to tell Beth not to let Mom do that again when Mom walked in the bathroom.

"What is it? I'm trying to study I have a test coming up" Mom said.

"I think I got my period and I need…."

Mom cut me of there.

"You think you got your period?" She was annoyed in my use of words. "You don't 'think' you got your period Jennifer. Either you go it or you didn't. If you have to question it you probably didn't. Let me know next month if it happens again. I'm too busy for this right now."

As she walked away I wondered what had happened to Mom. When did she become so apathetic? What could possibly be such a burden that she had become so distant?

I looked at Beth.

"This is the 3rd month in a row it's happened. It keeps getting worse. What am I going to do?"

"I know" Beth said. "Go in your room and get dressed I'll be there in a few minutes."

I went in my room and put on my pajamas. I was lying in my bed reading 'The Outsiders' when I heard a knock on the door.

"Who is it?" I asked getting up to open the door.

"It's me" I opened the door and saw Delia standing there with a large bag over her shoulder. "Can I come in?" she asked with a wink.

She put her bag on my bed and said "Well Beth called and told me you are officially a woman! Welcome to the club" she hugged me and I started to cry.

"Don't cry" she said. "There's nothing to cry about honey! You just need the right equipment."

She dumped her bag out on the bed. "This is all for you."

"For me? What's this?" I asked holding up a tampon.

Delia laughed and explained.

"Whaaaaat?" I was shocked at the horrific ideas coming out of her mouth.

"You can just save these for when you're ready" she patted my shoulder. "But, when summer time comes and all your friends are swimming, you'll be kissing my feet for giving you these."

She taught me all about how to use a pad and tampons and panty liners. She gave me Motrin for cramps and told me it was ok to wear sweats if I was feeling heavy. Beth listened intently to the whole thing.

"All part of becoming a woman" she said, "and that's a great thing."

I felt like a thousand pounds was lifted off my shoulders. She hugged me and said goodbye. Beth walked her to the door and then came back to sit on my bed.

"You called her?" I asked.

"I always call her if I need anything" Beth answered "she's nice."

"Thanks Buzz" I said.

"What's that book about?" Beth asked. She pointed to my book I had tossed on the bed. Beth loved to read as much as I did.

"This is a great book. It's all about kids who don't belong anywhere else but with each other" I said.

"Like us" she said without hesitation.

"Yeah just like us" I responded. "Want to hear some?"

"Yep" she answered.

We read that book a hundred times over the coming years. We watched the movie and quoted it regularly. Even Molly, who wasn't as into stories as Beth and I, could be easily persuaded to sit and read the story with us time to time. Other kids were probably still reading fantasy stories and fairly-tales. We were reading about the hard knocks in life and how sticking together makes it all bearable, easier in some ways. We were our own version of the outsiders. At least now, when my sister's periods came, I knew how to handle it and just like on my first day of kindergarten, I vowed that it would be better for them than it was for me. I wanted to make everything easier for them, but I just couldn't.

Molly and I began fighting more and more until we couldn't stand each other. She stole my clothes and my makeup constantly. She always wanted to hang out with my friends. She would purposely not do what I told her even when I was left home alone and in charge.

"Molly, get off the phone and come help me set the table" I hollered down the hall.

Nothing…nothing…

"Molly? Hello?" I repeated.

"What??!! She snapped.

"Dinners ready, can you help me?" I asked.

"Why do I have to help? I don't even want dinner" she would whine.

"Fine then, don't eat any," I said grabbing the dish out of her hand.

"You're such a bitch" she said.

I froze.

"What did you say?" I asked turning back around to face her.

"I said you're a big bitch" she said her eyes squinted right at me. "All you do is boss, boss, boss, all day and I'm sick of it! You're hardly even older than me."

"I don't want to babysit you! I don't want anything to do with you! You crazy little brat!" I quipped.

"Good cause I don't even like you anymore and no one else does either," she said.

I slapped her right in the face. She shoved me into the wall. I got up and grabbed her head by her hair and threw her down on the ground.

"You want to fight with me?" I screamed.

Molly started to cry. Beth started to cry, too. Soon we were all crying. I helped Molly up off the ground and started to put the dinner I had made into the fridge.

"Well what are we going to do now?" Molly asked.

"I don't know" I said quietly, "but I'm going to bed so you can figure out what you're going to do by yourself."

I put a plate of food down in front of Beth and put the rest away.

"I'll be I my room if you need anything."

I walked down the hall to my room like a wounded puppy. How did this happen? I thought. I was too stubborn to apologize and I really wasn't that sorry. She had pushed me to my breaking point so many times lately, and tonight I just snapped.

The next day after school, I went to talk to my Mom as she worked in her garden.

"Mom," I said "I don't want to be left home in charge of Molly and Beth anymore. It's too hard. Molly's almost my age and she doesn't listen to me at all."

Mom didn't look up at me as I talked.

I continued "Do you think we can go to Jamie's or something while you're in school from now on? We'll behave over there I promise."

"You don't have to worry about me going to school anymore. I quit last night" Mom said.

"What? Why?" I was shocked, and disappointed. We had all been counting on the day when Mom would finally finish and we could live a little more comfortably then we were presently.

"I'll tell you why." Mom looked at me "The neighbor called and told your Dad that all you girls do is fight at night. She said she can hear you through the windows when they're open. You said you say terrible things to each other and said you even hit each other sometimes. So, since my girls are little hell raisers, I can't go to school anymore. I have to stay home and watch over at night so you don't kill each other."

"Mom you don't have to quit" I started to say.

"Too late." She interrupted, "what's done is done. I made my peace with it. Just wasn't in the plan for me."

I was silent. I felt terrible. What had we done?

"I'm really sorry Mom," I said ashamed.

Mom tried to smile, but her eyes were full of sadness.

"It's ok" she faked a smile "Maybe someday you'll be a nurse for both of us. Lord knows you watched me study enough. Maybe some of it sank in your brain." She stood up and walked away.

Molly and I fought still despite Mom being home. Molly and I fought, Mom and Molly fought, Mom and me fought, then Mom and Dad fought about all the fighting. The only one who didn't fight was Beth. She stayed in her room playing with her Barbie's, or went to Delia's to play. In all of the fighting chaos swirling around her, she was a shiny little beam of light, and where there is light, there can't also be darkness. But she was such a little light, and the darkness was wide and deep. The light can still get lost.

During all of this turmoil, I made a friend at school. Something about this girl made me feel comfortable. Like I could finally just be myself and not worry about keeping up appearances or what others might think of me. If I said the wrong thing, she would just laugh and say 'you're crazy', but not in a mean way, in a fun way. Being friends with her changed my life. I spent more days at her house than I did at my own in the years to come.

Julia lived within walking distance to town. That made her house far more appealing than my boring country house. Someone is her neighborhood was always having a wild party or getting arrested. It was a place with more drama than my house, only I didn't have to be involved in any of it. I didn't have to worry about any of it either. We could just watch from the distance and then return home to our safe little bed in her room. This wasn't a nice part of town, and many of these nights that we "returned home" we actually had run home either escaping the police or a creepy van that had followed us a couple blocks before we got scared and sprinted all the way back to her neighborhood.

We learned how to pick locks and where we could get someone to buy us alcohol. I started smoking cigarettes. I wanted to forget about all the fighting at home, but I missed my sisters. At night I would lie awake after Julia had fallen asleep and wonder if Beth was awake thinking of me. I wondered if that little boy was creeping around our room, watching my sisters as they slept. I wondered if anyone even missed me there. I wondered, but I didn't ask. I didn't want them to know how much I wanted them to miss me, and how much I missed them.

On Saturday mornings I would walk to town where Dad worked at the Kids Club. I played games with the kids and used the time to check in on the happenings of the family. Dad was always happy to see me and every day after school, before the place opened, he would practice playing ball with me for an hour. One afternoon I finally got up the courage to ask him something I had been dreading mentioning.

"Dad? Are you and Mom going to let me go to Bournedale?" I asked.

"Say what?" Dad asked as if he didn't know.

"You know, Camp Bournedale?" I cued. "It's my classes turn to go for the weekend at the end of the month. I need the money soon or I can't go with everyone else."

"I see," said Dad. "Why don't you come home tonight and we can talk to your Mom about it?"

We threw a few more balls around and called it a day. I went home with him that night in a fairly good mood. We were singing to Tom Petty and the Warren Zevon on the way home.

"I'm making spaghetti," Dad said. "We can talk after dinner."

"Ok" I replied happily.

I went inside and headed down to my room. Molly was on the phone and Beth was on the computer typing away like a mad woman.

"What's up?" I said to them as I walked in.

"Nothing" they both said simultaneously.

"I'm starving" Beth said.

"Me too" I said. "Dad's making spaghetti. I'm going to shower I'm all sweaty from practicing."

"Want to use some of my new conditioner? It works really good." Beth got up and handed me her bottle of conditioner. She was growing so fast and was almost taller than me.

"Thanks" I said. "Guess it's a good thing that your mullet finally grew out."

"Ugh" she sighed. "Mom tried to give me a haircut again and I literally had to run up the street to Delia's to hide."

"HHMMM," Molly smirked. She had hung up the phone. "It was friggin' hilarious. You should've seen it," she said as she walked to her closet to get her pajamas.

'Yes,' I thought to myself, 'I should've seen it.'

"I'm showering first," Molly said walking off to the bathroom. "You're going to have to wait."

After dinner I sat at the table after the other girls retreated to their rooms.

"Can we help you with something?" Mom asked. "This is the most we've seen you in a long time."

"Mom I really want to go on the school trip for the weekend. I need the money by Monday," I blurted out.

"How much is it?" Mom asked.

"$180," I said "but, that includes everything."

"I have to think about it. What do you think?" she said turning to Dad.

"I think we should let her go," Dad said. "All the kids are going its chaperoned, it's safe."

I felt a glimmer of hope rise in my chest. This was going so much better than I expected.

"How bout we sleep on it?" Mom asked as she dried the last of the dishes. "Want to watch a movie with us tonight?"

I couldn't remember the last time I watched a movie with my parents.

"Sure long as it's not scary," I said.

"It's not," said Dad "It's some movie about rock climbers called "Cliffhanger."

I was white knuckled all night watching that movie with my parents. It was worth it. It felt so good to be home in my little house. No one fought that night. We all just hung out together, the way it should've always been. As usual, I fell asleep in Beth's bed, our feet hanging off the sides as we were both far too big to fit in her little bed now. Still, it was a great nights rest.

The next morning Mom called me to the kitchen after Dad left. She was scrubbing her combs in a bucket in the kitchen sink.

"Why are you still home?" I asked

"Just running late," she answered. "Listen, Jenny, I feel really bad, but I just don't think we can afford that trip."

I was devastated.

"What we can do," she bargained, "is let you skip school for the two days while you would've been away."

"What am I supposed to do all day? All my friends will be away!" I yelled.

"Don't you yell at me," she said calmly. "I don't know what to tell you, but you can't go unless you can pay for it. I'm sorry it's just the way it is."

"Fine," I said.

I gathered my things and got ready for school. I packed my book bag and then I packed an overnight bag for Julia's. I couldn't bear to go back there that night. I put cold water on my face and applied my makeup to hide the proof of my disappointment. I headed out the door.

"Hey wait for me," Molly said jogging to catch up to me. "Sorry, Jenny. I heard what happened."

"It's fine," I shrugged and just then I dawned on me that not ALL of my friends were going away to Camp Bournedale. "Hey you want to skip some school with me next week?"

"I can skip right now if you want" she laughed.

I missed her. I was glad she caught up to me, and suddenly, I was glad I wasn't going to Bournedale. I'd rather be home anyways than off with a bunch of people I hardly knew. I'd just make the most of it. It wasn't so bad.

It turned out there were other kids who didn't go, too. I wasn't the only one. I wasn't really that different from all the other kids. I had another girlfriend who stayed home too, and she hung out with us over the next couple days. She didn't have any sisters, but I did. Even if this friend hadn't been there, my sister would've been. I started to realize how lucky I was to have my sisters. Even though we fought so much lately, I knew they were always there for me. I never wanted them, any of them, to ever leave.

When you grow up really close to people through all your formative years; close in space, close in age, they become a part of you. The emotions that they feel become a part of your emotions. Their life directly affects your life. Their accomplishments enhance your life and their mistakes impact you negatively. It's all through love. You love them, and therefore, you sink or swim with them. The strange thing is, you don't realize when it's all happening how much you need these people. You don't realize that when they breathe, you breathe, but when they are drowning….you drown too. You just don't realize how much you lean on them for everything, until they are gone.

I got over the whole Bournedale thing and moved on with my life unscathed. Jamie had moved on with her life too. She had finished college like she said she would. She had become a nurse. She and Jacob had gotten married and both had graduated from college. He earned a degree in engineering and she in nursing. They worked hard. They loved together, cried together, and prayed together. Everything was together and we loved that. J.P. was like the baby brother we never had. We were very close; especially he and Beth. They were only 4 years apart and over the years had spent so much time together.

Jamie always tried to be good to us. Things weren't always easy for her, she had baby very young after all. But, she kept her priorities straight and she and Jacob were committed to each other and to finishing the family they had started. They had struggled for many years. After so long of saving and cutting coupons and studying and working double shifts, they were finally able to buy a house. Not just any house either, this house had a pool.

I remember going to their house after they had just moved in. I thought to myself 'J.P. is so lucky! I want to live here!'

J.P. had silk sheets on his big double size bed. He was a priority to them; he was the base of their relationship. We were all secretly jealous of him. His house was quiet and calm. He had so many toys. It seemed so perfect, but it was too perfect for misfits like us. We belonged in our little house together and it wasn't long before we proved that time and again. We just didn't fit in anywhere else, not like we fit in at home. Isn't that true for everyone?

Mom and Jamie took years to reconcile their differences but neither of them let it affect us girls. They were like their own entity. Mom had Jamie when she was just 18 years old herself. They grew up together. Mom worked so hard to raise her all on her own. Mom was a worker and no one could say she wasn't. She worked as a housekeeper in rich people's homes where she and Jamie lived in the attics or basements to keep the food on the table. She waited tables and tended bar, whatever she had to do, but it was always honest money. Mom wasn't one for b.s. or cheating. She was tough and she was a survivor. So was Jamie. They were more alike than either of them knew.

Jamie would get upset growing up over all the times she, or we, went without, but, looking back, we can see that that was what made us tough. Our struggles are what make us strong. They make us reach for more. If we are strong our struggles refine us. If we are weak though, our struggles define us, and that, that is not something that anyone wants. We must not let our struggles define us; we must not let struggle equal defeat. We must overcome. Mom was still trying to overcome, but Jamie had already succeeded. She had become an independent young wife and mother in a home we only dreamed of. She was our hero. Still, there was a rift. We were different and we all knew it.

Dad got cancer when I was in middle school. Once again, our lives were flipped upside down. The threat of losing Dad squeezed tightly around us each, as tight as a boa constrictor constricts its prey. "Jenny, what will happen if Dad doesn't get better?" Beth asked one day as we were sledding on a cookie sheet down the small hill in the back yard

"He will. Don't worry about that." I told Beth

I knew I was lying to her. I didn't really know that Dad would get better. I hated to lie.

"Amy says that when you have cancer you lose all your hair and throw up all the time," Beth went on as she huffed up the little hill.

"Beth, Amy doesn't know everything. Remember the other night at dinner? Dad promised he would never leave us, right?" I asked.

"Right. He promised he would make me a lemon cake for my birthday next year" Beth was smiling.

She loved cake. Dad knew just how to get her attention and make her remember his words.

"Then why are you questioning him? Dad wouldn't lie to us, and he wouldn't leave us. He will be ok. O.k.?" I asked pulling her onto my lap on the cookie sheet.

"Jenny, I really don't want Dad to leave us" she was serious.

"I know. He won't. He promised" I looked down at Beth's feet. "Where are your boots?"

"I couldn't find them so Mom put these plastic bags over my shoes," she said.

"After this we better go in. Your feet must be getting cold" I held her tight as we went down the hill together, feeling every bump in the ground below the thin metal sheet and snowy surface.

I remember how Beth's hair smelled in the cold snowy weather. I remember how when I wrapped my arms around her waist she would hold on to my hands. I remember her pale pink snow suit. I remember feeling how much she trusted me to protect her. I wanted so badly to always do just that, but I just couldn't always hold on tight enough.

Dad beat the cancer and came out on top like the champion he was to us. We adored him even more after we almost lost him. Once he was strong enough, he started looking for extra work and took a job on a large farm caring for horses and the pool grounds. It was an extra job on top of the Club to help with the mounting medical expenses. For three young girls, it was a dream job.

Like most little girls, we all loved horses. Mom traded haircuts for riding lessons for a couple years and we were fortunate enough to have the opportunity for some stable time. We cleaned the stables and brushed the horses. We earned our lessons, but we didn't mind. It was an honor to care for such majestic creatures.

When Dad took the job at the farm, we considered the possibilities for adventure to be endless. The owners were always away on business which left us there with Dad to care for the 160+acres of vineyards and horse pastures. We would take the horses out when Dad was busy cleaning the pool or tending the dogs, and ride for hours together through the old trails that wound throughout the property. We were transported through history at any given time. We would escape the harsh reality of real life where cancer and school drama tainted our thirst for innocent pleasures. We would ride all day until dusk. Then, we would turn back and ride under the fuchsia spring sunsets, confiding in each other parts of our days that we had kept to ourselves until this perfect moment for sharing presented itself.

If Dad had never got cancer, he may have never got that job. Sometimes, we have to struggle to keep faith that God does have a plan for everything. Those fuchsia sunsets, just like the beautiful ones over the pond, were our reminders that we were not forgotten or alone.

One Friday afternoon, I got home from school to find Jamie at the house.

"Hey," I said. "What's up?"

"Nothing, I just wanted you guys to come sleep over" Jamie said.

"I'm supposed to sleep at Julia's" I said.

"So cancel" Jamie said. "I miss you guys. Please come."

"Ok" I said not quite sure why the sudden urgency.

I called Julia and cancelled our plans and promised to sleep over the next night.

Molly was right behind me.

"Hey," I said "get ready we are going to Jamie's."

"Yeah" Jamie said. "Be quick, we got to get home to get J.P. from preschool."

"What about Beth?" I asked putting on my coat.

"Dad's going to bring her by after work. She has a doctor's appointment."

"OK." Molly said.

And we headed out the door. We went to Jamie's and got J.P. at school.

Whenever Jamie had us over for the night, she made it seem like a real big deal. We always went to the store and got all kinds of snacks and treats. This night started off like any other with a trip to the grocery store.

"You go get the ice cream and I'll get a movie" Jamie told us

She handed me some cash and we headed our separate ways

"Meet me at the door in 15 minutes" she instructed as she and J.P. headed toward the movie section.

Molly and I dashed off toward the ice cream freezers.

"Did you bring your Lactaid pills" I asked Molly

"Yep" she fished them out of her pocket "What kind should we get?"

"I don't know, something everyone likes" I answered.

"I like rocky road" Molly said.

"Molly, you know Beth hates rocky road. Pick something else" I said.

"I got to go look at something just pick what you want then" Molly said.

I turned to answer her and she was already out of sight.

"Great" I said to myself.

I grabbed the cash pocket from Jamie. I walked to the front of the store and stood in the line. I kept looking over my shoulder for Jamie or Molly but no one was coming.

"Where are they?" I thought to myself as I finished paying for the ice cream.

I walked to the front of the store and sat along the window edge for what seemed like forever. I was nervous that we would miss Beth getting dropped off if we didn't leave soon. Just as I was contemplating walking to the service desk to ask them to page Jamie (a trick I learned from my mother as she often paged us in stores which was terribly humiliating) I saw Jamie and Molly coming toward the front. Jamie had already paid for her movie and snacks and looked terribly disturbed.

She never even stopped walking as she moved by me to the door and said "Let's go."

We walked faster than usual to the car, J.P. jogging to keep up with his little legs.

"What is going on?" I asked as I buckled my seat belt. "Where were you guys?"

"Why don't you ask Molly?" Jamie answered adjusting her rearview mirror.

I turned back to glance at Molly in the back seat.

"What happened?" I asked.

"I got caught stealing," Molly said.

"What!?" I said "What did you steal?"

"Lipstick," she said.

"I don't get it," Jamie said. "I try to do something nice with you and you steal lipstick. Don't you know it's wrong to steal? You can't just take what you want! Why didn't you just ask?"

"All the other girls at school wear makeup and Mom and Dad won't buy me any," Molly said. "I didn't mean to get caught."

"It's not about getting caught!" Jamie said. "It's wrong! God sees you Molly! He sees everything you know that! If you can't buy it you can't have it. I'm sure this isn't the first time you've stole either, right?"

Molly didn't answer, neither did I. I knew she stole. In fact, she stole a lot. She stole clothes, razors, makeup, earrings, all of it. She wanted to fit in, and she always did. She looked fabulous all the time. Mom and Dad never questioned where the stuff came from. They must've known since they didn't buy it. Maybe she said they were gifts, who knows? All I knew was that I hated when she did that. I was always afraid she would get caught and this time she did. We rode the rest of the way home in silence. We pulled in the driveway of Jamie's house and Dad was waiting there with Beth.

"Hey" he said. "I'm running late I have to go meet Mom. I put her stuff on the porch I'll call you later, ok?"

"Ok sure thanks," Jamie said he drove off in a hurry. She didn't have time to tell him even if she wanted too.

Molly had narrowly escaped Dad's wrath. Dad rarely got mad but when he did it was awful. He had the hardest hands and a spanking from him made a harsh impression. We would be fools to repeat an offense and risk a 'Dad' spanking. Maybe if Molly had gotten one, her pattern would've broken.

We went on to have a great night at Jamie's complete with ice cream Sundays and nerf gun wars. We fell asleep on the pull out couch watching 'Mrs. Doubtfire'. I woke up late to go to the bathroom and heard Jamie and Jacob talking in the kitchen as I walked down the hall. Jamie was crying.

"I just don't know how I never noticed before. Of course she steals! There's no way she pays for all that stuff she has. I just don't know what to do' she said sadly.

"Just talk to her," Jacob said, "you're not her mother, you're her sister. Be there for her and try to help her."

I did not want to hear more. I went back to bed and decided to wait till morning to go pee. I didn't want to disturb anyone's night more than it already had been.

The next day we learned why Dad was in such a hurry the night before. Dad came to pick us up at the scheduled time, only he wasn't in his old big green truck. He was in a brand new minivan.

Mom had quit nursing school a couple years earlier because it was too much time and commitment with us all being so small and her still needing to work. But, Mom definitely wasn't a quitter. She still wanted better opportunities for us so she instead went on to get her real estate license. It was a great time to sell real estate because property values had sky rocketed. Mom was good at it too. In her first 6 months she made more money than she had made in the last two years. It was a good time for us. Mom and Dad were happier than they had been in a long time.

"Jamie, can J.P. sleep over tonight?" Dad asked as he put our bags in the new spacious car.

We were all piling in and exploring all the fancy shiny buttons and controllers.

"Dad this is great" I said. I was so happy for my family to finally have a nice car.

"Wait till you see what we have at home," Dad said.

"What? What is it?' we were all exclaiming.

"You'll have to wait and see," Dad said smiling.

"Where's Mom?" Jamie asked suspiciously.

"She's at home finishing setting up the surprise," Dad answered.

"Ok" Jamie said. "I want to see what this is all about so wait a minute and I'll get J.P.'s bag and I'll drive over and meet you there."

"Great" Dad said.

"What do you think the surprise is?" Beth asked.

"I have no idea," I said "but I can't wait to see."

Dad climbed in and told us to put on our seat belts. He backed out of the driveway.

"Wait till you girls hear the stereo on this baby," and we were off on our first ride of our new chapter in life.

The car ride home was amazing. Molly and I decided not to ruin the day with mentioning the trouble she had started the night before.

She promised she wouldn't do it again. She knew she got lucky escaping Dad's punishment this time, and she wouldn't get so lucky next time.

We pulled in the driveway and Jamie pulled in behind us.

"Where is the surprise?" we were all asking.

The yard looked the same as usual. We were perplexed.

"Go find it," Dad said laughing.

We all ran in different directions. Beth and J.P. ran around to the backyard and Molly and I to the side yard by the big cherry blossom tree that was in full bloom. We climbed to the top for a better view of the yard. The only place we couldn't see was the back corner.

"You see anything? I asked.

"Not yet," Molly said as she climbed higher.

Just then we heard a loud scream.

"That's Beth!" I said. "She must've found it!"

We jumped down out of the tree and followed the sound of Beth's joyous shrieking. As we turned the corner to the back yard we saw it! It was huge, blue and beautiful! It was a trampoline.

It was the perfect gift. We were beside ourselves with happiness.

"Mom sold a big house" Dad said proudly.

"Do you love it?" Mom asked excitedly. "Watch, try to do this."

She showed us how to jump high enough to see over the roof and how if Beth and J.P. curled up in a ball, we could bounce them like popcorn kernels. She was wearing a huge smile with her blonde hair bouncing as she jumped higher and higher. She was just as happy as we were.

"And, after you jump you can go cool off in the pond," Mom suggested.

That's exactly what we did. That trampoline gave us one of our most innocent summers of fun. We had the perfect summer hang out spot. Our friends always wanted to come to our house. I didn't need to go run around town like a wild girl on a Friday night this summer. Julia would come over and we would bounce and jump and swim. Some nights when we stayed up later than usual we would steal people's paddle boats around the pond and take them out to the middle of the glassy waters. On a clear night the sky over the pond was magical. We would float out there and talk and float for hours. Sometimes Molly would come but usually she was sleeping. We would talk about our dreams for the future and where we wanted to travel. We talked about the boys we liked and the girls we didn't like. Sometimes we would go night fishing, praising each other for our hidden talents that no one else knew about. No other girls knew we could hook a worm or take a fish off the hook. We were each other's soul mates, as close to sisters as you could be without being born into the same family. Julia knew everything about my family, good and bad, and I knew everything about hers. We were each other's chosen family. Over the years, we spent thousands of nights together under the night sky, cloaked in the starlight and protected by the darkness. These nights though, of this summer, were special. They still had innocence and childhood in them. The moon watched over us and held our secrets safe as we grew.

One afternoon was hotter than usual and I decided to run on the treadmill that I had bought with babysitting money instead of running outdoors. I had an all-star game that night and wanted to get a good burn session in. I had the radio up loud and was oblivious to any other happenings as I ran. Julia came in the room and turned the radio off.

"Hey!" I said annoyed.

"Molly got hurt on the trampoline come outside" she said as she ran outside.

I ran outside behind her and could see Molly lying flat on her back on the black netting.

"What happened??!" I asked.

Molly was crying too hard to answer. As she sobbed her head and neck stayed very still.

Julia answered "She was doing her back flip and she landed wrong. She hit her neck on the bar on the edge and her legs just went limp."

My heart sank. This was one of the scariest moments I can remember. 'Oh my God please don't let her neck be broken' was all I could think.

"Julia, go get the phone," I ordered. "Molly, can you feel your legs?"

She just looked at me wide eyed "I can't feel anything" she said "I can't move"

Julia came out with the phone and I tried calling Jamie. No answer, she must've been at work.

My fingers fumbled the number as I tried Dad's work number. I knew Mom was on the road showing houses and there was no answer at Dad's work either.

"Julia, go get ice for her neck," I said.

Julia went in the house and came back out.

"I just saw Beth going to the pond with Delia. I'm going to go get them." She threw me the ice pack and she ran off.

Delia came running around the corner a few moments after.

"Molly, can you move?" she asked "if you can't move we have to call an ambulance so you got to try."

"I don't want an ambulance. Please don't send me to the hospital!" Molly begged.

"I know you're scared Molly, but this is really serious, honey, so try to wiggle your toes" Delia urged.

Beth and Amy came around the corner with little Susie. They ran over to see what was happening.

It was a miracle that Molly could move her toes. Slowly Delia instructed her to move areas of her body slowly so she could see that she wasn't paralyzed. Julia brought her out more ice and Molly started to feel better.

"Want to try to get up?" Delia asked.

"O.k." Molly answered.

She slowly made her way to a sitting position and then slowly made her way off the trampoline.

"There's no way I can catch for you in the game tonight" she said to me with tears rolling down her cheeks. She had a large purple bruise already over the back of her neck.

"I don't care about that" I said. "You need to go lay down."

We put her into bed and Julia and I went over to the pond with the others. Delia told Mom what had happened when she came home from work. That night Mom and Dad took the trampoline down, despite our pleas, and sold it.

The rest of the summer we spent most of the nights at Julia's. Molly came with us some nights. One night Julia and I were at our girlfriend Karen's house and her older sister left a half bottle of tequila on the kitchen counter.

"Oh, my word! What is that?" I said pointing to the worm.

"That's the worm," Karen said. "Supposedly it's a wild time if you eat it."

"That's nasty," Julia said.

"Want to try some?" Karen asked.

"No, but I will," I said laughing.

We set the bottle of Cuervo on the table and sat around it.

"Ok I'm not doing this alone" I said.

"We will each take one at a time," Julia said. "Karen, it's your house so you go first."

Julia poured her a shot and she took it.

"Ahhhhhhhhhh, oh my gosh, that's gross!" Karen said. "You guys better do one now."

Before we knew it we had each had our fill and the bottle was empty. We made mashed potatoes and ended up having a food fight. We were delirious. We sat on the roof smoking cigarettes and yelling at people walking on the sidewalk below.

The night didn't end well as one could imagine. We were doing adult things at an adolescent age. This seemed so normal for us. We thought nothing of our behavior. We never thought about the future consequences.

Of course when Karen's mother came home, heads rolled. She kicked Julia and me out into the dead of night after she came home from her business trip. She was tired and jet lagged and had no patience for her own child's stupidity, never mind ours.

She threw our clothes at us and told us to get out with some choice profanities.

"Its 2:30 in the morning" Julia said.

"Well, you think you're so grown up! You kids are so stupid! If you think you're old enough to drink booze, then you're old enough to walk home!" Karen's mom yelled.

We threw our clothes on and scurried out the door like little mice. Karen stayed behind. I was glad Molly wasn't with us. This was scary.

"I'm so dizzy" I said.

"My mom's going to be furious" Julia said "I don't even have a key to get in"

"I think your window might be open" I said. "I smoked a cigarette out of it earlier I can't remember if I closed it."

"Good thing" Julia said. "We will just have to climb up onto the roof and go in. I think there might be a ladder beside the neighbor's house."

Julia's whole neighborhood was made up of duplex's that all looked the same. It was a residential housing neighborhood that ran parallel to the down town area. You could get to anywhere in town by cutting through one of the paths from her neighborhood. Her dad was a fisherman and was away for weeks at a time. When he returned it was reason for celebration. A good trip meant a good paycheck. He would stay up all night after returning and soak in tub after tub to get the fish smell off of him. When we got up in the morning, there would always be a Dunkin Donuts ice coffee and bagels waiting for us. Then he would sleep for about three days straight. He had just returned yesterday and we didn't dare knock on the door tonight and risk waking him to get in the house; especially in our condition.

We stumbled up to her house and saw that the window sure enough was open to her room. After unsuccessfully trying a locate a ladder, we decided our only choice was for me to try to let Julia climb on my shoulders and pull herself up to the awning outside of her roof. We hadn't gotten very far into our plan when we heard a voice from behind us.

"What are you doing?" he said.

We turned around, startled at this voice out of nowhere in the middle of the night.

Standing there was a new boy who had just moved to town. We hadn't really met him, officially, but we had seen him around. There was a lot of talk about this new boy, actually. He was very good looking; tall, tanned from working in the summer sun with golden high lights in his hair. He had slightly mismatched eyes, one hazel and one more green. We had overheard some boys we knew saying they didn't care for his cocky attitude, but the girls seem to swoon for him. Supposedly his parents had lots of money, too, which added to his appeal with the girls. They lived in an old farmhouse on the outside of town. His grandfather had made a fortune whaling and invested in shipping companies. He had just moved home from private school, somewhere out of state. No one seemed to know much about him, or his parents. They were supposedly 'away on business' a lot, but there were rumors that those 'business trips' were sometimes his dad's stints in rehab. This boy's older brother had been a football hero in some fancy school out west and reportedly had joined the service after high school. From what we had heard, this boy was now coming home to take over the family business, if he could stay out of trouble. His name was Benjamin.

"We are locked out" Julia explained.

"Can you lift her up onto that awning so she can get in the window?" I asked pointing to her window that was left open.

"I can just get up there myself" he said, and in a second he had pulled himself up onto the roof.

"You don't have to make it look that easy," Julia said sarcastically.

"Be real quiet" I said in a hushed tone. "Her dad's sleeping. Just go down the stairs and let us in."

He slipped through the window like a pro. In no time at all he was opening the front door.

"Thanks," Julia said slipping by him.

"Guess the dog didn't worry about the guy climbing in your window." I laughed as we went in the kitchen.

"He's so old, huh Max?" She bent over and let her golden retriever lick her face.

"See ya later girls," Ben said. "You should probably close and lock the door. It is the middle of the night after all. Not all guys are as nice as me." He winked and closed the door.

Julia went over and locked it.

"That was good timing" I said.

"No kidding. We would've still been out there probably" Julia replied as she bent over the stove to light her cigarette. "Want some Pepsi?"

"Yes please" I said. "I'll meet you upstairs I got to go use the bathroom."

We ended that night the way we ended almost every night; lying in bed in Julia's room, watching the X-Files, drinking Pepsi and smoking cigarettes. We talked and laughed. If it were ten years later that all this was happening I could've texted my sisters to say 'goodnight I love you.' I could've FaceTimed then to include them. I held them in my heart these nights when we were apart though. After Julia fell asleep I wondered where they were, what they were doing, who they were with. 'I'll call them in the morning', I'd tell myself, 'I'll call them and plan something fun with just them'. Time just goes by so fast. Things come up and life gets in the way of the important things. I felt guilty a lot of the time. Guilty that I didn't spend more time home with them or doing anything with them.

Sometimes we look back on life and say all the things we would've done differently. But the truth is, anything done differently would have changed the course for everyone. We can't think that way. I can't think 'if I were home more we would still all be together'; cause I don't even know if that's true. I do wonder about it though, late at night when I still miss my sister, wishing I could call her to say I love you. I wonder if I could've just dealt with the craziness, the fighting the frustrations and tension that hung so thick in the air you could cut it with a knife, would she still be here?; my beautiful, funny, sweet sister.

Mostly, I wonder about why things turned out so differently for her than for me. I ran around and did things I shouldn't have, too. I made bad choices. My life didn't get the best of me though. I didn't become an addict. Why does it happen to some people and not others? Why didn't I become an alcoholic? How come I could stop the things that I experimented with, but she couldn't? That's what keeps me up at night.

I hated the fighting. It's not that I'm 'not confrontational' or a 'bad communicator' it's that I take on everyone else's worries and frustrations as my own and one person can only bear so much. When we were all teenagers it was tough. We were all hormonal and moody. We were needy, as girls are, and demanded attention and time and money. None of which there was much of at home. We fought with each other and especially with Mom. We fought over chores mostly; whose turn it was to do them, why there were so many of them, who didn't do them good enough or at all. The chore load was heavy, time consuming and daily. It was a huge burden for young teens to carry. We should've made better plans to get it all done in a way that we could all work out. We should've stayed a tighter team, but we were selfish as kids at that age are. We wanted desperately to be relieved of the burdens at home. The house stopped being our place of refuge and rest, and acceptance of who we truly were when the rest of the world was gone. It became a place we all tried to avoid.

Mom wanted a tight ship, everyone up early doing our chores and reading and being quiet. We wanted to be young and carefree. It wasn't a good mix. We didn't want to worry about the windows or floors being clean. We wanted to just look pretty and be smart enough to be respected. We wanted to play softball and stay up late talking and hanging out with our friends. We wanted to go shopping and seek adventure. We were young girls caught between womanhood and childhood. We still had dolls in our rooms, but we also had bras and Bonnie Bell lip gloss. We worried about our figures and what we would be someday when we grew up. We worried about how we would spend our summer vacations and how we would cover our babysitting shifts and still have weekends with friends. It should've been a beautiful time in our lives. It should've been all dreams of the future and school dances with loving support from our family to make us strong and capable. It should've been a great with three sisters there all going through life's trials together, but it wasn't. It was hard.

As we grew older we became very independent of our parents but remained close to each other. I was especially independent. I started working at age 14 and liked the feeling of never having to do extra chores at home for money. I earned my own money and with that earned my own freedom. No one seemed to question where I had been or what was happening in my life. I just stayed out of any trouble that would get anyone in my 'business'. I maintained honor roll, and played my sports and showed up for work and that seemed to satisfy my parents. Long as I didn't seem to be in trouble, they didn't pay me much attention. I did pretty well with independence. It seemed to please my parents that they didn't have to be concerned with me and I liked that. It made me feel like I was contributing something to the family, even if it was just not causing any drama. I spent almost all my free time at Julia's house. I did my best not to be a burden there, too. On pay day I would pick up a bottle of shampoo or toilet paper to leave there. Her mother told me repeatedly that I didn't have to. I just couldn't help but feel like it was necessary. I couldn't even risk her parents not wanting me around as much; it was my home away from home.

Every Friday I took the bus to her house after school. I would have one book bag full of clothes and one book bag full of school work. I would get off at her house with her and then we would walk to the Kid's Club where we usually both had to work. My dad knew the best way to keep us out of trouble was to schedule us both for Friday night and Saturday shifts. We didn't mind either because we were together. The work there was fun. Most of our friends that we hung out with went to the Club too so we were able to maintain our social life in a somewhat supervised setting. My dad insisted on keeping up with my practicing softball even through high school. I loved it. It was my alone time with him. Julia was usually there too, watching and supporting. Molly was there once she came to high school and was able to take the bus with us. I thank God for the Club. It was the only thread of consistency and normalcy in my teen years. Our job was to run games and homework clubs. We were responsible for maintaining a positive influence to the younger kids. We volunteered at the Salvation Army for the holidays and organized toy drives. We raised money for under privileged kids to play sports and for the fields to be maintained. We learned an appreciation for what we had, no matter how little it was, it was more than what some others had. In the summer, we worked the summer camp and got to take tours of Fenway Park and the Boston Garden. We brought the kids to the beach and day trips all over New England. It was the best job in the world. It filled our days and evenings with structure. If it weren't for that Club, and those jobs we would've hardly even seen each other. It helped to keep us close when we were away from our little house on the pond.

Our little house wasn't really so little anymore as we continued through high school. Mom was doing well in real estate. She and Dad had built on to the house and there was a bedroom for almost all of us now and two bathrooms instead of one. Things had been updated, but they were just things. The laughter and imagination that filled that house when we were little was gone. Secrets started to fill the space where loyalty and love once lived. We were hardly ever all home and the emptiness festered. Idle space, like idle hands, can be dangerous. I wasn't the only one who had made a home outside of home. Molly made a close friend too where she chose to spend most of her time. Beth continued to spend as much time as possible with Delia and the girls at their house. They had moved out of our neighborhood by now and into a beautiful large house a couple miles up the road. They both had friends in a higher class than what we lived in. They took day trips to the camp or the city and celebrated holidays lavishly. Julia and I ran wild in town.

Our days and early evenings had structure but nights were another story. We drank liquor and smoked. By the age of 15 I could down ten shots of tequila in a night without it affecting my performance at work the next morning. We hung out at places that kids don't belong in. We regularly were hiding behind shrubs and telephone poles as the police drove slowly by with their search lights looking for the kids who were disturbing the peace at 2 a.m. We never committed any major crimes; we were just young and dumb and hung out in all the wrong places. We, for some reason, gravitated toward trouble instead of away from it. More than once we had just left a residence to get an ice coffee or a soda only to learn that as soon as we left, the home had been raided and everyone arrested. Unfortunately, we became very desensitized to this. We stayed out too late and slept too little. We didn't have cell phones yet, but we had beepers. Molly would occasionally page and we would walk across the highway through town to meet up with her and party. We would walk anywhere. Some of our friends drove, but we liked to be independent. We walked all night until our legs just about carried us back to Julia's to plop on the bed and watch our shows before catching a few hours of sleep. Again, I look back and wonder how I grew up like that and never turned into an addict myself. Is it truly nature or nurture?

Beth was not around much during this time. She was different than Molly and I. She had a much more timid soul. She could never have run from the cops and kept her cool, she would've cried. She couldn't plow over the catcher to steal home plate and she certainly couldn't drink tequila without getting sick. These were all facts, tried and true. She was our gentle Buzzy, Boo Bear, as we called her. She still liked to dress up and live in her fantasy world of prince and princesses. She took vacations on planes with Amy and her family. She wore expensive, nondrug store, makeup. She wore brand names and played tennis for school and ran for student government. She sang in the chorus. She was beautiful and popular. She was different than us. We never worried about her. We adored her. She was our baby, our princess. We would've never guessed she had the strength of a bull inside.

The summer before my junior year of high school was a hot one. Julia and I walked down to the park regularly to put our feet in the cool ocean water when we were away from the pond to cool us off. We were down there one day when we saw that boy again who helped us get into Julia's house the night we were locked out. He had started coming around our usual hang outs and we had become familiar with him. He had a lot of jobs around town but fished mostly. He was mysterious. Despite his family having money, he was fairly independent and I liked that. He came over and said hi to us.

"Where are you going off to?" we asked.

"I got to work till midnight at that new restaurant on the pier," he said.

"What are you doing there?" I asked.

"The boat I work on delivers fish there. They offered me a job in the kitchen a couple nights a week. I'm pretty quick with the fresh stuff, you know taking apart oysters and shrimp, stuff like that" he said.

"Have fun with that," we said as we packed up our clothes and put on our flip flops, trying not to act interested.

"Hurry up I got to pee," Julia said as we gathered our things.

"Hey my parents just let me start to renovate an old garage on the edge of our property. It's not done yet, but it's good enough to hang out in" Ben said. "Here's my number. Come by and check it out if you want sometime. I think it's going to be a great party spot. I put in a fridge and a couple couches, a radio, you know, the good stuff."

He wrote his number on a piece of scrap paper and handed it to me. I paid it no mind and put it in my pocket. We said good bye and went on our way.

"I don't know how I feel about that kid," Julia said as we walked down the sidewalk to go get an ice coffee.

"What do you mean?" I asked.

"Well clearly he likes you" she said. "I always see him around and he looks like he's staring at you. You think he follows us?"

"Be real" I said. "I never see him around. But, the two different colored eyes thing is kind of intriguing. I mean how freaky is that?"

"That's because you don't pay attention," she said. "He's always walking down the street at the same time or in the stores where we are, and yes the one green and one brown eye thing-very odd. I can't tell if I love it or hate it."

"Are you serious? He's always around?" I asked fixing my pony tail as we walked.

"Yeah! I'll show you next time" she laughed. "Either he just happens to be in the same area as us a lot, which I suppose could be, we do kind of work in the same area."

"And it is summer. Everyone is out around town," I added

"Yeah it could be coincidence," she said as we turned the corner into Dunkin Donuts. She opened the door "Or he could be a freakin' psycho."

I laughed as I walked through the door and turned to her, "Let's just hope not, but I have no intentions of calling him anyways. I started talking to that guy who lives up by grandmother and I kind of like him."

"Oooh. Let's go up there tonight. There's nothing going on around here just the same old stuff every night. You know where he hangs out?" Julia asked.

"Yep I do" I answered they're always at the beach by my Grandmas. We can park there and walk down. They'll all be there."

"Does he have a lot of friends? Cute ones?" Julia questioned

"Yeah. We should see if Molly and Debbie want to come, too" I said.

"You think Tammy will drive us up?" Julia asked.

"I don't see why not we are together every night driving around here. We got to get out of town. It's so boring here. I'm sure she won't care we can call her when we get home" I said

"Sounds like a plan" Julia said. "We should find a buyer now though."

"He's 21" I said.

"What?" Julia said

"I know he's wicked old," I said. "But, who cares it's just for fun."

We spent many nights that summer being young and free hanging out at beaches and partying with boys, men, way too old for us. It's a wonder we never got hurt, but we never did. People did start to wonder though where we were all the time. Not our parents, but our friends. One afternoon as we were getting ready to go out, a friend of ours pulled up in Julia's parent's driveway.

"Hey!" she yelled. "Where the heck you two been? We've hardly seen you all summer!"

"What do you mean? We've been around," Julia said.

"Well there's a huge party going on tonight and you better be there," she said.

"Where?" I asked.

"At Ben's garage. It's amazing out there. There's light's strung in the trees, even an above ground pool. Everyone's going. I'll be here to get you at 7," she said getting back in her car. "Oh, and by the way, why haven't you called him?"

"What do you mean?" I asked.

"Ben said he gave you his number weeks ago and you never called," she said putting on her mascara in the visor mirror. "It's all he talks about now, how you blew him off."

"Oh," I said, "I didn't think he was actually waiting for me to call."

"Well, you can make it up to him tonight, if you want that is." She laughed and backed out of the driveway. "See you at seven," she called out the window driving off.

"I told you," Julia said. "Psycho."

"Eek" I said. "Oh well lets go everyone's going to be there besides I'm sick of driving all the way to Scituate all the time. He's going off to college next week anyways that's not going anywhere."

"Fine by me," Julia said. "I'm always down for a good party."

Sometimes in life there are moments that change the whole course of our future. Moments that determine not only our paths, but the paths of those who are around us. This night was one of those nights. I could look back and say I wish I hadn't been there to start dating that boy, Ben. I could say I wish I was home in my little house doing chores, sweating in the August heat and cooling off on the outside shower. I could say I wish I had run and gone to Jamie's for a sleep over with my sisters to go night swimming and eat ice cream sundaes with J.P. But, if I did that, my life would be completely different today and after all is said and done, I love my life. All of it except the one part that this night somehow didn't seem to affect. The one part I would change if I could, had nothing to do with this night, at least not that I'm aware of.

Julia and I got all ready and were done by 7. We loved summer. We had amazing tans from playing out in the hot sun all day and a great night life as the sun stayed up with us extra-long during those months. Prep was easy in the summer-cutoff shorts, flip flops and a tank top with some sunglasses and bracelets and we were good to go. I grabbed my back pack and threw in a hoody to make sure we could carry discreetly whatever paraphernalia we needed without worrying about bottles breaking/clanging etc. We were pros at this after all. We kissed Joy goodbye and said we'd be home by 12:30.

"Do not stay out past 12" Joy said. "Not 12:30! 12!"

"Ok," Julia said, "might even be home before that. Relax. Love you."

And we were off. Just like that. Life changed.

We pulled up to the garage and ran in to some friends outside.

"Hey, girls! We are hitting the packy, you need anything?" they asked.

"Yeah wait, here's $20. Get us a bottle of tequila please and a bottle of Pepsi to chase it." Julia handed him the money.

"Tequila?" he asked.

"Yes, yes, we know gross" I said.

"You girls are nuts" and off he went.

We through the huge double doors and walked inside. The music was so loud and there were so many people there we had to hold hands so we didn't get separated as we walked through the crowd. The air was thick with cigarette smoke.

"Oh my gosh, Julia, I can't breathe already," I said with my shirt over my face.

"Stop you'll be fine once you get a couple shots in you" Julia answered.

Even though I smoked, I hated sitting in a room of smoke. I also truly was a homebody. I was never one for going to parties or big events. I liked to just stay home. Julia liked to be social. We were a good balance for each other. She kept me from self-isolation and I kept her from getting into too much trouble.

"I don't want to stay too long, I have a bad feeling" I said.

"Fine," she said. "We will leave in an hour. Can you just stay for an hour? Uh oh, here comes Ben, get ready."

"Where?" I turned to look and when I turned back Julia had disappeared into the cloud of smoke.

"Hey, you came," Ben said approaching.

"Yeah, nice place," I said. "We can't stay long just stopping by."

"That's cool. Hey your drinks are here. They're in the ice box" he said.

"Finally," I said.

We went around to the back and got the drinks. There was a beautiful garden back there. I was shocked.

"Want to sit out here? It's not so smoky out here and the flowers look nice in the moonlight" Ben said.

"That would be great, but I got to find Julia," I said.

"She'll be fine. Just come have a seat" he said.

I really shouldn't have. I had no business being there at this place at 15 years old. I should've got Julia and just left. Something inside me though said to go sit with this boy. He had a kind of sadness in his big mismatched eyes that pulled me in. I had heard that his life at home was less than ideal despite the appearance that things were perfect. His parents, supposedly, were pretty tough people in business and in private. I was slightly intrigued. I also was a fixer; could I fix that sadness in his eyes?

We went out onto the bench into the thick, hot, July night air. I took a couple shots and started to loosen up quickly. He asked me about school and my grades and softball. He said he had seen me around town and heard I came from a big family. He had one older brother who was serving overseas. He told me how his brother had refused to take on the family business, and had left after an awful fight with his parents to enlist in the army. He said he doubted he'd ever return, even if he could, the fight with his parents was bad, and damage was done that couldn't be erased.

"You really shouldn't smoke" he said as I lit up a Parliament Light.

"Thanks for the tip," I said smartly. Who did this kid think he was telling me what to do? "I got to get going. What time is it anyways?"

"12:00" he said checking his pager.

"Shoot we are dead. I got to find Julia." I said turning to go inside.

"She went for a ride to the beach with a couple others. Should be back soon," he said.

"What? How do you know?" I asked.

"She came out to tell you when you went to the bathroom earlier. I told her you would stay," he said.

"Hey! You don't get to answer for me" I started to get angry. "I decide what I do, not you."

Just then I heard a car pull up out front. Julia stumbled out.

"Jenny c'mon we are gonna be so late!" she hollered.

"Yeah by the way she's a mess," Ben said. "They all are. I tried to keep her from getting in the car with them but she wouldn't listen. I was just trying to protect you."

He got up and walked inside. I was confused. I was also starting to spin and knew we had a good 3 mile trek to get home if we took the shortcut through the pasture and then the graveyard. I gathered up what I needed. There was only a little bit of the tequila left. Had I drank all that? I decided to leave it. In our condition there was good chance we were going to at least be questions by the police if they saw us and I didn't want anything on me that could get us in trouble. I walked downstairs and caught up with Julia.

"We are sooo late," she managed to get out.

"I know" I said "We got to walk quickly. Here take a chug of this."

I handed her the water bottle I had packed.

"Ugh no I'm too nauseas" she said.

"It'll help you sober up faster if you puke, remember?" I said handing it to her.

She knew I was right. I was the fixer. She took the bottle and chugged half of it before running to a nearby push to puke. She came back a moment later wiping her mouth.

"That's much better," she said.

"Here" I handed her the little travel bottle of Listerine.

"Thanks," she said taking a rinse and spitting "What are you going to do?"

"I don't know I can never throw up," I said. "I wish I could."

I took a rinse of the Listerine and spit it out as we started to approach the main road. I put some lip gloss on and tried to look decent.

"We are going to have to cut across the graveyard," I said.

"Yep" she said. "Let's do it."

We darted across the street and tried to get far inside where we wouldn't be noticed by cars passing by.

"I saw Molly at the beach."

"Oh, yeah? What's she up too?"

"Nothing, the usual, dancing and putting on a show. She is a funny one. I told her we'd call her tomorrow."

"Kind of late for her to be out."

"She's fine Jenny. She's practically our age."

"Ugh I feel like crap. Tomorrow's going to suck getting to work. Can't you walk any faster?"

"Um, no. My legs are shorter than yours dummy. I got to find a bathroom soon or my bladder's going to explode."

"We are not peeing in a graveyard."

"Jenny, they're dead it's not like they know."

"I know that but it's so disrespectful."

"Ok, let's go in that gas station over there."

"K" I said and we made our way to the gas station.

After our stop we still had to cut up the hill and through the woods to come out behind Julia's neighborhood. There was a small creek we would have to jump over to get through. She was always much better at that than me and as usual she made it across no problem. When my turn came, I was spinning just enough to know I wasn't going to make it.

"C'mon you've done it a hundred times," Julia said. "Just go."

"I'm trying sshh," I said and I lost my balance and fell into the cool creek.

I was laughing so hard I couldn't get out.

"Get up!" I could hear Julia saying over the water trickling past my ears.

I tried but I just couldn't I was too disoriented. Julia reached in and grabbed my arm. Adrenaline must've kicked in and her tiny frame was suddenly strong enough to pull me out.

"Oh my god we are so stupid" she said.

"Why?" I asked standing there soaking wet.

"It's only knee deep! If I had known you were going to go swimming I would've suggested we just took off our shoes and walked through" she said.

"Oh, oh yeah" I burst into laughter as we both look at the shallow water slowly trickling by.

It was a very shallow stream. It was really only an obstacle in the winter when the water was freezing. Why it was such a challenge that night was surely due to the alcohol.

"Oh well. My soaking clothes are a dead giveaway of our condition now. Joy's going to kill us," I said.

"Yeah well we are also 1 1/2 hrs. late and she's paged me 50 times," Julia said.

We walked up the steps and before we could open the door it flew open.

"Get your little asses inside right now!" Joy yelled.

We had it coming. We took it without complaints. We showered off and went to Julia's room to settle in with our show.

"Oh yes! It's a new episode tonight" Julia said excitedly with the remote in one hand and a butt in the other.

"Awesome" I said toweling off my hair.

"Hey was Molly going back to Debbie's tonight?" I asked.

"Yes, Mom," Julia said sarcastically. "Don't worry I told her to page me when she got home with 143 so we knew she was safe and she did while you were in the shower. I knew you'd be asking" Julia laughed.

"You're the best," I smiled.

"I know," she said, "and I'm tired hit the lights."

We went off to bed and I wondered where Beth was. I wondered about Ben, too, and what was happening over there and what he was doing. I fell asleep to the sound of Julia's dog snoring beside me.

The next few weeks were the same as usual. We went to work we went out at night. We went to the pond and spent some time swimming with Molly and Beth and their friends. We walked in the July 4th parade celebration as we did every year with the Club. We dreaded the restart of school. Julia and I officially enrolled in Drivers Ed. I was thrilled that my mother had agreed to pay for half; I had been expecting to pay for the whole thing.

We were walking out of class one night when Ben came walking over.

"Girls going to be driving soon?" he asked.

"Why don't you drive?" I asked. "We always see you walking."

"I spent most of my life getting driven around by drivers" he said defensively. "Everything I need is in walking distance. I prefer to use my two legs. Besides I can drive a boat, that's more useful to me."

We didn't know what to say. We just stood there in awkward silence.

"Anyways, come by later having another party" he said.

"When aren't you having a party?" Julia said.

"Going to be a good one" he said walking away.

We stood there for a moment perplexed.

"I don't get that kid" Julia said. "Sometimes I like him and sometimes I think he's pretty cocky."

"You want to go tonight?" I asked "We haven't been there in a while. I hear everyone saying it's the new place to hang out."

"Whatever I don't really care" Julia said. "Let's go swimming first it's so hot!"

"Sounds good, I know Molly and Beth are home I'd like to see them" I said.

We went to the house but didn't stay long. Mom was in a mood and didn't want anyone walking around in her house that she just spent the morning cleaning. I wanted to at least peek in on Beth. I felt like I had hardly seen her all summer.

"Hey" I said. "Where are you going?"

"Anywhere but here," Beth said packing her suitcase.

"Seriously," I said.

"I'm going to Florida with Amy for the long weekend. Her dad has a conference down by Disney," Beth said.

"You're so lucky" I said giving her a big hug. "Will you say hi to Tinkerbell for me?"

She laughed. "Seriously, Jenny, I hate it here. I hardly ever come home and I'm starting to think that's how everyone likes it, especially Mom."

"That's not true, she's just stressed" I said trying to give her from comfort.

"From what?" Beth said looking expectantly for an answer.

"Oh I don't know, life I guess," I said with a sigh. "Well, I love you Boo Bear."

"I love you too," Beth said.

I looked through her suitcase a little when she went to get her shampoo.

"Hey when did you start smoking?" I asked holding her pack of Newports as she reentered the room.

"I don't know about 6 months ago. I didn't want you to know" she said as she grabbed her butts and threw them in the suitcase. "Can I borrow these?"

She held up a light coat and a pair of sandals of mine.

"Go for it," I said. "Look at you Miss Fancy. Where'd you get all this?"

She had all Victoria's Secrets lotions and undies in her suitcase with Paul Mitchell hair products and Gap jeans; very high end for our blood.

"Delia gets a lot of samples and coupons and she shares with us" Beth said.

"Well don't forget the little people," I said. "Hey, slow down I want to see you."

"Sorry" she said. "I'm just trying to make sure I'm on time. I can't find my sunglasses."

"That's because you already packed them." I laughed pointing to her suitcase.

She looked radiant. Her tan skin was gleaming with summer kisses from the sun. She had clearly recently dyed her long, waist length, shiny hair chocolate brown and her makeup was on point. She had a million megawatt smile and the voice of a song bird.

"I miss you," I said guiltily.

"I miss you too" she said. "I hear you been hanging out with that kid, Ben."

"I wouldn't call it hanging out. We hung out once. He's kind of sketchy. How'd you know?" I asked.

"I've been dating Eric. His older brother knows Ben. Says he really likes you. You haven't had a boyfriend in forever it would be good for you, but I agree; he's kind of a mystery, be careful."

"When did you get so smart? And when did you get a boyfriend?" I asked

She laughed and gave me a big hug.

"Think you can give me 2 French braids?" she asked "really quickly though? It would be nice to have some beachy waves tomorrow when I take them out."

"I'd love too" I said.

Beth had the thickest hair of us all. Her hairline was uneven though and one side was thicker than the other so one braid always can out bigger. She was perfectly imperfect.

"Who's this kid you're dating?" I asked.

"Eric. He's a good kid. He goes to private school. He's a junior. Wants to be a Navy Seal so I don't know where it's going to go but he's good to me" she said.

"Good to you?" I said pulling her head so she was facing me. "What do you mean 'good to you'?"

She laughed. "He's real nice. He calls me and tells me nice things, buys me little presents. He tells me I'm smart and pretty, you know all that good stuff."

"Have to say, I'm impressed," I said.

I put her elastics in and kissed her on the cheek.

"Have fun," I said. "Let's do something when you get back."

"Sounds good," and with that she was out the door.

"Shut that door! The AC is on," Mom hollered as I waved good bye to Beth.

I didn't go back in either. I had plenty of clean stuff at Julia's. I'd get a ride with a friend back over to her house and get ready there.

We got ready as we usually did. I thought about Beth and watched the planes overhead as we walked and wondered which one she was on. I wondered about his boy she was dating and wished her a lifetime of happiness in my head. I prayed for a safe journey for her. I missed her. I missed curling up with my baby sister at night. She wasn't a baby anymore. She was starting high school in just a few weeks with Molly and me. At least then I could keep a better eye on her, I thought to myself.

We walked up to the garage where the party was supposed to be but no one was around. The door was locked.

"That was a waste of time" I said to Julia as we started down the path toward the road.

"What was?" Ben asked leaning on a nearby tree.

We jumped a mile.

"Where the heck did you come from? I asked holding my heart from the startle.

"I'm just sitting here, minding my own, locked out. Where the heck did you come from?" he asked smartly getting up and walking toward us.

"We came by for the 'party'" I said. "But, it looks as though that's not happening tonight."

"Not so" he said. "I'm just locked out so everyone's meeting back here in an hour. My key will be here in a few."

"Oh" I said looking at Julia. "We can come back in a bit"

"I wish you'd stay and keep me company" he said.

I tried to think of an excuse why I couldn't, but nothing came to me. I just stood there awkwardly.

"Ok" Julia said "I'm going to walk down the street and try to get a ride to town. I need to get a few bucks from my mom at work then. I'll be back in a bit"

"No you shouldn't go alone" I said to Julia.

"Huh? Broad day light, Jenny, I think I'll be ok" she winked and started off.

"In that case get me an ice coffee" I hollered after her.

"Yeah, yeah" she waved me off as she walked up the drive toward the main road.

"Don't be afraid I'm not going to bite," Ben said.

"Oh I'm just really tired, sorry, I'm not trying to be rude" I said.

"If you're so tired sit down beside me" he said pushing over on the bench.

"I think I'll just sit on the grass" I said sitting down beside the bench.

"Whatever" he said.

"So how did you get locked out?" I asked.

"My dad wasn't in a great mood today when I went for the monthly business meeting. We didn't have the best financial month. We ended up in a fight. My key must've fallen off the key chain. I couldn't find it when I got home," he said.

"Oh sorry," I said.

He just looked at me.

"You're lucky, you have a nice family. That's a blessing. Not everyone has it, you should cherish it," he said looking to the distance.

"A blessing?" I asked

"Yeah you know from God. Don't you believe in God?" he asked. "You never heard of a blessing?"

"No, I have I just….you just caught me off guard," I said.

"It catches you off guard to talk about God? You should think about him all the time. Like today when my father was flipping out and my mother was crying, I was thinking about God."

"What were you thinking about him?" I asked uncomfortably.

"I was wondered where he was, why he wasn't making it stop," he answered quietly.

My head was spinning. What was this kid talking about? Where was Julia? I was getting desperate for a coffee and someone else to break up this intense conversation. I felt really uncomfortable.

"Yeah I believe in God," I said, "and I keep a relationship with him actually if you must know. I don't just believe in him. I can believe in anything. I love him. That's the difference. He was there with you; we just don't always understand his ways. You need to have faith."

"You have faith?", he asked me.

"Yeah I do! I have lots of it, what's your point?" I was getting annoyed with the seriousness of this conversation.

"I knew I liked you" he said "you're deep. I like deep. You know what my point is? I'll tell you. Everything you do is a test. It all comes down to the end. The end of days when it will be good against bad, God against the devil and every move you make your whole life will count toward one side or the other. It's the whole purpose of life. Some people think they just drift through aimlessly, but we don't. We have a purpose."

"Ok" I said ". "This is getting a little too intense."

I laughed nervously trying to lighten the mood.

"There's always someone watching you, Jenny. You can't hide anything. But if you go through life with the right person you'll have nothing to hide," he said.

I did like the idea of having nothing to hide. I wanted a clean conscience. I always felt guilty about smoking and drinking and swearing. He sounded crazy but I couldn't help but feel like he had the right idea, and the right intentions, under the crazy. I wondered if I could get through the crazy, or if I really even wanted to try.

Julia came walking up ice coffees in hand "You're still sitting here?" Just as she approached a car drove up.

"Finally, the key's here. He works for my parents. I'll be right back" Ben said walking toward the car.

"Damn dude you been out here stuck, huh? That sucks in this heat" the man in the car said tossing Ben the key. "I'll be back in a couple hours."

"Thanks" Ben said.

As he bent down to catch the key I noticed a purple bruise in the shape of some fingers on the side of his neck under his shirt.

"What are you looking at?" he asked as he stood and caught my stare.

"Nothing," I said. "You should put some ice on that though."

"You want to come inside and put some ice on it for me?" he asked grinning.

"We actually have to go," I said looking at Julia. "We'll see you soon." Julia followed as I turned to walk away.

"What the heck was that all about?" she asked.

"I don't know I felt panicky all of a sudden. He's so intense," I said.

We walked back to her house and I called Dad at work for a ride on his way home. I told him I had a stomachache and wanted my own bed. I really was suddenly feeling very homesick, a very unusual feeling for me. I wanted nothing more than I wanted to go home in that instant to my own home with my own family. We may have fought and had our own problems, but no one put bruises on my neck. Ben was right, it was a blessing and I felt bad that I took it for granted.

I spent the next two days hanging at the house. Molly and Beth stayed home too. It was the first time we had all spent so much time together in years. We watched Dirty Dancing, The Outsiders, and Willow and Honey I Shrunk the Kids, all our favorites from growing up. J.P. came over and swam and caught frogs with us. We had so much fun. I went to bed with a happy heart each night.

One night, I heard a tapping at the sliding door in mine and Molly's room. This was not a totally unusual occurrence as friends often stopped by late at night. I expected to see Julia or Amy when I opened the door, but instead it was Ben standing there.

"Hi," I said. "What's up?"

"Where you been?" he asked in a far too entitled manor for my liking.

"I've been here at my home," I said. "Who are you to ask?"

"You made me nervous. I didn't see you at all the usual places," he said.

"Do you follow me?" I asked directly

"Don't flatter yourself," he said. "You aren't that special. I just like to know you're ok. I wanted to see if you'd be my girlfriend, but maybe you think you're too good for me now that I think of it."

"Why would you say that? I'm not a snob I just wanted to come home. You're kind of rude," I said.

"Yeah, see ya later, sorry to wake you," he turned and started to walk away.

I felt guilty, but I shouldn't have. I was the one being young and stupid. I should've seen the sign and told him to kick rocks, but I didn't. Instead I justified this odd behavior; after all, no one else was showing any interest in my whereabouts on a daily basis. He seemed so sad and lonely. Didn't he have anything else to do besides worry about me? Did he really like me that much? Maybe he was a really good kid but just had a crappy support system at home; maybe someone just needed to give him a little support. The boys had warned me though, the boys I grew up with from the neighborhood. They saw us talking and they told me to stay away from him, that he was bad news. It just drew me in more, it was a challenge. Besides, it's just a couple dates, I thought, it's not like I'm committing my life to him. What could be the harm?

I went to my closet and fished out a sweatshirt.

"What are you doing? Molly groaned her eyes still closed.

"Be right back. I got to go get that kid and talk to him for a sec," I said throwing on my hoody.

"Shut the door behind you. Don't let any bugs in," she said and went back to rocking herself to sleep.

I slipped out the door and caught up with Ben about halfway up the road. He had his headphones on so he didn't hear me coming. I tapped him on the shoulder and he turned around with his fist raised.

"Jeez, girl! Don't sneak up on me like that!" he snapped.

"Are you ok? Are you nuts or something?! If you're going to be hanging out with me you need to relax a little" I grabbed his headphone and took a listen. I couldn't date someone with crappy taste in music. I was relieved to hear it was The Lost Boyz, Renee, I loved that song. "Hmmm" I made the Rogers sound all us girls made when we had a comment on something that we kept in our head.

"Ok" I said.

"Ok what?" he answered.

"Ok I'll try this dating thing with you" I answered. "But, don't be a jerk. I have kind of big plans for my future that don't include rotting in this town."

He kissed me and it felt right

"I coach a kid's baseball team. We have a game tomorrow night. Want to meet me at the field at 7 and then we can grab a bite after?" he asked.

"Sure but I'll probably have Julia with me. Bring a friend," I said and turned head home.

I was happy to hear he coached a kid's team. He must be a good kid, I reassured myself.

"Hey wait. I'll walk you back," he said.

From then on we were together most of the time. It's hard to be young with a best friend and a boyfriend. It's hard to balance your needs and your best friends needs and manage your relationship while maintaining a boyfriend. It becomes stressful after a while, and there were times I just wanted to run away from everyone.

I couldn't deny that Ben was good for me in the beginning. The changes made to my life all seemed positive to me. I had quit smoking cigarettes with his prodding and a financial bribe from my mother. I started going back to church on Sundays. I had an exercise buddy built in, and we spent a lot of time jogging and working out. We focused on improving ourselves physically, mentally and spiritually. He helped my dad with projects around the house and seemed to be making himself a welcomed figure in our lives. I started waitressing, too, at a local ice cream diner. Ben had worked in restaurants and told me how much money waitressing could bring in compared to my minimum wages I made currently. They didn't serve alcohol there so I could start at 16. He taught me how to properly load and unload a tray so I didn't spill drinks on my customers. We even took a few trips with his family and got to do some traveling. Even my sisters, although weary of this new boy, were mostly accepting and enjoying having him around. We seemed to be achieving our goals together and things seemed really good. I was quickly falling in love with him and all the new adventures that he brought into my life. I didn't see past that to the control he also was waging over me. Nevertheless, I wouldn't change anything. It all played a purpose in my life. That waitressing skill was what led me to financial independence and is how I met some of the best friends I would ever have. For a time, life was good. Julia was my best friend since middle school, and she wasn't about to give up on me over some boy and I wasn't going to walk out on her. We made time for each other. I was also home more than I had been in years, back at my little house on the pond. I thought it kept me out of trouble being in a relationship with him, and it did for the most part.

Ben renovated the garage on his parent's property into an apartment and we were basically living together by the half way point of my junior year. I stayed over there most nights. It was so much fun to design and decorate a place of our own in the beginning. It was nice to have my own space and play house, but I did secretly long for my independence back. I didn't mean for it to get so serious so fast, it just happened. I wanted to have my own space and my own bed. I wanted to climb back in bed with Beth for a night like when we were little and life was so simple. I stayed focused on graduating and tried not to notice all the little red flags that were popping up everywhere.

I started to plan for my future and hoped to go to college and travel. I studied Spanish and kept my grades at honor roll status. I didn't pay much attention to the fact that Ben was drinking more and more and doing drugs when he thought I wasn't awake. I tried not to notice that his temper had gotten short with me and he seemed to get to the point of shouting, over minor things, every day and even in public. We started to keep to ourselves more too. It wasn't intentional. Looking back, I can see that it was fear driven on my part. I was afraid of him yelling at me and humiliating me in front of my friends, or even worse, my sisters. Ben also started fighting with his bosses and friends more. He didn't coach the kid's teams anymore or make time for his family like he should've. He and his father met frequently to go over the business, but he didn't see his mother much and when he did he was often short tempered with her. I tried to tell him he should better to her, that family was very important, but he blew off me advice. His mother started to blame me for his distance and before long, our relationship was strained also.

When time came to get my license I had a car waiting. Mom and Dad had taken all of my, Molly and Beth's bonds out of the bank back when they were losing the house and now that things were better, they promised us each a little car when we got our license for repayment. Mine was a little sky blue K car. It was 15 years old but had low miles. I didn't care what it looked like. It was mine and it was freedom. I could get in that car and escape to anywhere. I was responsible for all the gas insurance and upkeep and I maintained it well. Ben hated that I kept it for myself. It was something he couldn't control. We would have fights over it regularly, but I didn't care. I wasn't giving in. I needed something for myself at the age of 16. Ben's behavior was becoming more and more unpredictable.

"You're a selfish bitch" he would sneer at me when I picked him up for work. "You look so stupid driving around in this old lady car."

"Umm, you want me to pick you up or not? Cause I can easily find something else to do. You can have mommy's driver get you," I would sarcastically say.

These fights were a regular occurrence. The fighting was exhausting. Trying to hide the fighting from everyone around me was even more exhausting.

I had just pulled in to the driveway at my parent's house for a visit when Ben started one of these typical arguments.

"Ben, go take a shower and relax I'm too tired and hungry to argue" I had started to say when he got out, slammed the door and stormed inside.

I was standing in the kitchen cooking eggs when he came out of the bathroom all clean and calm. I was relieved to not have any fighting occurring. The front door opened and my mom walked in. She didn't say anything, just walked to the bathroom and shut the door.

Beth walked in behind her. She looked pale and tired. It was only late morning but she looked like she'd been up for days.

"What's wrong with you? You look like you've seen a ghost," I said.

She turned her teary eyes to me and I could tell immediately this was no laughing matter.

"Delia's dead," she whimpered. "She's dead!"

She started bawling and ran down to her room and slammed the door.

Mom emerged from the bathroom. Her eyes were red and puffy too. I could tell shed been crying, and Mom never cried.

"Mom, what happened?" I asked choking back tears myself.

"Beth went to sleep over Delia's last night, as usual. Then she called around 6 and said that Charles (Amy's dad) had called and wanted to take them to the family camp in Connecticut for a couple days. We told her that was fine and Charles picked them up as planned. Delia stayed behind." She had to stop to wipe her nose and then continued "Charles got a call at 2am that there was a fire at the house. By the time he got back there was nothing left but ashes. He called me from the neighbor's phone and I drove right over around 6am. The girls were all there, Amy and Susie were screaming and Beth was hysterical. The whole house completely burned down. She couldn't get out. The neighbors tried to get her but they couldn't….. and the girls they would've been there if Charles hadn't gotten them. Thank God they weren't there! We would've lost them too!"

I couldn't believe my ears. How could this be? Delia had been a huge part of our lives for so long. She was Beth's second mother, Mom's best friend. Why did this have to happen?

Mom went on "Amy will be here in a couple hours. Charles is dropping her off. She's going to stay with us a while so Charles can handle matters. This is so unexpected there's so much to deal with."

"She's staying here?" I asked. "What about Susie?"

"She's going to stay with her dad at their aunts. She's too little. Beth and Amy wanted to stay together." She turned and went to the bathroom and turned on the shower.

I hadn't noticed until now that she had soot all over her clothes. She had been at the scene of the fire for hours with girls, consoling them and Charles, trying to ease their pain. She looked distraught.

Molly came walking out of her room crying.

"I heard. I can't believe it" she sobbed

She turned and ran to Beth's room.

Ben hugged me, "Are you ok?"

"I'm worried about Beth. I have to go to her," I said.

I went to Beth's room to find her sobbing into her pillow. Molly was rubbing her head.

"What am I going to do?" she kept saying.

"Beth we love you. We will get you through this," I tried to comfort her.

"No, No, no, no. You guys don't understand she loved me and now she's gone. She's gone." Beth was inconsolable.

We sat there with her in her room of Barbie dolls and childhood memories until Amy arrived. The two of them shut themselves in that room for 2 days, coming out only to use the bathroom. A love had formed through the years between them, and now strengthened through this tragedy that affected these two girls like no one else. When they came out they were older and wiser than they were when they went in. They had a new life, with new fears and challenges. They were not our "little girls" anymore. They were young women. They had suffered a massive loss that could never be replaced. They were fearless, now.

We got somberly through the next few months. We tiptoed around Beth and Amy, trying to be sensitive, but not too sensitive; caring but not intrusive. Things slowly started to return to normal, but Beth's normal was never the same. She suddenly was home more. She went on the big old box computer we had and instant messaged people all night when she couldn't sleep. Her insomnia had gotten worse. We figured it was part of the grief she felt.

The school year started to wind down. I had quit playing softball, a heart breaking decision. Prom season had come and gone and I didn't go. I wanted to, but was told I'd have to pay for that expense myself since it wasn't "necessary". I didn't want to part with my hard earned money that it had taken me months and months of sacrificing my weekends to save up. I decided if that was the way it was to be, then I needed to increase my earnings so that the next milestone that rolled around, I'd be able to attend. I still wasn't over missing out on Bournedale years before and I was angry that after working and keeping my grades up and staying out of trouble, I still would have to miss out on prom. So, I decided I had no more time for childish things like playing ball. I had already played varsity my sophomore year anyways. That goal had been achieved. I needed more time for working, a terrible decision for a 16 year old to have to make. I remember dreading telling my dad that I wasn't going to play anymore. I finally told him at the Club one afternoon.

"This is a mistake" he said sitting at his desk, shaking his head. "You're going to regret this for the rest of your life."

He didn't talk to me or look at me for 2 days after that. I let him down. It wasn't just quitting playing ball; it was that I gave up on a piece of freedom and childhood that he was trying to preserve for me. I let it go and he was holding on so tightly. He was right, too, in a way. I don't regret the decision I made, because I didn't see any other way. It's more that I resent having to make it. It wasn't fair. Life's not fair.

I helped my girlfriends get ready for prom. Julia and I went shopping for makeup and shoes. Her dress was beautiful. One Friday I walked in the front door at home and saw Beth holding a baby pink gown up to herself in the bathroom mirror. She was all tan and her hair was done up gorgeous.

"What are you doing?" I asked her.

"I'm going to prom" she said cautiously. "Are you mad?"

"You're going to my prom? No I'm not mad I'm just confused…" I started to say.

"No, no, not your prom. I'm going to the Duxbury prom with this boy I've been seeing. He asked me to go and I'm so excited. Do you like my dress?" she asked.

"How…?" I started to ask but then I stopped.

I could see the excitement in her eyes. I knew she must've lied about her age, but I didn't want to call her out on it. She looked happier than I'd seen her in a long time. She loved to dress up and tonight she got to play princess. I wasn't going to take that away from her.

"I love your dress. I can't wait to see it on you. Can I help you get ready? I have about an hour before work. I'll put on some tunes and get this party started."

I went to the stereo system we had all gotten as a shared Christmas gifts and fought back the lump in my throat. I was so happy for her. I told myself to stop being pitiful and put on a smile for her and that's what I did. I put on some Tom Petty and we got her all fancied up to 'Last Dance with Maryjane'.

Ben came in to pick me up for work. Sometimes I liked when he picked me up in one of his parents fancy cars. It made me feel hopeful for a solid future. We were young after all, everyone does dumb things now and then when they are young.

"You sure you don't want to go tonight?" he asked.

"Yeah I'm totally sure it's fine. I'll see everyone after if they come in for food anyways. Maybe we'll go to an after party or something."

I walked out with him knowing what I had just said was a lie. I did want to go, but definitely not with him. I also knew I wouldn't go to a single after party with him. He'd ruin it for everyone. He fought with people more and more, and although I had never physically caught him, I was pretty sure he stole from people too. Everywhere we went people would end up missing something. A watch would be missing, or a $20 bill. It was too much of a coincidence to ignore. No one was missing things when he wasn't around. Even I had started to miss things. Gift certificates I had gotten for Christmas were just suddenly gone, or my huge jar of change that I had been saving from my tip money. Little things like that which wouldn't be noticed right away and I'd have no way of tracking. It didn't make sense because it's not like he needed the money. It made me start to think that he had something to hide. I wondered how many secrets he kept from me. I had no one to ask for advice, he had no real close friends and I could never talk to his mother about these things. If I told my sisters how angry he could get they would hate him, and then there would be no turning back. I wasn't ready for anything that permanent. I just tried to stay focused and concentrate on the positive things about him. He was very handsome and could be really thoughtful and sweet when he wanted to. He was a hard worker and had a good education. Maybe he'd go back to college. Maybe his temper would even out as we got older. Still, there was just something off.

As I drove to work I saw the limos in front of people's houses and kids posing for pictures for their parent's on their front porches. I desperately wanted to be a part of it. It just wasn't part of the plan for me. I justified it all in my head- think of all the trouble I'll not get into and I'll have my own money for my car repairs when they come up. Maybe I'd even get a new car. I pulled in to work, put on my apron, and a smile, and started my shift. I still liked to be independent. I would never be dependent on a man; my gut told me that, and I listened.

My birthday rolled around at the end of my junior year and Ben took me out to dinner. I was quiet most of the time. I really had nothing to talk about.

"So, I have two things I wanted to discuss" he said.

"Ok" I said.

"First of all, I got us our very own apartment" he said.

"I'm not moving out of my parent's house" I remarked immediately "I told you before I'm going to college. Besides, I'd never really leave my sisters just yet."

I could see where this was going. End up depending on him for every need I had and with his mother watching over how I raised our children and critiquing my every move? No thanks! I wasn't falling into this trap.

"I knew you'd say that, so I have the perfect plan. You don't have to officially move out of home just yet, but....." he said.

He got up from his chair and got down on one knee and asked me to marry him. I had to swallow the vomit that was rising in my chest. He even had a ring. I felt for a minute that I might pass out. I took a couple deep breathes and stared over the box at the ring. It was actually beautiful.

"Where'd you get that ring?" I asked suspiciously.

"You're mother. It was your grandmother's. I had the setting redone" he said.

'Oh my God' was all I could think. My mother already knew of this? But I had so many plans, secret plans but still plans. I could see that he was certain I'd say yes and he did put a lot of planning and effort into the evening. I decided to say yes to keep the peace for the moment. Besides, I would do anything to avoid a car ride home during one of his fits of rage. I'd barely made it out of the car with him alive more times than I cared to count. We'd even been pulled over a few times for his unlawful driving, but every time he got into trouble his parents got him out. Then there was our living situation. What would happen if I said no? He had a key to my parent's house and almost everything I owned was at the garage. I was so immature, all of that stuff is replaceable-safety is priceless.

I went home that night and couldn't sleep. I tossed and turned for hours reliving the night in my head. When I finally fell asleep, I dreamt I was walking along a road on a clear summer night with a bag over my shoulder. I could hear the peepers chirping loudly as they did when I was little over the little pond out back. In the distance was a train. I started to jog to catch up to it, and when I finally did I jumped into one of the carts. I threw my bag down into a pile of hay and fell asleep. I awoke with the sunrise as we approached a farm area. I threw my bag out and jumped. I walked up to an old barn as if I'd been there a thousand times. It looked like the one from Little House on the Prairie, a show my sisters and I spent countless mornings watching together as little children. The simple innocence of that show resonated in my dream and I felt a sort of peaceful contentment that I had been longing for so long in my young life. I walked into the barn and washed my face in a cool bucket of water and started brushing a beautiful yellow horse. I turned to the sound of feathers ruffling, and saw a beautiful red hawk sitting just above us on the rafter. The horse suddenly reared up on its back legs, neighing loudly. It landed and looked me right in the eye, huffing aggressively. I woke up with a startle.

I sat up straight in bed and looked around. It was the kind of dream that you leaves you deep in thought. I lay back down and started to cry quietly, being careful not to wake anyone. I tried to calm down, but all I could feel was the ring from my birthday dinner proposal. It wasn't a large ring, but it felt like a thousand pounds crushing my finger. I started praying to myself and felt the tension inside diminishing. As I lay there in the silence I suddenly was very aware of the keyboard tapping coming from Beth's room. I got up and walked in to see her.

"Beth? Its 4:00 in the morning. Who could you possibly be talking to?" I whispered.

She closed out of her screen before I could see what she was doing.

"Hey" she said. "I'm happy to see someone else is awake. What are you doing up? I usually have the house to myself at this hour."

"Don't you ever get tired?" I asked her as I looked through her impressive closet of designer clothes.

She came over and shut the doors.

"Jenny can I tell you something?" she asked sitting on the bed. She looked sad.

"Of course Boo Bear you can tell me anything, you know that." I answered as I rubbed her head.

"I'm so tired. I never sleep. I always have this sense of unrest and I don't know why. I'm just so, so, tired" she started to weep.

I didn't know what to say. I knew the last year had been really hard for her, but I hadn't paid her enough attention for it. She was obviously still hurting so much. She was so delicate.

"I've been writing a lot" she picked up a notebook and handed it to me. "It seems to help with the pain."

"What's the pain, Beth? Can you tell me?" I asked

She shook her head no "Each time I try it comes out wrong or something gets in the way...."

"What do you mean 'in the way'?" I started to ask.

"Never mind," she said, "it is so late now. Maybe I can rest a couple hours at least. Want to sleep in my bed tonight?"

She pulled down the covers and stared at me. I could see the circles under her eyes and she looked thin.

"I'd love to sleep with you," I said as I climbed in her bed.

She went over to the TV and turned on her usual Nick at Night. I Love Lucy was playing, it was the episode where Lucy and Ethel had to stomp the grapes to make wine.

"Oh yes I love this one" she said excitedly.

She climbed into bed and I felt I was right where I needed to be at that very moment. Snuggling my baby sister, laughing with her as only sisters can at our little inside jokes that came with commercial breaks and morning breath.

I decided I needed to have more faith and just hold on for the ride. 'God helps those who help themselves' I could hear my mother's saying in my head. Everything happened for a reason, after all, and everything was going to be o.k. As long as I did what I needed to do for myself and my family, God would watch over us. I fell asleep with the comfort from this in my heart. Most times though, God's ways are not our ways. Sometimes we have to walk through the forest to find the meadow.

Senior year was uneventful. Ben moved into his own place off of his parent's property, which I was incredibly grateful for, although I tried not to show it. We had started getting along better. He seemed to feel proud at having his own place for a time and that gave him a sense of independence I suppose. I worked, went to school. Beth and I started writing a lot together and we both found it very therapeutic. She still stayed up late, too late, but was starting to show signs of her old self more and more. Molly got her license and, true to form, backed her car into a dumpster the first week she had it. Dad was beside himself.

"How do you miss an entire dumpster? You obviously weren't looking where you were going!" he exclaimed.

"Dad it was an accident. What do you care? It's my car you don't have to drive it," she wisely replied.

Molly had become quit the tough little nut to crack. She was often unforgiving and abrasive with her words. She would do the very opposite of what you told her just to get a rise. But in the moment when you really needed someone, or something, she was old reliable. She always pulled through in a pinch, and she'd make sure you knew how lucky you were to have her services. She had grown up beautiful. She was the darkest of us all, very Portuguese looking but tall. Her trademark long Rogers hair was dark and shiny and she had a glimmer of mischief that twinkled in her eye. She would try anything once, or twice, or even three times to make sure she really knew how she felt about it.

Dad sighed "I just wanted you to have a nice car and it was the best I could do. Now it's all banged up."

It was an old silver Buick, a boat. It was nice though, clean, low miles and good brakes. Until now the body and interior were in perfect condition. He had put a lot of time into finding this one.

"Dad, it's fine. I'll fix it don't worry," she said and walked down to her room.

I rolled my eyes as I remembered all the things she still promised to pay me back for. I looked over at Dad. He was shaking his head. He looked tired too. The years of chasing after all of us girls were exhausting.

We had also learned that Danny had been in and out of jail and drug rehabs over the years. I knew this bothered Dad more than he let on. He, like Beth, was often up late at night watching TV all alone. When I waitressed a closing shift I tried to bring him home a late night snack to offer some comfort from whatever was bothering him. There was so much unrest in that little house. The air was thick and almost suffocating some nights. There was a strong undercurrent, pulling us into discord that none of us could see, but we all could feel.

I was terrified of ending up like Danny. No family, no home to go to when I needed rest from the world. This fear is what saved me from myself. Most kids I went to school with were starting to use Oxycontins, Percocet and Cocaine on a regular basis. It was rampant in town. I never asked which of my friends did it or didn't. I didn't want to know. All I knew was that I wasn't going to take a chance on any of that junk. I figured out that Ben had been doing cocaine, though. He promised me he stopped, but now that he was really out on his own I had a strong suspicion he was doing it behind my back. His mood swings became worse than ever. I tried to keep peace and just wanted to get through my senior year. Maybe then I could go off to college. One thing I knew, drugs were not for me. I didn't mind pot, but that was it. No speed or anything up my nose. I just didn't see the appeal. It wasn't worth the risk. Whenever I would ask Ben about his habits, he would start a fight with me about something else. I didn't know much about manipulation back then.

When Molly's birthday rolled around we went for our yearly trip to Aunty's to celebrate. Ben came along. Beth and I were in the dining room most of the afternoon visiting with Mom and Jamie and Grandma.

Molly kept getting up to go to the bathroom and we just figured she had an upset stomach. Ben was watching TV and dozing in and out on the couch. Beth and I helped clear the dishes and cleaned up and were ready to start packing up to leave. I saw Ben coming in from being out on the porch with Molly. He had a stupid grin on his face and I knew he was up to something. I grabbed my coat and went outside. Molly was sitting outside a big smile on her face wide eyed and holding a poinsettia leaf in her hand.

Ben came out on to the porch

"What's with you" I asked Molly but got no answer, just giggles. "Hello?"

"She's rolling," Ben said.

"Rolling what?" I asked annoyed.

"On ecstasy. She's high. It'll wear off," he said and turned and walked away.

I was livid.

"Molly snap out of it," I said lightly slapping her face.

Molly couldn't even tolerate milk! If there was a germ within 10 miles she caught it, every time. I knew this would end badly. I pushed her along and packed her into the back of Mom's minivan hoping her strange behavior would go unnoticed and maybe she would sleep it off. We packed up everything else and left.

"What do you know about this?" I snapped at Ben in the car.

"Nothing," he answered slyly, "your sisters a big girl she makes her own choices."

I wanted to punch him in the face.

Sure enough a couple hours after we got home Molly was throwing up and had a fever. Mom was concerned and wanted to take her to the hospital.

"She hasn't looked right all day," Mom said.

"I think she'll be ok" I said trying to avoid Molly getting found out in the hospital and shaming my parents.

"No, I better take her in something may be wrong," Mom said gathering her purse and health cards.

"Mom I really thing you shouldn't" I said sternly.

"Jenny cut the crap, ok? If you know something you better just say it. I'm too tired to deal with this right now," Mom said.

"If I tell you, you promise you won't rat me out and say where you heard it?" I questioned.

"You better tell me what the heck you are talking about," Mom said.

I told her. I didn't know what else to do. If Molly went to the ER and they found out she was on drugs, which I had a pretty good feeling they were going to do, I didn't know what would happen then. She looked better to me now, the vomiting had slowed and her temp had broken from the Tylenol. She needed to stay home and sleep it off.

Mom stared at me blindly for a minute after I told her Molly was high on ecstasy, not sick.

"Mom," I said, "you can't tell her I told you."

She turned around and marched right into Molly's room.

"Serves you right" I could hear her saying.

I ran down to Molly's room to get Mom out but I was too late. As I entered I could hear her saying "Your sister told me."

From then on I was not to be trusted. Molly and Beth kept anything they didn't want Mom and Dad to know from me, and that was a lot. It took a long time to earn trust back, rightfully so I suppose. I tried to explain to Molly that I was only trying to save her from a possible DSS interview or another hospitalization, especially for psych if they suspected she was on drugs, but there was no reasoning with her. I had betrayed her in her eyes.

I stayed away a little more than usual for a few months. I went to Julia's whenever I could escape Ben's control. I figured every so often he'd need a fix and would gladly take space from me so he could get it. Julia and I were looking forward to graduation and had big plans for the summer. We talked of driving cross country and living the gypsy life.

One night Julia and I were at my house for dinner. Dad was making chicken, ziti and broccoli, Julia's favorite. Mom announced that she had some exciting news.

"I sold a big house" she said excitedly. "My commission is going to be great and that's on top of an already really good year."

The real estate market had been fruitful for Mom. She was almost over not finishing nursing school. She still did hair on the side, but her main income was now from selling houses. It was a good job for her. She had the freedom to make her own hours and got to dress up nice. It was much nicer than working in a hot smelly nursing home for lousy pay. The changes were positive and visible.

"So Dad and I decided that we are all due for a nice vacation to Florida!" she announced proudly. "We leave the first Saturday of April vacation and Julia, you're coming too. I've already worked it out with your parents!"

We were ecstatic. Beth had been to Florida a few times with Amy and her family, but none of the rest of us had even ever been on a plane! This was very exciting news.

We wished the days away until finally the day of departure was here. We woke up early and headed to the airport. I was thrilled to have a whole week off from school, work and Ben. I had a whole week to myself with my family and my best friend in the happiest place on earth. What else could I want?

Molly still was giving me a bit of the cold shoulder. When we finally arrived to our beautiful villa in Florida, Julia had a little chat with Molly.

"What's it going to take for you to trust her again?" Julia asked frustrated that this had gone on so long

"I don't know. She needs to do something to prove she's trustworthy far as I'm concerned," Molly replied.

"Don't you think you're being a bit ridiculous? She did save you from getting into trouble and your Mom was already on to you" Julia pleaded my case.

"Well, we will just see" Molly said "I'm almost over it anyways"

That night we went out to dinner and made our plans for the following day with the family. After dinner Molly Julia and I went out to "explore" the grounds. Beth stayed behind to go to a late show at the theatre with Mom and Dad.

"You have 3 rules tonight" Dad explained "1. Don't leave the grounds of the hotel 2. Don't get in anyone's cars! 3. Don't take any alcohol"

"Dad, ok, what do you think we are?" Molly joked as she followed us out the door

We walked to the end of the drive and noted all the pools, the gym area, the restaurants and made our way to the highest point in the path to where we could see the strip below that ran through Orlando. We climbed on top of the stone wall and looked below.

"I see a couple liquor stores, a tattoo parlor," I said.

"A couple outlet stores, a video store," Julia added.

"Let's head back soon I'm getting thirsty," Molly said.

Julia and I hoped down and we started walking back to our building. Just then, a white Infinity pulled up alongside us. There were 2 men inside.

"Hey ladies what are you up to tonight?" the driver asked.

"Just out for a walk" Julia replied. "What are you guys doing? You live down here or just visiting?"

"We work here," the man said from the back seat.

"Are you lost?" asked the driver

"Do we look lost? We are just looking for some alcohol. The restaurant is closed and we haven't rented a car yet," Julia said.

'Oh no,' I thought to myself, 'don't do it Julia please'. But, of course she did.

"Can you guys run to the store for us? Do you mind helping out some of your guests?" Julia asked

The driver replied "How old are you girls?"

"How old do we look?" Julia laughed. "Honestly we are both 21 and she's 20"

Julia pointed Molly out as being 20.

"No biggie, I'll go to the store for you guys but you have to come for the ride," the driver said.

"Kind of risky there, we don't even know you guys for 5 minutes," I interrupted.

'Go home. Go home now!' The little voice inside my head was screaming. Why do we never listen to that voice when we are teenagers?

"Look here's our work ID's," they both handed us there photo work card.

"I'm sitting in the front, and you have to give me something of yours to hold, like a watch or a necklace" I said

"Why?" the driver asked smiling.

"Cause if you try any tricky stuff with us I'm going to grab the wheel and crash your pretty car. I need something of yours to hold cause I'm going to keep it for collateral in the hopes that there might be a hair fiber or something on it that's going to trace you back to the crime should you try to assault us," I said.

"Take my watch," he said as he threw the gold and diamond watch over the passenger seat to me.

It definitely wasn't bought on wages earned at that hotel.

"Thanks" I said putting it on. "Now open your glove compartment and show me there's no gun in there."

He laughed and did as I instructed. He patted himself down so I could see he had nothing concealed.

"I'm not trying to hurt you girls, I'm just out tonight with nothing to do," he said smiling.

"Ok," I said, "I think it's safe enough."

I climbed in the front and Molly and Julia got in the back. I was terrified the whole ride to and from the liquor store. We got small bottles each so we wouldn't ever leave our drinks unattended and we were careful to note landmarks on our way to the store to make sure we were being brought back to our resort. Miraculously, everything went smoothly and we returned to our resort unharmed. We hung with those guys all night in one of the outdoor gazebos, finally admitting that we weren't the ages we attested to being when we met.

"How old are you really?" the driver, Leonardo, asked in a very concerned tone.

"We are 18 and she," I said pointing to Molly, "is 17."

I lied again. Julia and I were still short of 18 and Molly was only 16.

"I think you should have to do something to make that up to me, you know to prove we are good friends now" Leonardo said.

Instant panic ran through me. I immediately thought the worst.

"What are you thinking" Julia said

"There's a tattoo/piercing shop down the street that stays open all night. One of you should get something to commemorate our night together. You know something to remember us by," he said laughing.

I already had an eyebrow piercing I had gotten when Julia got her tongue pierced on her neighbors couch, we both had tattoos from a tattoo party in sophomore year and Molly had a nose ring. I really didn't want to go home with something that Ben was going to demand an explanation for, the thought of that alone sent shivers down my back.

"I'll do it," Molly said from around the corner where she was relieving herself in a bush. "That is, if no one tells on me."

She walked by me with a sly look on her face.

"What are you going to get?" Julia asked.

"I'll get a tattoo. I've been wanting one anyways and the legal age is 16 down here so I'll be covered," Molly said gathering her things.

"You won't be able to swim the rest of vacation." I tried to talk her out of it.

"Jenny we live on a pond I can swim anytime," she said. "But, I'm sure this is going to cost money so who's going to pay for this?"

Leave it to Molly to get exactly what she wants for free.

"I'll pay up to $100," Leonardo said. "You guys were fun tonight and we didn't even have to buy you dinner."

"See? Perfect! A free tattoo what could be better?" Molly said. She couldn't have planned it any better herself.

"You know what you're going to get?" Julia asked.

"I'll get the man on the moon on my back" she said pointing to the moon.

All night we had been remarking about how we actually could finally see the man in the moon that night. I couldn't find a good enough excuse to talk her out of it. We had already left the park once with these guys, we felt pretty safe with them and we were going to a legit parlor. Besides, I could see she was testing me.

"Let's go then. It getting super late" I said.

The rest of the night went off without a hitch. Molly's tattoo came out nicely and we stopped at the video store on the way home and rented movies. We stayed up all night watching Casino and The First Wives Club. Beth joined us for movies and snacks when we got back.

"I can't believe I'm the only one without a tattoo now," Beth said peeking under the bandage on Molly's back.

"When you're older we can take you if you still want one," I reassured her.

"No way, I'm terrified of needles," Beth said.

"Don't let Mom and Dad know," Molly said. "Jenny and Julia already promised not to tell."

I walked into our room we were sharing and found my engagement ring in my top drawer. I had taken it off before we went out. I hated wearing it. I decided to leave it there the rest of the trip. I also decided that when we all got home, I was going to call off the engagement. He'd get over it. I was enjoying my freedom too much. I wasn't ready to give it up. I went back into the living room and spent the rest of the week laughing and dreaming under the hot Florida sun with those I loved most.

When we returned, I did call off the engagement. I did it over the phone out of fear of his wrath. He had started throwing things and breaking things when he was angry when I told him, he didn't take it well and of course told me how awful I was and how I'd regret this. I didn't agree.

"I just think I'm too young and I'll only resent you if we go through with this. I'm still in high school!" I argued.

"What do you know? You're such an idiot. You were probably out whoring around down in Florida, too. Don't come crying to me when you need something you stupid ugly whore" he screamed before hanging up the phone.

This had become more and more usual. I wondered if his father treated his mother this way. The more I'd try to distance myself the more he'd creep me out. If I went somewhere he'd show up there, or he'd spread awful rumors about me. I used to argue back, but I'd learned that just letting spout off all his anger and keeping quiet reserved my own energy and sanity much better. I planned on ending it for good with him soon enough. I just wanted to get a couple things secured first so I could make a safe move with him interfering too much. He'd already told me that if I tried to break up with him, he'd call the school and have them review all my attendance records. I had missed a lot of school, but my grades were great. All my work was always done and my teachers liked me. They let me slip through the attendance cracks. I think they knew my circumstances outside of school were less than optimal. They would often ask me why I wasn't at prom or homecoming or going on the class trips. I usually saw them after big events when I was waiting on them at work. They always treated me kindly and offered an ear if needed. I would kindly thank them and move along to the next table. Polite enough to ward off just enough suspicion, a little smile goes a long way I had learned.

Ben had shown up at my work a couple of times and started making a scene when I didn't get out on time and he was waiting in the parking lot. He came in yelling about how his fiancé must be having an affair with the cook. Soon as he started I'd slip into the storage cellar and act as though I was just stocking. I pretended I didn't hear him. I pretended a lot.

The cook or manager would eventually get him to leave. I'd reemerge with a smile, as if I knew nothing of what was happening, and no one made me feel bad about it.

One night as we were closing up the cook asked, "Why don't you just leave him?"

It was an excellent question. I did care about him, for a time I thought I loved him. Another part of me felt as though to walk away would be to admit it was something I couldn't fix, part of me was afraid of what he would do if I did leave-report me to school, rob my parents, hurt me, and still another part of me wanted desperately for him to just go away and leave me alone.

"It's better now than it was," I answered the cook, "and besides I am going off to college soon hopefully."

"Well I think he's an ass. I just hope you know you can do better," he said sincerely at the end of our night.

The cook was a nice kid. I think he actually had gone to school with Ben when they were younger.

"Ok thanks," I said and I headed to the car.

I drove to Julia's house most night after work now. I didn't want to go home in case he showed up there and I didn't want to go to his apartment and spend the night arguing with him. I needed to be left in peace and that was the only place I would get it.

Graduation came and went smoothly. One more thing was checked off the list. I was officially 18 and a high school grad. I had officially made it past the ages of my Mom and sister when they had their first babies. I was going to be alright.

There was an Applebee's being built in the lot off the highway. This would be a huge money maker for Plymouth as there were no other chain restaurants around besides Friendly's, and Friendly's didn't serve alcohol. I went for an interview and immediately got the job. We were scheduled to open in September and training would be held in August.

I had also applied to a community college and was accepted. I decided I needed my Associates Degree before taking on too much with student loans at a big school and really didn't want to leave my sisters. There would be plenty of time for that, I had told myself, and with the money I saved going to a smaller school I would hopefully be able to buy a newer car soon and maybe take a nice trip.

When I started my training Molly took my old job over as a camp counselor with my dad at the Club. I was going to miss that job and those kids, but it was the perfect job for Molly. She was great with the kids. We didn't see much of Beth that summer. She had been spending even more time with Amy and had gotten a job at a little boutique store in the mall.

One random afternoon she came walking through the front door of Mom and Dad's as I was peeling potatoes for dinner that night.

"Hey" I said running to her for hug.

She smelled like coconuts and pineapples.

"Where you been? You look so dark!" I exclaimed examining her bronzed skin.

"I just got back from the Dominican," she said pouring a glass of water.

"The Dominican? With who?" I asked

"Me and Amy went with Charles and Susie on business" she said. "It was gorgeous, but I'm so tired. I got to go lay down I have to work tonight at 7."

She gave me a big hug and a kiss on the cheek "I miss you. I got you a coconut."

She reached in her oversized pocket book and pulled out a plastic furry coconut.

"It opens into a cup." She took it apart and showed me grinning proudly.

"Cool. I love it thanks," I said taking the cup.

"I got Molly and J.P. one too," she said. "I figured we could take some cute pictures with them in the pond or at Jamie's pool."

"Ok" I said.

"I got to lay down I'm so tired. Wake me up by 6." She headed down to her room and closed the door.

She was getting more and more mysterious. I didn't even know she had a passport. She suddenly had albums full of pictures of fabulous places she'd been and people she'd met. She loved people. She was a people person. She was magnetic and charming and beautiful. She had a smile bright enough to excite you and dark dreamy eyes. She was a beautiful creature with a beautiful soul. Her writing was just as beautiful as she was. She was deep. Deep and lovely like the ocean, her moods changing like the tides.

I didn't like to ask too many questions. I didn't want to seem distrusting or nosey. I did have questions though; like, how did she pay for all those trips? Did Charles pay? Did Mom and Dad know that she was going on all these trips? How did she manage to keep her job and grades and live this lifestyle? Did she sleep? Most of all I wondered if she knew how much I missed her and how much I loved her.

The summer rolled on as usual. The sun rising and setting over the pond, watching us as we were becoming little women and the family was evolving. It watching Mom go out to show her houses each day then come home to cool off in the pond before heading into the garden to work in to the dusky evenings. It watched Dad coming home each afternoon, usually with a fresh piece to the dinner he was about to prepare in a paper bag from the store. It watched us all come and go in and out of the driveway as we quarreled, played and rushed around. It shined on the garden and gave life to Mom's work. The garden was huge now and bloomed from the start of April to the end of fall. It was Mom's trophy, proof of her dedication to this home she had bought so many years ago with Dad and little ones, Beth still in her belly, Jamie and Danny running wild. It was a piece of the family legacy, her footprint on her land.

When training started at Applebee's I couldn't have been happier. I was about to be more financially independent than ever. Independence to me was freedom, and I desperately needed freedom. I wanted so badly to make my own mark on the world. I was nervous at first but learned that I was good at sales. This was going to work out well. I was proud of myself for stepping out of my comfort zone and learning something new all on my own.

After our first week of training was complete, some of the girls had a drink out back behind the kitchen to toast the opening and new friends. They let me sip off their Bahama Mamas and margaritas. I liked these girls. They were smart and mostly my age in college, too. They invited me to go out with them but I couldn't. Ben had insisted on driving me in, so I had to wait for him to pick me up. I wasn't old enough to get served in a bar anyway.

I went out front to wait for Ben. As soon as I got in his car, my excitement diminished. I could smell the alcohol on him from the passenger seat.

"What? No kiss hello?" he slurred as soon as I got in.

I kissed him hello. His lips were hot. I could tell when he had been drinking because his skin always felt hot when he drank. He became moody and easily irritated. I didn't even know why he drank, it just ruined everything now. I sighed and said goodbye to my happy mood after a good week. I again wished I was out being a carefree girl. I deserved a nice Friday night after a long week of work and school, I thought. I knew to keep these thoughts to myself. Ben would just turn it around on me saying I was a snob or selfish for wanting such things. I had started to truly try to plan a break up with him, but I didn't know how to do it. It sounds silly now, but at the time I was a naïve 18 yr. old kid, and all I had been with him for 3 years. I felt oddly indebted to him, like I owed it to him to stay with him until he got himself squared away. I worried about him, who else would go to his therapy with him or make sure he didn't have too much to drink? Who would be there to comfort him when he fought, so awfully, with his dad? These shouldn't have been my concerns at this age, but they were. I don't know how or when it became like this, but it did, and I hated it. He had set some goals and was making small strides in achieving them. He wanted to work in carpentry and become a contractor or maybe buy a small café on top of running the family business someday. He had dreams, he was a person too, and deserved someone to invest some time and love in him. I felt this was my duty for some reason. It seemed like he was always living in his older brother's shadow at his own house. He was like second choice and everyone there knew it, including him. It gave him pain. He had been loyal to me up to this point, far as I knew. He had taught me how to waitress, helped me quit smoking, went to church with me. He wasn't all bad, but I didn't want *any* bad. I just wanted to worry about myself. When he was 'bad' though, he had become very bad. He would yell at me, name call, throw things and lose control. I would tell him he needed to get control of himself-that if he didn't he would end up his own worst enemy, or worse, like his father. He protested the idea of self-implosion, said he was determined to be a great husband and father someday. He said he wanted to do everything his parents didn't. Sometimes I believed he would, but mostly I had doubts. There was something off about him and my deep down gut told me to get out. I did care for him though, I loved him, but I wasn't in love with him. There's a difference.

I was having anxiety in the car. What if we got pulled over? What if he got arrested for DUI? What did he have on him? Pot? Would I get arrested too? I just wanted to get out of the car and be home, then, I could breathe easy.

"You smell like alcohol," he sneered. "I thought you were training not boozing it up."

"Nice attitude Ben," I replied. "I had a couple sips of one of the girl's drinks after work. Is that ok with you?"

"Don't be such a tramp! I didn't have to come get you. I could've left you there," he replied.

Great, I thought to myself, this night is going to suck.

"Ben, let's just go home and have some dinner," I suggested trying to keep the peace.

"You make me sick you're going to make friends with girls who give you booze now? They know you're underage? I don't know what's wrong with you. You just keep screwing up!" He was getting louder and louder and hardly looking at the road.

"OK, Ben you drink with me all the time so what's your point? Besides I'm not even buzzed you on the other hand are clearly in no condition to be driving so why don't you just pull over?" I suggested.

"You little bitch! I'm not pulling over for you. I don't need you to save me. Go screw yourself!" He was screaming at me now.

'Please God just get me home safely' I prayed to myself. Luckily, Ben's studio apartment was close by and we made it back safely. Every time we made it home safely, I was grateful. This, too, was becoming a usual occurrence.

Ben's apartment was small, cute and simple. It was centrally located which was great in the summer especially. It was an old Victorian house that had been turned into a bunch of small apartments. It smelled like a mixture of moth balls and chicken broth when you opened the front hall door. It was homey and affordable. It gave us some freedom to come and go and not have anyone questioning us. It also gave him freedom to drink and party without anyone else interfering.

I hurried up the gravel drive, hoping to get inside quick enough to escape a scene in the driveway for the neighbors to see. Ben followed behind, taunting me and antagonizing. I went inside and shut the door behind him.

"Enough! I get it! I suck! Just stop!" I finally started to argue back.

He grabbed me by both arms before I could finish. He squeezed and pulled my face close to his.

"Don't you talk to me like that you wretched witch!" He was spitting when he talked and his eyes were bulging. He was walking in circles and pulling me with him. "You think you're going to leave me behind? You think I need this crap?"

I had no idea what he was talking about, as usual. He threw me on the bed and turned away. He took off his shirt and threw it at me.

"Go take a shower you smell like booze and grease from that sleazy restaurant," he said.

I got up to go to the bathroom.

"Hurry up, too. I need to get in," he called after me.

In the shower I wanted to cry, but I couldn't. I was running out of tears. What was happening? How had this become my life? I looked at my arms where he had grabbed me. They were red but I didn't see a bruise. I walked out of the bathroom to find Ben sitting at his kitchen table smoking a joint by the window.

"Hey," he said.

I just kept walking to the couch. I made up a little bed. There was no way I was sleeping with him tonight.

"I'm sorry. I never meant to put my hands on you. It will never happen again. I promise. Please, you've got to believe me." He was pleading with me.

"You need to stop drinking," I told him.

"I just got too angry. I can control myself. Just don't make me so mad, help me" he answered. "I need you."

"I have needs too, Ben. I need to feel safe, and lately I don't feel safe with you." I was walking a dangerous line with these words and I knew it.

"I'm sorry. Please forgive me, please."

The begging was so pathetic.

"Just go to bed," I said.

I lay on the couch and turned my back to him. I closed my eyes and pretended to sleep again, but I didn't sleep. I laid there awake listening to him as he thought I was sleeping. He poured himself more alcohol and talked to himself as he looked through old pictures. He opened the door and left around 5a.m.. I had no idea where he was going. I knew he didn't have to work. I finally fell asleep while he was gone. I awoke around 8:30 and he still hadn't returned. I quickly got dressed and left. I knew my dad would be at the Club. I walked down there and hung out with him. I had to get away while I could.

A few weeks later the restaurant was up and running. I was at the drink station with my new friends Khloe telling her what had happened. I liked Khloe from the moment I met her. She felt like home. She was like me and my sisters, down to earth, deep, and real. She was like family, only better because I had her all to myself. She listened without judgement. She never made me feel bad, or stupid. She knew how complicated things could be. She had a little boy of her own that she was trying to navigate through life with. I liked hearing her stories about her and little Corey. I liked how her face lit up when she talked about him. She was a great mom and I held her in the highest respect for that.

"You know, he is a little crazy." She smiled pouring her Shirley Temples.

"That's what my sisters say, too. It's like sometimes he's totally normal and then other times he's a whole different person. It's so confusing, makes my head spin," I said.

"You're going to have to eventually break up with him. I know you already know this. It's going to get harder the longer you wait," she said.

"That's what I'm afraid of. It just seems like every time I'm ready to do it, he does something that makes me change my mind. Plus, I can't move back to my parent's full time. It's not peaceful their either and I'd feel like I took a step backwards if I moved back home. Does that make sense? It's like I need a positive to balance out the negative. I need to keep moving forward in life. Sounds crazy right?"

"You don't sound crazy. You just sound like you know what you need in life. Besides, there's no rush" she loaded up her tray.

"I guess, hopefully I can just get my own place soon or transfer to a better school, maybe live there. Hey, I'm thinking about nursing school, you should come with me. We can be study buddies!" I said.

"I don't think Corey would let me study enough for nursing school," she laughed. "Besides, nursing's definitely not my thing, but thanks. Ok I got to go, talk later," she smiled and walked around the corner with her tray and chip basket.

I loaded up my own tray and headed to the bar. Khloe was there too getting a smoothie for her table and flirting with the bar tender. She turned and winked at me before walking off with her order. I smiled at her and thought 'if I can be like her someday, that'll be enough for me.'

Jamie had another baby, also named Corey and I nannied for him twice a week while she and Jacob worked. We all adored Corey. He was just like J.P. as a baby. He even looked like him with blonde hair and big brown eyes. His chubby cheeks smiling at me became my favorite parts of every week. There hadn't been a baby in the family in so long and when he came we spoiled him. Jamie would leave me a car seat and when the weather was nice we would go on walks and to the park. Sometimes I would bring him to Mom and Dad's for a visit. He was such an easy baby. The days with him at Jamie's house were great. We had space to play and laugh. The furniture was soft and cozy. I loved to be hanging with him, nowhere else to be, no one else to please - just us. I wanted my life to be like this someday.

I had stayed for dinner one day after babysitting and Jamie and I were talking while she cooked. I was playing with Corey in his swing.

"Why don't you just start taking nursing classes?" she asked.

"I don't think I could do that. It looks really hard… and kind of gross" I said.

"If I can do it, you can do it," she said.

I hadn't thought of it that way before. That's when I had first considered the idea about becoming a nurse myself, but I doubted I could do it alone. After asking Khloe though, and she declining, I put it out of my head.

A couple days after my conversation with Khloe, I was taking Corey over to visit at my parents. It was a Saturday morning, not my usual day with Corey but Jamie had picked up an extra shift. I thought Molly and Beth would be psyched to get some time with him. I packed up his stroller and baby bag and headed home.

As I got out of the car to get Corey's carrier out, I could hear arguing coming from inside. I opened the front door to see Mom banging on the bathroom door.

"Molly, get out you've been in there 15 minutes! I've got to get ready for work!" she was yelling.

Each time she yelled, Molly just turned her music in the bathroom up louder.

"Hello," I was saying behind Mom, but she couldn't hear me.

I walked over to Beth who was sitting at the kitchen table and put Corey down beside her.

"Hi" I bent down to kiss her cheek. "I wasn't sure you'd be up."

"Like anyone can sleep here" she said.

She bent down to nestle Corey's face. "Hi, beautiful boy."

Mom walked over "It's time to get up anyways Beth. You can't just sleep all morning. Hi Jenny, nice to see you," she kissed my cheek. "You brought Corey, great!"

"Mom it's a Saturday, sleeping isn't really unusual for kids my age." Beth pressed putting her dish in the dishwasher.

"Molly get out!" Mom was back to banging on the door.

The phone rang and Beth answered "Hello?"

'Please done let it be Ben' I thought to myself.

"Yes she's here. Hang on" she handed me the phone.

"Hello?" I asked.

"Hi!" it was Khloe.

"Hey what's up?" I was so relieved it was her. "I was actually going to call you. I have Corey want to do a play date?"

I walked into the living room so I could hear her better.

"Yes. Definitely. Let's go for a ride to your school, too. I decided I want to do that nursing school thing with you if you're still considering it."

"No way!" I said

"Yeah, I decided I don't really want to be a waitress my whole life," she laughed.

"I'll be there in 20 minutes," I said.

"We'll be ready. See you in a few." She said and hung up.

Molly came out of the bathroom in her sweats with a towel on her head.

"Corey!" she exclaimed when she saw him.

"Molly Jeanette Marie. Get in here and clean up this mess," Mom was yelling from the bathroom.

I could see this day was going to be full of the regular bickering and petty arguments so I scooped up Corey in his carrier and headed on my way. I stopped by the fridge on my way out and grabbed my usual hard- boiled egg and an apple. Then I remembered I had wanted to cash in some change, quarters, I had been saving for months from work. There was a new pair of running sneakers I wanted and there should've been enough in the jar.

"Beth. Watch him for a sec? I asked putting Corey back down beside her.

I ran down to my room and looked on my shelf where I was certain I had left them. They weren't there. I looked all around, thinking maybe the cat had tipped the jar over. They were gone. There must've been $100 in there at least, I was certain of it.

This was starting to drive me crazy. I constantly was missing things. What started off as a CD here and there, a necklace, $20 was turning into much more substantial losses. I had $75 missing the prior week after my shift and a gold necklace was gone from my room. I had absolutely no way of proving who had taken anything. Ben came and went frequently, my sisters were here, and their friends were around. I didn't know who I could or couldn't trust. So I started to trust no one. It was the only option I could see that made sense. I couldn't accuse anyone without proof, that could backfire and it would be hurtful to them if I was wrong. I decided that until I could move out, I needed to buy a safe and lock up my valuables. Sometimes you can try and try with all your heart to change your situation, but things and people still get in the way and crowd your path to victory. You have to try harder, and choose carefully who you want around. One of Beth's favorite quotes seems so appropriate now when I look back:

'The truth is, everyone is going to hurt you.
You just have to find the ones worth suffering for'
-----Bob Marley

Frustrated and annoyed, I walked back out into the kitchen.

"Has anyone seen a giant jar full of quarters around?" I asked sarcastically.

"No, why?" Mom asked.

"Cause I can't find mine. Shocking I know," I quipped.

"I keep telling you to put your stuff in the bank," Mom said walking by with laundry.

"Haven't seen it Jenny, sorry," Beth said.

"I haven't seen but if I find it I'll put it aside for you, after I take a couple bucks that is" Molly joked.

"It's really not funny" I said. "It's actually really annoying that I can't leave stuff here."

"Hey we didn't take it!" Molly snapped. "Ask Ben, I'm sure he has an idea."

I left annoyed. Part of me knew Molly was probably right, but I couldn't directly ask Ben he'd flip. I'd just be more careful from now on. I really needed that safe.

I went over to Khloe's and we went to the school to register. We had to wait for the next fall to take pre-recs, and we had to pass a test to even apply for the nursing program.

"Ugh, I hate taking tests" she said carrying her Corey down the steps to the car.

"Me too, but I guess we better get used to it" I said putting Corey's car seat on the base.

"Want to grab a coffee before we head back?" Khloe asked.

"Sure, actually, do you have time to stop at the store? I need to buy a safe," I said.

"Why a safe?" Khloe asked intrigued.

"Someone in my house keeps stealing from me and I have no idea who it is," I said.

"Someone in your parent's house?" she asked.

"Yes," I answered.

"Jenny, that's so weird" she said. "That's not normal."

"I know, I know," I said

She rolled her eyes and I pulled in to the little parking lot.

"I'll be right out," I said shutting the door.

I returned a few minutes later with a very small safe. Khloe laughed when I put it in the backseat.

"What?" I asked

"I'm just not certain that someone wouldn't easily steal that whole thing. It's so small!" She burst out laughing.

"Shut up" I said punching her arm. "It's all I could afford after they stole all my quarters."

I was laughing now too, the whole thing was pretty ridiculous. I started the car and pulled out, still giggling under my breath.

"Someday" I sighed "Someday I'll be a nurse and have a big house with a security system and I'll live there all alone."

"Me too" Khloe said. "Sounds great. Count me in."

The next year and a half was kind of what I'd call a flat line between my sisters and me. There was a shift that occurred; I was out of high school and they were in their junior and senior years. They were concerned with school parties and Beth's student government trips. I was worried about building a future and staying awake for full time school days followed by double shifts at work.

I had moved out onto my own. First, I lived with Khloe in the house she rented from her dad with her and Corey. My first night away I cried all night, but it got easier and easier. Then, I lived with Julia and her boyfriend for a while. I was so happy that I at least got some of the 'college experience'. I got to be young and free; on my own with no one else's rules to follow, even if it was for a short time. It was a great time, the greatest, for me anyways.

It didn't take long before Ben had enough of my freedom run though. Before long, he couldn't take it. I think part of him expected me to fail. I think he figured I would go running back to him, needing him like I did when I was younger. Only, I didn't need him anymore. I liked being on my own and I was good at it. My bills were paid on time and my grades were good. I was making it happen for myself. He couldn't take that.

"You need to clean up your act" he said to me one night driving home from dinner.

"What?" I asked "where are you driving to? I need to get back I have a test tomorrow."

"You need to pay me some attention. I've been waiting for you all the time, helping you have time to study, putting you before me-your work, your career, your school. What about me!? Who the hell is looking out for me?" he was furious without warning.

"Ben what are you talking about? You work, you went to school, and you chose to quit. This is my life if you don't like it, you don't have to be a part of it." I was so tired of our nights ending this way I just wanted it to end.

"Oh, really? Well maybe you don't have to be a part of it either. Maybe you just need to friggin' die! Maybe then you'll be grateful" he clearly had gotten high on something while I wasn't paying attention.

"Ben, I think you better bring me home. Everyone's going to start looking for me soon," I said cautiously.

"Everyone? Like who everyone? Oh all your friends? Your friends that just want to use you and then leave you for dead." He was hysterical now and I was starting to get truly frightened.

Ben was driving way too fast down very dark and windy roads. I knew where he was going. We were in the state forest. I started to plan my escape. I had been running and I was pretty certain I could escape him, as long as he never got a good hold on me. I had told Julia I would be home after dinner, it wasn't a lie that they would be looking for me soon. Ben's abuse had turned more and more physical and I couldn't always hide the evidence of his outbursts anymore. My friends had seen my battle scars, and they were officially concerned; and angry. I sneakily dug my fingers through my purse for anything I could find to use as a weapon in case I needed one. There wasn't much in there, a set of keys, a lighter, my cigarettes, a few bucks I had brought for emergency. I grabbed my money and stuck it in my pocket in case I needed it.

"O.k. Ben let's just go home, come on we had such a good night" I tried to coax him.

"Don't mess with me you conniving slut" he said.

We drove out to a deserted area. He put the car in park and took out a blunt.

"Ben lets go. If we get caught out here we are in big trouble" I pleaded.

"You think I give a crap about getting in trouble?" he said inhaling deeply. "I been in trouble my whole life."

He calmed down after he smoked, per usual. I tried to get him to let me drive but he flat out refused.

"I'm sorry I get so angry. I don't mean it. You know I don't" he said. "I just don't feel like you love me, no one does, and it makes me crazy. You know I'd die if I ever lost you?"

"Yeah" I said "you're not going to lose me. Everything's fine."

"You say that," he said, "but how do know that it's true? I need a bigger commitment. I need you to move in with me."

My heart sank. I had been dreading this moment since I graduated high school.

"Ben, you know I want my time to be myself. I'm not done exploring the world yet. I don't want to resent you someday if..."

"Resent me? You're going to resent me?" he screamed.

He reached across to the passenger seat and grabbed me by the back of the neck. He squeezed so hard that I couldn't move. I couldn't even speak.

"You're going to move in with me. You hear me? Unless, you want me to destroy you, and your family" he laughed. "I know way too much about you and you know it!" he said wisely.

He let go of me and pushed me into the door. Part of me wanted to jump and take my chances I just stared out the window. I had started turning numb to avoid feeling pain and hurt. It kept me from being a pitiful emotional mess. I watched the scenery pass by like memories of my life. 'How did I get here?' I thought to myself, 'How did this happen?'

I thought about the 'me' I used to be; playing at home with my sisters, laughing with J.P. at his silly stories, planting flowers with Mom and playing catch with Dad. I couldn't let him ruin them. I had to protect them, he would lie. He would lie, and I knew it. He ruined life for all of us. He would turn them against me. His family had too much power, they could even make Mom and Dad lose their jobs, and they had worked so hard for so long. I couldn't let that happen. I needed to just get through school. Then I could leave and take them with me. I'd think of a plan by then.

"O.K. Ben," I said. "You win."

"Damn right, I win. You got till the end of the week" that was all he said for the rest of the ride home.

"You got one week" he said again as he drove off after dropping me off. I went inside and told Julia what had happened.

"I seriously hate him" she said. "Just leave. He won't do anything."

"It's not worth it. He'll just make every second of my life miserable. Believe me, I'd love to get away, I just don't know how. Maybe he'll be better if I pay him more attention" I said.

"He was pretty plastered at Ryan's party last weekend I heard. I heard he was trying to get with every girl there. He's a pig. At least you're in school, I know you're not dumb, but I have no idea why the heck you're with him" and she walked out.

"Hey," I yelled to her down the hall, "pour me a drink. I didn't move out yet."

"Now you're talking," she said and she blew me a kiss.

I was gone by the morning. I wasn't good at goodbyes, and I couldn't say goodbye to her, it was too painful.

I hated living with Ben. It was like a hell I couldn't escape. Every night I heard the phone ring continuously only to hear the machine pick up to one person or another yelling at Ben for owing money or ripping them off. I couldn't turn down the volume or unplug the phone. God forbid he caught me; I'd have hell to pay.

I took advantage of every opportunity to escape to Jamie's house or Khloe's and even my parents. I saw Julia less and less and I hated that. Even Molly would get so angry

"Jenny just leave him he treats you like dirt!" She would spit the words at me like she was punishing me.

At least, that's what it feels like on the receiving end. Beth was always kind though. She would always hug me and say 'don't cry Jenny' or 'it's ok Jenny you always have us'. She was so much gentler, so much more forgiving. It was as if she knew what it was like to have a horrible pain inside that you just couldn't bury. It was like she could see my heart and she was trying to protect it. She just got it. She got me. I clung to her and her love.

That fall I had just started my junior year in college. Khloe and I were going to the city 5 days a week and working full time waitressing still at Applebee's. Molly was a hostess there with us now, too, and Beth had applied for some hours after school. It was better than it had been in a while and I started to regain hope that everything was going to work out ok.

One September morning Khloe came running through the front door of my tiny apartment. "Are you watching TV?" she exclaimed breathlessly.

"What?" before I could answer her she grabbed the remote and turned on the TV.

"Oh my God!" I sat on the couch "What is that?"

"I don't know. No one knows if it's a prank or real," she said.

No sooner did the words come out of her mouth than right in front of us a huge jet drove right into the second tower.

"Oh, my God!" I shrieked covering my mouth. "Is this a joke?"

"I don't think it is, but I don't know. It just doesn't make sense," she said.

"If it was real they would be sounding a siren or something, right?" I said.

"I guess we should go to school. Let's go. If it's real we will find out soon enough," Khloe said sensibly.

We went to school to find everyone huddling around a television in the book store. The President was on the television addressing the nation. We were so far in the back we couldn't see what was happening or hear what he was saying. Everyone was crying and talking on their phones.

We walked over to the counter to the side of the store to ask the clerk what was going on.

"The Pentagon's been hit," she said covering the receiver of the phone with her palm and sniffling through tears. "We are under attack. School's closed girls, everything's closed!"

"We have to go! I have to get Corey! Corey's at school!" Khloe was crying and so was I.

"OK, it's ok, let's go right now," I said.

The world changed that day. Everything was changing and faster than we knew. Our quiet little town was changing too. There was an evil creeping in under the harbor and behind the quiet streets, infiltrating the peaceful life that we all knew. That's the thing about life. You never really appreciate what you have until it's gone. You don't appreciate the stars until it's cloudy and you don't appreciate the rain until a drought. We take for granted the delicate balance that makes our life so beautiful and so unique. We take for granted those we love and love in general. We don't realize how special it is just to call someone and say "I love you" until we can't call them anymore, and then it's too late. The end never comes with a warning bell, it just comes, and all good things come to an end.

# HER-oin

"Owe! What was that? Something just bit me!" Beth swatted the back of her arm.

She was standing in a line outside of the bathroom door at a house party. It was the Friday before her high school graduation. The music was loud and there were wall to wall people. Beth looked stunning as usual with her nails and tan freshly touched up. Her teeth where newly whitened and her Tiffany necklace perfectly accented her Louis Vuitton pocket book.

"Something bit you alright," Nate said with a sleepy grin on his face.

"What was that?" Beth demanded.

"Don't worry about it. Just tell me if you like it," Nate said lighting his cigarette.

The world turned to a foggy, still, blur and a peaceful wave of rest swept over Beth. She was happy and relaxed enough to float up to the clouds. Her life was changed and so was ours, in that split second, forever more. That was the end of Beth being her own self, free to make her own decisions. She would spend many years bound by the chains that enslaved her that night. Secrets too big to bury would resurface no matter how hard she tried to bury them, and the pain, the pain would grow and gain strength from her weakness, always chasing and nipping at her heels, even when she had the lead, she was never really ahead. None of us were. We went down together.

The next morning was hot. I was always hot these days it seemed. My belly was huge with my growing baby inside of it and the summer was sure to be a hot one. I was sweating and the day had just begun. Ben and I were running around our tiny apartment trying to get ready to Beth's graduation. Mom and Dad and Molly were coming to park in our driveway so we could walk downtown together and avoid the traffic.

"Hello," Mom said walking through the front door.

"Hi" I said walking to her to give her a hug.

"Getting harder to hug you with that belly" Mom said rubbing my 7 month tummy. "Can you believe our Beth is graduating?"

"I really can't" I said.

"Helloooooo" Molly bellowed poking her head in. "Let's go we don't want to be late for Boo Bear's graduation!"

We gathered up our cameras and tissues and got to the hall just in time to see Beth and Amy walking in with their caps and gowns on.

"Wait, wait," Mom said. "One picture. Quick, get together. Say cheese."

They were beautiful and smart. They had the world had their fingertips. I remember feeling so proud. She was going to have the life I only dreamt of, I was sure of it. I rubbed my belly and whispered a prayer for my sister.

We piled inside the auditorium and when they called Beth's name we erupted in applause. Our baby sister had made it. The last of us had finally graduated. I was about to enter my senior year in college and had a baby boy coming. This was the beginning of our new life. We were going to make it. We were going to be o.k.

We went back to Mom and Dad's for a cookout that night. The fireflies were just starting to show themselves when I started to yawn. I suddenly felt very sleepy and wanted to put my feet up after a long day.

"Come on. All you ever want to do is sleep what's wrong with you? Such a pain in the ass" Ben whined.

"O.K. Love you guys. Beth I'm so, so proud of you Boo" I hugged her, ignoring Ben's comments.

"Love you Jenny. Thanks for coming. I'm leaving soon too, got some serious parties to hit tonight" she smiled.

"Be careful" I said heading out the door.

"Bye Mom and Dad, love you" I said and we headed out.

I went to bed that earlier than usual that night and Ben was gone when I got up to use the bathroom. I looked around to see if he left a note, but of course, there was nothing to explain his disappearance. I looked out the window. His car was gone.

I headed back into my bedroom and had just gotten comfortable when I heard a faint tapping at the front door. At first I tried to ignore it, but then I heard a familiar voice quietly pleading for my attention. "Jenny, please, Jenny answer" the quiet little voice was saying while quietly knocking at the door, which was right beside my bedroom window at the head of my bed.

I sprang to my feet. I looked out the window, but I couldn't see anyone. I ran to the front door and opened it to find Molly curled up in a ball lying on my front step.

"Oh my God" I knelt down beside her and examined her as best I could in the moonlight. "What happened are you hurt?"

"My stomach, Jenny, my stomach hurts so badly," she was sobbing.

She looked so helpless all curled up in a ball. I hated seeing her like this.

"Can you get up? You have to stand up" I said taking one of her arms and putting it over my shoulder. "What happened did someone hurt you?"

"No, I had a couple drinks, I don't know, maybe I ate something but my stomach hurts so badly," she whimpered.

"Is it the usual pain? Does it feel like it usually does?" I asked walking her to the car.

"Where are we going?" she asked ignoring my questions.

"I'm going to take you to the hospital, hang on I need to get my keys and shoes." I slid her on the backseat so she could lie down and ran inside.

I grabbed my keys and shoes. I looked at the clock 2:20am. It was going to be a long night. I rubbed my belly and grabbed an apple and a bottle of water and threw them in my purse for a snack and headed out to the car.

I sat with Molly in the little ER room when we got inside. The nurse put an IV in her arm and gave her some fluids. She went down for an ultrasound and a few hours later the doctor came back in the room.

"So, you don't seem to have any issues with your gallbladder or appendix, which is good. You do have some inflammation in your colon, but that should resolve with bowel rest. So clear liquids only for the next couple of days. I would like to talk about your alcohol level though. You are obviously under age. Do you need help finding treatment for your drinking?" he asked.

"Oh no. that's ok. I was just celebrating my sister's graduation. I feel better now thanks" she started ripping out her IV and putting her shoes on.

The doctor tried to convince her to stay, but true to form, Molly refused to listen.

She was halfway to the door before I could even grab my things.

"Wait up, jeez I can only waddle so fast" I said with my apple in my mouth.

"Seriously hurry up that guys totally lecturing me right now and I'm so all set," Molly said rolling her eyes.

"He's just doing his job," I said starting the car. "Where to?"

"Can you just bring me home? I'd like the privacy of my own bathroom" she said.

"Ok" I said. "Are you sure you're ok?"

"I'll survive" she gave a half smile with her head resting on her hand against the window.

I was relieved when I pulled in to see Beth and Amy's cars both in the driveway. I noticed Beth's bedroom light was on, but I didn't think much of it. At least they were home safe.

"Hey did Beth get in to any schools?" I asked Molly as she got out.

"She's "slumming" it at Quincy with us this year. Says she and Amy are applying at some big school in New York next year, they're going to get their own apartment" Molly said rolling her eyes.

"Fancy" I said. "Good for them. Maybe we can visit"

"Yeah, thanks Jenny. Call you tomorrow. Love you." She shut the door and went inside.

I drove home with the windows down and the music loud so I didn't fall asleep at the wheel. The sun was rising and the sky was a beautiful pink grapefruit color. I looked at the clock 5:40 am. I had a doctor's appointment at 10:00am.

"Just enough time for a nice long nap, baby" I said rubbing my belly.

My hopes disintegrated when I pulled in my drive way and Bens car was there. I realized that I forgot to leave a note where I had gone, not that I got the same courtesy. I could see him pacing through the living room window.

I got out of the car and took a deep breath. I was sure there was a battle waiting for me on the other side of the door. He hadn't put his hands on me since I had gotten pregnant, but his temper was still irrational and unpredictable. I hesitated as I approached the door. I reached my hand out for the knob but before I could reach it the door flew open. Ben was standing their sweating and panting. He reached forward, grabbed my shirt and flung me inside.

The scene in the apartment was disgraceful. I had left it perfectly neat and tidy. He had destroyed that. He ripped through everything, all my school files and car loan papers were thrown all over the place. The phone was ripped out of the wall. I could see I'd have to buy a new one of those. I took a quick inventory of the damage, nothing too serious that I could see.

"Where the hell you been you little whore?" he yelled at me

"Ben please I can't fight I'm so tired. I drove Molly to the hospital. Here I brought in her discharge paper work she left in the car. See for yourself" I handed him the papers.

He looked at them suspiciously. "So you've been up all night in your condition? What kind of mother are you?"

I couldn't win, I knew that. I was so desperate for rest. "Please, Ben I need to lay down. I have a doctor's appointment and then work tonight. Let's just go to bed."

I don't know what made him relent so easy, but I was so thankful that he did. I couldn't even imagine staying up another minute longer. He went to the couch and started flicking through channels. I went in my room and kicked my shoes off. I don't even remember my head hitting the pillow.

About 6 weeks later, I was working at Applebee's with Molly. I was only a few days off of my due date and I couldn't wait for this little guy to come. My sisters and Khloe had thrown me a beautiful baby shower at Jamie's house. We had great friends and family who spoiled us and we were all set up and waiting for our little bundle to arrive. I started feeling a lot of pressure this one particular night. I was certain that the baby was coming. I tried to work through it, but the pressure was unrelenting.

"Molly, you got to come with me in the bathroom" I said quietly at the hostess station.

Molly was wiping down menus. "Um, why?" she asked.

"I think the baby's falling out," I said.

"What?!" she exclaimed putting the menu down. "What am I going to do? You need to go to the doctors!"

"I'm afraid it's a false alarm. You need to check" I said pulling her arm toward the bathroom.

"Tell me you're kidding!" she stopped short.

"I'm serious. I'd do it for you" she knew she couldn't argue and came with me into the bathroom.

Once inside, I put a chair under the knob of the door so no one else could come in. I pulled my pants down and lifted one leg up on the toilet.

"I can't believe your making me do this," Molly said.

"Just tell me if you can see the head" I said.

Molly bent down "nope no head, just your gigantic stomach" she laughed. "Can I go now or do you need something else."

"Wait till I get myself together" I said zipping up my pants.

"You have a name picked out for this baby yet?" Molly asked rubbing my belly.

"I want Dylan but of course Ben wants Ben, so I guess it's just baby for now. I really don't want to name him Ben" I said.

"OK, weirdo. I got to go back to work," Molly said as she fixed her shirt and removed the chair from under the door.

"OK" I said.

"Don't tell a soul about this! I mean it," she said squinting and pointing her finger at me.

"You don't have to worry about that" I said and off she went.

I fixed my shirt and my apron and took a good look in the mirror.

"OK baby anytime now you can come meet mama. I got to get you settled and get back to school. I have a life to build for us, so let's wrap this pregnancy up here" I whispered to myself.

I put on some lip gloss and headed out the door.

The next week I was still pregnant.

"It's so hot!" I whined while floating in Khloe's above ground pool.

"Hey, enjoy your last days of being able to float without a little one to watch over" she said as she swirled Corey around in the cool water. "But, I hear you. Plus, we got school in 2 weeks! Clock's ticking here. What's the doctor say?"

"She said I'm ready to go anytime now. She said I could take a couple teaspoons of castor oil if I got really desperate" I answered.

"What are you going to do?" she asked.

"Well, if this August sun ever cools down tonight, I'm going to go for a long walk, then eat some extra spicy Mexican food and then if still no baby, I'm going to drink the castor oil" I said.

"Bottoms up" Khloe said.

I went home that afternoon and tried everything I could think of to get that baby to come. When there was still not a single contraction at 10pm I went to the bathroom and took the castor oil. I poured it in a champagne glass mixed with orange juice and did cheers to the end of my childless life. I went to bed and settled in.

An hour later I awoke with the worst cramps ever. I ran to the bathroom and made it just in time. I lost just about everything inside me except the baby. I started contracting, but my water didn't break. It just felt like someone had a wrench and was clamping down on my back tighter and tighter. I paced the halls and timed the contractions until they were regular and only 3 minutes apart. I called the doctor's office and she told me to meet her at the hospital. My bag had been packed for weeks and sat waiting by the door. I went in the bedroom and woke Ben up. He was frantic running around getting changed grabbing odds and ends for himself, he never asked if I was ok or what I needed. I didn't care though, I had learned to know what to expect. I had already made arrangements for Mom and Jamie to meet me at the hospital.

"Did your water break?" Mom asked.

"No but the contraction are close and regular for the last hour" I said.

"OK ill meet you there. I'll call Jamie" Mom said.

We headed to the hospital and started in on what was to be one of the longest nights of my life. 22 hours later, my baby finally came into the world with my mom and Jamie there waiting to greet him, but he wasn't breathing when he came out. There was no typical baby cry that came out from this baby to cement his arrival in to the world. He came out and was immediately placed on the table in the corner of the room. I was hardly awake but I could see that something wasn't right. We all sat silently as the nurses and doctors hurried about running in and out of the room.

"What did the mother have for drugs?" the doctor was yelling. "Go, now we have to go."

And they started to run out of the room, collecting supplies and going toward the door.

"Wait, hey!" I was trying to yell, but I had no breath. "Hold him up! I want to see him!"

They kept going, working frantically. I was desperate for a glimpse. I knew if I could just see him, he would recognize me and be ok.

"Hold him up" I tried to yell but the words wouldn't come out.

"Hold him up!" I finally yelled out.

One of the nurses heard me and as she ran by she held up my little naked blue baby so I could catch a glimpse of my little miracle. As he went by I could see his color was bad, but he opened his eyes and saw me. He had eyes as blue and deep as the ocean. I saw life in them. I put my head back on my pillow. I could feel in my soul that he was going to be ok.

"Did you see those eyes?" Mom said. "He's going to be ok, don't worry Jenny. I always wanted a blue eyed boy named Benjamin. At least consider it. You have to name him something."

"You did so well! You did it!" Jamie was saying.

Mom and Jamie were hugging each other excitedly and making phone calls to announce the baby's arrival. Ben went for a walk to 'get some air'. I laid in bed and waited for my baby. A short while later, the nurse brought him in and put him in my arms. He reached up and grabbed my finger. I never knew this kind of love and I couldn't wait to share him with the rest of my sisters. I made him a promise as he slept on my chest. I promised him that I was going to take the best care of him and that I would never ever leave him. I took that promise very seriously, and started planning the rest of our life immediately.

Molly and Beth came to visit the next morning and stayed the whole day. They were very interested in this little baby that had suddenly blown in to our little circle. Ben's family came and showered him with love and gifts. Our friends came, too. Khloe came and brought me some clean new sweats and helped with the baby so I could shower.

"Have you heard from Julia?" Khloe asked.

"Not since the shower. I've tried to call her but her numbers been changed. I hope she reads it in the paper and comes to see him," I said.

"I'm sure she will" Khloe said. "I'm sure she's just going through her own stuff."

"I know. I just miss her," I said taking the baby back in my arms.

"I'll let you get rest. Call me when you get home I'll help you settle in. How's Ben been?" Khloe asked.

"He hasn't been here much, which is fine. I just hope my house isn't torn apart when I get home" I said.

"By the way what are we naming this baby?" Khloe asked turning back from the door.

"Benjamin Royal" I said.

"Royal?" Khloe asked.

"It's a family name and besides, he's officially my little prince" I said.

"Love it! And love you, see you soon" Khloe said.

My fears were for nothing and when I returned home everything was as I hoped it would be. The baby things were all assembled and waiting. Jamie had made a huge grocery delivery. Aunty Rose and Uncle Rob brought over a couple weeks -worth of formula. Molly and Beth came over to help with the baby so I could nap and Ben's mom, Evelyn, came over and help clean the first few days as I was recovering. Mom stopped by every day with a hot coffee for me and a new gift for the baby. The warm August air drifted through the windows as I lay lazily with my littlest love listening to lullabies and snuggling away the hours. That was one of the happiest times of my life, the calm before the storm.

I had so much going on in my life that I didn't notice how much I didn't notice. Twice a week, on the days I had to do 8 hour clinicals for school, Molly would watch Benjy for me. I would drop him off to her at 5:30 am when she would take my sleepy baby and cuddle him back to sleep and then keep him happy and safe for the rest of the day into the evening hours. Most days, Beth wasn't home still. She was either at Amy's house, or out of town visiting this friend or that friend at college. She started being more secretive. She stopped going to classes by her second semester of college. Her friends were changing and she was more moody than ever.

One afternoon I stopped over to visit Mom and Dad after work and brought some appetizers. I walked past her room and noticed the computer screen was left open. I walked in her room and found it a mess. Her clothes stunk like cigarettes badly, and she had a suitcase half unpacked with clothes thrown all around. Her coat lay crumpled on the floor and looked like it had blood down the sleeve. This was very unusual for my sister who took exceptional care of her belongings usually. Even more unusual was the large wad of money I could see in her top door that was left half open. I walked over to the computer and started to read what was on the screen. I didn't get far. I could just about make out that I was looking at airline tickets when she found me. She wasn't happy.

"Hey!" she yelled to get my attention.

I whipped around, startled at her tone. She stormed in front of the computer and closed at the window.

"Do you mind? This isn't for you!" she snapped.

"Oh excuse me. I didn't know you had such needs for secrets. Nice to see you too," I said as I left the room.

I stopped half way to the door to see if she would stop me, or apologize, but she didn't. She was frantically putting things away and sorting out her clothes. I walked out to the dining room to find Mom sitting at the counter painting her nails.

"Soon as these dry I'm taking Benjy for a cuddle," she said.

"Ok" I said bouncing my boy on my knee. "Mom, where has Beth been? Now that I'm thinking of it, I haven't really seen her much these last few months. Since Benjy was born, actually."

"She comes and goes. She has a new boyfriend. I think he's occupying most of her time," Mom said.

"Seems grouchy, too" I said.

"You all get grouchy time to time" she laughed. "She's just getting older, spreading her wings, you weren't around much when you were her age either, remember?"

"I guess. I just get a bad feeling" I said.

"That's because you love her and you don't want to let her go and grow up," Mom said taking Benjy in her arms.

"You think she's ok?" I asked.

"I think so" Mom said.

I let it go. Who was I to really say anything? I had made less than great choices in my own life and still had no idea how that was going to turn out. I figured Mom was right, I was just being overprotective. Besides, I had to stay focused on finishing school and taking care of Benjy. Beth was smart, she would be o.k. She would come to me if she had a problem.

I pushed through the next few months, determined to graduate and give Benjy a solid life. It was incredibly difficult with a baby, and I often times wanted to quit. I leaned on Khloe when I needed an extra push. I spent every minute I had studying and working and when I wasn't doing that or taking care of Benjy, I was exercising to clear my head and de stress myself. Our day started at 4am and finished around midnight. I kept this pace through the whole year. When finals rolled around I was exhausted in every way. I had sunk 20lbs below my pre baby weight. I hadn't seen my family, except for baby drop off or pick up at Mom and Dad's or Jamie's, in months and I was ready to just quit.

"You can't quit," Khloe would tell me. "You're going to finish what we started."

I could barely hold my eyes open most nights to get Benjy to sleep. Then I still had studying and house work to do. The exhaustion was physically painful. I remember one night coming home from waitressing a double shift. I can still hear the sound my keys made when the door knob unlocked in that apartment. I pushed the door open and prepared myself mentally for a long night of studying for midterms. My feet were aching badly and I desperately wanted a long hot shower. I entered through the door way and saw Benjy sleeping in his swing. I should have known it was too good to be true. I quietly put my stuff down and looked in the bedroom for Ben. He wasn't there. I walked around the corner into the kitchen and found him sitting on the floor in an absolute mess of shredded paper, my papers- my school papers.

"What are you doing!?" I cried.

There was paper thrown all about. My empty book bag was lying empty on the table.

"I know you're hiding something, I know it!" he was in a delusional state again.

"What have you done?" I was in a panic.

All my study guides, all my notes, months of work, all ripped up like pieces of trash.

"That's all you care about of course" Ben said.

The alcohol was heavy on his breath.

"What do you care about besides ruining my life and Benjy's life? This is our future!" I fired back

I wasn't letting this go

"Of course, YOUR life! What about me?" he yelled and pushed me on to the ground.

I tried to get up but he held me down on my stomach with his foot, my face smooshed into the cold linoleum floor.

I remember thinking 'Please God don't let this escalate! Not with Benjy here.'

"Ben, please, please stop!" I was saying but he wouldn't.

This is what addiction does.

"I said 'what about me,' you piece of trash" he was bent down saying it right in my face with his hot breath stinging my eyes.

He loosened his grip long enough for me to turn on my side and he kicked me right in the stomach. I was breathless. I thought my rib was broken for sure. I lay there whimpering like a wounded puppy. He grabbed my keys and left in my car. He always took my car, so I would be trapped there. This was the usual routine these days. I looked around through the tear filled eyes at the mess of papers all around me. I could hear Benjy starting to stir in the living room. I made my way up and rinsed my face with cold water. I didn't want my son to have the image of my tear stained face in his brain, ever. I went in the living room, but he had fallen back to sleep. I went in the bathroom to shower and when I took my clothes off I looked in the mirror at myself for the first time in a long time. I was frail and had bruises and cuts all over my back and arms. This was not how I pictured myself when I was a little girl. The girl I used to be would not stand for this.

I made a decision that night, looking in the mirror that I was not going to become this woman; I was going to overcome this. I was going to achieve the goals I had set for myself and for Benjy, and if Ben was going to treat me this way, I was going to leave him as soon as I got a nursing job. I decided that after finals, I was going to the court house to find out my options. I had called the police on Ben before when he did this to me, but they always said if I wanted to leave, I had to leave Benjy behind with his Dad. I couldn't do that. That wasn't even an option. So I never left or pursued legal action. The risk of losing Benjy's custody to Ben, or his parents, was more than I could bear. I would rather have my son and take a beating, than not have my son and not get a beating. That's a choice no woman should ever have to contemplate. No, this was not the life that was meant for us. I made up my mind and got in the shower.

When I got out, Benjy was still sleeping. I poured a coffee and looked at the time: 1 am. He probably wouldn't be back tonight. I assessed the damage in the kitchen and started talking out loud to myself, like a crazy person.

"OK," I said "he ripped up your papers. What are you going to do to fix this? I think it's easy. Tape them back together."

I'd be lying if I didn't admit that I started to cry more than once during this process. Tears of exhaustion, frustration, of mourning for the life I used to have. There were at least 40 pages of handwritten notes to go through and they were ripped into tiny pieces. Shred by shred I found the systems that went together, the anatomical pieces that matched and the true false keys and put them all back together, every single one. This was not how I pictured my night going. This was not how I pictured my college experience to be. But, these were the circumstances I had, and I would not become a victim of my circumstances. I completed my task, and strangely enough, felt as though I had done a great deal of studying by the time I was done I got Benjy from his swing and brought him into bed with me. He was a great sleeper and I was incredibly grateful every night for that.

I tried not to cry anymore as I fell asleep, not wanting my face puffy and swollen for church in the morning. I couldn't help but worry about everything going on. I knew Ben was up to no good. He was disappearing more and more now and I shuddered when I had to leave Benjy alone with him. I worried he would get into a car wreck or a fight, and kill himself or someone else. I worried about my sisters and hoped they were ok. I worried about what would happen to Benjy and me if I couldn't finish school and get a decent job. I worried about letting my parents down and burdening them with my troubles. I tried to think of all the blessings I had in life- a big loving family, a beautiful healthy baby, great friends, school….

Next thing I knew I was driving along a very narrow road on the ledge of a beach. Khloe was driving and Benjy was in the back seat. We were sliding all over the road and it was snowing hard. The waves of the beach were crashing all around us and soon our little car was being pulled out to sea. We were in a panic. I swam into the back seat and loosened Benjy from his baby seat. I was trying to get out of the car but my coat kept getting stuck on the broken glass of the window. I couldn't free it unless I let go of Benjy, and I couldn't do that. I was twisting and turning trying to get free. It was so cold and everything was starting to go quiet when I felt a hand grab on to my coat from above and pull me and Benjy out of the car. It was Khloe. She brought us up to the surface. We took a big breathe and she held me around my neck.

"Just hold on to me, I have you. Hold on to me, hold on to Benjy" she was saying over and over.

That's what I did. I held on as she pulled me into shore.

I woke up that morning feeling surprisingly refreshed after just a few hours of sleep. I got a coffee and looked outside in the driveway - still, no Ben. I looked in the bed and saw Benjy's sleepy blue eyes looking at me with nothing but love and adoration. He smiled and all my fears from the night before vanished.

"Hi baby" I said to him and gave him a big kiss "we are going got be ok. In fact we are going to be great" We got dressed, had breakfast, and headed out the door for church. I packed a bag big enough so I didn't have to return for the whole day. I had everything I needed with my baby and my friends and family. Everything was going to be ok.

The next few months went by even faster and when Ben ripped up my study guide for the year end final, I was prepared with a copy hidden at Khloe's house.

"What a jerk. I can't believe he does this stuff to you" Khloe sighed as we reviewed the material for our final.

"I know but I'm almost in the clear. Once school is done I can get a job and then separate and provide for Benjy on my own. Then I can afford a lawyer and get custody," I reassured her.

"I know you're smart but just be careful. I agree with your mom, he's the type that will try to trap you and you'll end up like that girl we saw at the courthouse that day with the two crying babies. Remember her? She was trying to get a restraining order?" Khloe said

"How could I forget her? She was crying so hard. I felt so bad for her" I answered.

"You have a plan right?" Khloe asked

"Yep, already started saving toward first, last and security somewhere. I'm hoping since he's had little offenses and I've never been arrested that will work in my favor, character wise. I know he'll lie. He'll say I use drugs, run around all night, you know the usual" I laughed.

I always tried to laugh it off, but it really wasn't funny. The truth was most nights at home were much worse than I let on. I feared for my life on multiple occasions and had started sleeping with my keys in my pockets so he wouldn't hide them on me. Many times I had woken up to find my cash, keys and telephone all gone. I would be left stuck at home unable to make appointment and work on time and having no way of calling to even plead my case to whoever was waiting for me. He would often keep me up fighting all night long depriving me purposely of sleep, an essential ingredient to a healthy life.

This is what addiction does.

When it came time for graduation, I couldn't have been happier to move on with my plans for life. Getting through school had been incredibly difficult, but I clung to the hope that is I just got through it, I could finally be free. Khloe and I got ready and drove up together. We had to wear the old fashioned white nurse's dress and cap to the pinning ceremony. We wore them proudly.

Looking out in the audience, I saw my sisters, all three of them and I waved excitedly. I was so happy they were there with my parents and Jacob and J.P. to see me achieve my dream of finishing college. I felt like I was setting a good example for Molly and Beth too, like I was doing something right. But, the best part of it all was looking out and seeing Benjy sitting on Ben's lap, clapping for his mama. Khloe could see Corey, too from where we stood. We felt like super women. We had gotten something that no one could ever take from us, and we had done it together. We had worked so hard, and accomplished something that would change our lives against our odds.

We continued to waitress and eventually passed our boards. Molly, Beth and J.P. all worked with us and I loved seeing them more and more. It was like 1,000lbs had been lifted off my shoulders now that school was done. I took Benjy to the pond every chance I got. He loved to splash in the shore and hunt for frogs and turtles just as my sisters and I did for so many years before. Most days Molly would come out and hang at the pond with us. Benjy adored her. He had gotten so close to her while she babysat during the school year. He adored his Grandma and Grandpa too. Everyone had played a huge role in getting us settled into a good position for life.

I did notice some things about Beth though that had me troubled. I tried to push them off as no big deal, but I couldn't shake the feeling that something was wrong.

"What's up with Beth?" I asked Molly as we sat with our feet in the pond watching Benjy splash around.

"What do you mean?" Molly asked.

"I never see her and whenever I do it seems like she's running off somewhere. She seems moody and just, I don't know, different" I said.

"Different, how?" Molly asked.

"Just grouchy, and what's with the boyfriend she has? He never comes inside he just sits and waits in the car all the time, and his cars are super expensive. He drives a Cadillac? No one thinks it's strange that a 17 year old drives a loaded Cadillac?" I asked.

"I guess it's weird. I just assumed his parents were rich" Molly laughed.

"I guess. I just feel like something's off," I said.

I decided to let it go. Molly didn't seem to know anything, or if she did she wasn't talking I would have to go straight to Beth if I wanted answers.

I made myself more visible at Mom and Dad's that summer, trying to catch a glimpse of Beth whenever possible. Khloe and I had started waitressing at a popular new bar down on the waterfront at night for more cash. I saw just about everyone we knew there on a nightly basis, everyone except Beth and her friends. They were up to something, I just knew it. It was like they weren't even around. They just drifted in and out of town without being noticed, like ghosts.

When I finally saw her at Mom and Dad's I jumped at the chance to confront her about where she had been and what she was up to.

"What do you mean where do I go?" Beth quipped

"Where do you go? It's a simple question. I never see you around, no one does. I feel like you're up to something no good and I'm worried you're going to get into trouble" I said.

"I don't 'go' anywhere except the beach or a friends pool, what are you talking about. Sorry I don't hang out here or at the pond all the time, and I'm not legal so I don't go to the bars. Jeez, Jenny get off my back, mind your own business. I think you have your own problems to deal with." She nodded at me and I noticed my bruises on my arms were showing.

"Don't pull your sleeves down, now, either like I don't see those bruises all over you. Don't you think it's odd that you wear long sleeves in the summer? Or can't go swimming past your neck because the makeup might wash off and show your dirty little secrets?" She was being mean now on purpose.

"Hey! This is about you. Don't deflect back to me!" I shot back.

"Don't use your fancy words on me. Ben's right, you are a snob now" she said.

The words cut like a knife. I was stunned for a second. She had been hanging out with Ben? That was bad. He had nothing good to offer her. I couldn't go on after the hurtful words she had just fired at me.

"I have to go. This isn't over!" I stormed out.

It wasn't over. It was just the beginning. That night Ben and I had a terrible fight. I didn't want to tip toe around him anymore. I went through his dresser and found all kinds of evidence of his double life while he was gone that day. He didn't have to live a life in secret like I did. He didn't have to hide everything to protect it like his keys, wallet, phone, papers. He just left it all there, like he wanted it found, or he didn't care. Either way I had had enough. I had Benjy's bag in my car and he was sleeping in his car seat. Soon as Ben walked in the door of our little apartment I jumped at him.

"What the hell is going on with you?" I demanded.

"Excuse me?" he said.

"I said what's going on with you? You take off and I never know where you go. You never have any money, or pay any bills for that matter, yet, you "work" all day. I found pictures of other girls in your drawer and a bunch of random phone numbers on paper. There are people calling here all the time looking for you saying you owe them money, and now you're hanging out with Beth behind my back? I find it all very odd." It all came pouring out.

I couldn't even finish before he flew at me. He stopped me dead and threw me into the wall beside the couch where I laid at night to get Benjy to sleep. Everything flew off the end table before I landed on top of it. I tried to brace myself before he got hold of me again, covering my head with my hands. This time he threw me to the floor and threw anything he could get his hands on at me. I laid there motionless for a second until I got my wits about me. I tried to crawl away toward the door where Benjy was in his seat, waiting for me to take him wherever I was going. I could see his little eyelids starting to flutter with all the commotion. Benjy jumped at me and pulled me back by my back leg.

"Oh, no you don't. You're not getting off that easy," he was laughing.

It was funny to him.

He grabbed me by my hair and pulled my head back tight. I didn't make a sound. I wasn't going to give him that satisfaction. He grabbed his pocket knife and held it to my throat.

"You have something you wanted to ask me about? Or how about I cut up your pretty little face, right here?" he held the knife right under my eye.

I just kept staring at Benjy, praying that he wouldn't wake up. I couldn't move a single inch, or I would have my flesh pierced. I don't even remember breathing. The phone rang and he was distracted for a quick second. I jumped forward again, but he caught me immediately.

"You know what your problem is, Jennifer? You don't listen, you never do" he was whispering in my ear.

He had me from behind, his arm around my neck squeezing tighter and tighter.

"I should've listened when everyone told me to get away from you. I should've listened then!" I couldn't help myself. I was enraged now. He was threatening my son, risking that he would awaken and witness this abuse. He was trying to take his well-being away, and that was the only thing in the world that mattered at that moment. I wouldn't let Benjy fall into this cycle. I'd die first.

He squeezed tighter. I couldn't talk anymore. I could feel the breathe escaping me. I used every ounce of energy I had to reach my toes far enough in front of me to cover Benjy's face with the visor of his car seat. All I could think of was him. I couldn't let him see this, and he was waking up.

I awoke to Jamie standing in front of me.

"Oh my gosh! Oh my gosh! Are you ok? Wake up! Wake up quick!" she was saying.

I opened my eyes and sat straight up "Benjy!"

My eyes searched the room frantically.

"He's in the bedroom, he's fine" Jamie said "I came over to bring Benjy's formula, you left it at my house the other day, I figured you'd need it. Ben saw me and ran out the front door. What the hell happened?"

Just then I heard sirens in the distance. I knew it. I knew she called the police.

"You called the police? Why?" I asked

I had become so numb.

"Because I thought you were dead until I felt you breathing. What do you mean why? I called Dad, too. What the hell happened?" she demanded.

"Crap, help me clean up quick. The cops will take Benjy if they find all this!" I was frantic.

I jumped to my feet and sprang into action. I threw all the broken picture frames and candles, any evidence of our fight in the trash. I ran in the bedroom to grab Benjy, he was playing quietly with some toys in his seat still, unharmed, unaffected, I hoped.

"Jenny, you got to do something. You can't live like this, he's getting worse," Jamie was saying.

"I know I have a plan I just need a little more money saved. If he would stop taking my credit cards, I could get out faster," I said rushing around.

I threw some water on my face and looked at my neck. At least I had a few days off from work. They had some time to heal.

"Come on lets go before the cops get here. Hurry!" I said pushing Jamie out the door.

Ben had already warned me that if he got arrested, he would turn it around on me, and make sure I got arrested too. I knew I could never get a nursing job with an assault charge against me, and he knew it. I wouldn't put it past him to go give himself a black eye just in case the cops were here, so he could say I hit him first and plea self-defense. As ridiculous as it sounds, that's the way it works.

Dad pulled in the driveway just as I was walking out.

"Dad its fine I'll meet you at the house. Please! Go quick" I said and jumped in my car.

When we got to the house, Dad was less than pleased.

"Jenny, I don't want to get these calls anymore. Figure this out."

That was all he said and he walked away.

I knew things had been getting hard with Molly and Beth, and my parents couldn't take on any extra stress. I brought Benjy to the pond and buried my pain inside. I pretended nothing bothered me, even though inside I just wanted to run away, far, far away and start a whole new life. I couldn't do that anymore, now that would be kidnapping. I thought of that as I sat and watched my beautiful baby play in the shore and wondered why God put him here with me. Why where things unfolding this way? Why did I have to stay here and go through all of this?

This is what addiction does.

I hardly saw Beth that summer. She would stop over here and there to say hi to me and Benjy. A couple times, I came home after work at 2am and she was there sitting on my couch watching TV with Ben. I never questioned it, I had learned my lesson, and that would serve no purpose. I knew that she would never let anything happen to Benjy; so long as she was there he was safe. I worried more that Ben would get her in to bad things that he did, introduce her to the scummy men he hung out with, steal from her and treat her badly like he did to me, but he didn't seem to, at least not that I could see. If I tried to ask anything or make sense of anything, somehow I ended up being the one that felt stupid. I remember one night asking how she drove such fancy cars and who the cars belonged too.

"What do you mean?" Beth asked like it was a nonsensical question.

She and Ben looked at each other and then me, both grinning ear to ear, like there was some secret they weren't going to let me in on.

"Well, how do you drive those cars? I see you usually in the Cadillac, but the other day you were in a BMW" I said.

I wanted some answers and I wasn't going to let Ben chase me away from protecting my sister, but of course she had an answer. She could charm anyone.

"Jenny, don't worry. Have you been worrying about this? Thinking I'm up to no good? Jenny you're so sweet" she was smiling and holding my face in her perfectly manicured hands. "That's part of J's business. He rents out his car to people and he makes money, it practically pays for itself. The beamer was his Dad's. This is the new thing everyone does it. Haven't you heard of entrepreneurs? We are creative with how we earn our money."

"What about your weight loss? You look so thin?" I went on.

"Thanks! I've been trying to lose some weight" she smiled and winked.

I guess it makes sense. She was off to the porch for a cigarette and I followed behind. I asked and she answered. I didn't want to dig too deep. I just wanted to enjoy her company. I wasn't in any position to ask about the bruises either, we both knew that. Once I was out on my own, I could ask her to live with me. I would take her in and she would be fine.

I had noticed that she was looking thinner and thinner. I noticed she started to have bruises on her, too, also in places that were easy to hide. She startled easy and she cried when she thought no one was watching. I hated seeing her like this. I was careful what I said to her though, because I wanted her around as much as possible. I wanted to put her in my pocket and keep her there, but that wasn't safe for her either, and we both knew it. We would stay up together sometimes all night and talk, sitting outside on summer nights and enjoying the warm breeze. Then, just like a ghost, she would be gone. She would disappear for days, sometimes weeks and we wouldn't hear from her or know if she was ok. The worst part about it was that we all got so used to it. We became desensitized to the signs that were right in front of us. If we had only known then, what we know now, we would've done things differently.

It wasn't long after that that I passed my boards and got a job at the local hospital. I was over the moon. My plan was coming together, finally, after years of planning. I made some great new friends at the hospital, too, mostly women, smart, real women, who were living life and understood where I was coming from and where I wanted to go. I stayed in touch with Khloe and we were still having dinner together a couple nights a week. I got to see Molly all the time and she continued to watch Benjy regularly for me so I could work. She even lived with me time to time when she needed a break from Mom and Dad's, or they needed a break from her. Life was on the upswing, for the most part I still had so many worries over Beth, and I missed Julia terribly. I wondered about them both all the time.

One evening in late fall, something made me drive to the drug store. I had been feeling nauseas and couldn't remember the last time I had my period. I dreaded taking the test, but I knew it had to be done. I went home and took the stick out of the wrapper. Ben was going to be home soon; I wanted this done before he got home with whatever drama he would bring with him. Benjy was sitting quietly with his trains watching TV.

"Stay there buddy. Be a good boy. I'll be right out" I said from the bathroom doorway.

I took the test. I tried to convince myself I was just being paranoid, but I knew in my heart it was going to be positive. I could feel the life inside me.

I knew no one would understand how this could happen. No one understands that sometimes it's easier to just give in and let him have his way then to put up a fight. I wished then that I had put up a fight, but it was too late now.

I looked at the test on the counter and saw the two pink lines. I threw my cigarettes on the back of the toilet in the trash and walked out of the bathroom. Ben was just coming in the front door.

"Hey, babe, what's up? Happy Friday" he was in a good mood.

I walked right up to him and threw a punch. He ducked out of the way. Luckily, he was sober and took it well.

"Hey, what's wrong with you?" he said.

"I'm pregnant" I said.

"No you're just paranoid; I told you we use protection. It's impossible" he said.

"Is it?" I said throwing the test at him.

"Well, I use protection. I know that, but I don't know who else you screw around with" he answered.

I figured this was the route he'd go. I wasn't surprised. I grabbed Benjy and my keys and went to Khloe's house.

Khloe hugged me and told me it would all be ok when I told her I was pregnant. Beth did the same, of course, when I told her. She always understood. Molly wasn't so understanding, but she promised to help in any way she could. Those were the only three people that knew for a few months. I hid it as long as I could.

Ben was much better behaved while I was pregnant. He didn't put his hands on me, and he got us into a bigger apartment for when baby came. His parents offered us money, but Ben wouldn't take it. He was determined to prove that he didn't need his parents. He wanted to earn a position in the family company instead of being handed one. I respected his ideals, but I knew he wasn't capable of truly earning it, at least not in his condition. I started to wonder if anything would ever make him get help.

One day, Evelyn showed up to surprise Benjy with a new bike. She brought a new stroller for the baby, also. Ben let our secret out to her as soon as I told him. She was nice to me while I was pregnant, though. She adored Benjy. She fussed over him and even Ben's dad would show up now and then to take him for ice cream. I could see glimpses of kindness in them at these times, but those were the only times. They were mostly cold to me, and even more so to my family. It was no secret that they had wanted Ben to marry a girl from a privileged family, a blue blood. He didn't though, he chose me, and that made me feel indebted to him. I tried my best to be thankful for Evelyn's generosity. She didn't have to make the effort, but she did. As the mother of a boy myself, I could respect that she wanted the best for her son. She clearly didn't think that was me. Still, on the occasions that she stopped over I was polite and made small talk. This particular day was no different. She made her way down to the storage cellar to help me put the stroller away. Ben was due to come home from work soon. She said she'd stay and help me get dinner ready.

We turned on the light and there he was. Ben wasn't at work at all. He was passed out cold on the floor. An empty bottle of whisky lay beside him. I was so angry I dropped the stroller and turned and stormed up the stairs.

"Jennifer! Where are you going? Help me get him up!" Evelyn chased after me.

"I'm not doing that! He's supposed to be at work! We are behind in the rent and I'm about to be out of work! Why does he do this?" I was fuming and I wasn't trying to hide it.

"He's sick Jenny. He can't help it" Evelyn started.

"I know he's sick. We all know he's sick, but we never talk about it. Do you know I spend two afternoons in therapy every week with him? Do you know I drove him to detox and he promised he's stay… and then he left! He left before I even got home Evelyn! I beg him all the time to stop and he just won't even try!" I was furious….and heartbroken.

Why did he have to do this? This time should've been so nice for us. This is what addiction does.

"Maybe if you were a little older you'd understand better. It's your job to take care of him," Evelyn raised her voice to me.

"It's my job to love him Evelyn. You're his mother, you take care of him. I'll take care of him when he takes care of me. I have babies to care for!" I turned and walked away.

I left and took Benjy for a walk. When I returned, Ben was gone. I never asked what happened. I never mentioned the incident to him at all. I only confided in my sisters.

"They're so messed up Jenny. What did she expect you to do? Nurse him back and play pretend that everything's ok?" Molly was her usual tough self.

"I don't know what she expected but I can't do this anymore. I deserve peace and the kids deserve better. I certainly don't want to be married to him, I know that much. He can't even take care of himself anymore." I was so upset and I couldn't hide it any longer.

I just wanted to run away.

"Maybe after this new baby he will be better. Don't give up hope Jen. It's going to be o.k." Beth said

Beth always had the words to make me feel better. Her tone was gentle. It was like a little hug from heaven.

Ben and I moved on and continued to work on our relationship. We went to the ultrasound and let Benjy come too. We found out it was a girl and Ben cried. He promised that things would be different now. He apologized for his shortcomings and even went to detox out of state. I was full of hope and thrilled to be having a girl. My sisters were, too. They immediately started shopping for dresses and hair bows. We picked out names and dreamt of what life would be like for her. Despite all the day dreaming and high hopes though, I still had secret fears. I couldn't help but put my ear against the door and listen every time Ben took a call in the other room. I discretely searched his pockets while doing laundry. Something inside me was still screaming that something was wrong and that I needed to be careful. The screaming got louder and louder as I got to the end of my pregnancy. The warning bell in my mind was now ringing like an all alert alarm. In the back of my mind there was always the lingering question of what kind of monster Ben would turn into when the pregnancy was over.

I had been so caught up in my own issues that I had stopped focusing so much on Beth and her odd behaviors, although they didn't stop either. I was sitting at home one day after work when Mom called crying.

"Can you come over? We have to do an intervention with Beth" she sobbed.

"What do you mean an intervention?" I asked getting my things together.

"The neighbor just called. She caught Beth up the street in J's car. They were shooting up" Mom was hysterical.

I stopped dead in my track. Shooting up? Heroin? No, this couldn't be.

"No Beth hates needles" was all I could say.

"Just come, come now" Mom pleaded.

When I got to the house only my parents were there. They couldn't find Beth. J must've driven off soon as he knew Mom's neighbor was onto them. Mom couldn't reach her anywhere. She wouldn't answer her phone. I tried calling her, but it was no use, she wouldn't answer. Molly had gone out in her car to try and find her. I couldn't believe this was happening. I looked at all the pictures of us as little girls hanging on my parent's walls and felt sick. I ran to the bathroom and started throwing up.

"You're still not feeling good?" Mom came in and handed me a towel. "Maybe you should cut back on your hours at the hospital."

"Mom I'm pregnant." I could hardly get the words out between my deposits into the toilet bowl.

Mom sat down on the floor beside me.

"I don't know what I'm going to do. This wasn't in my plan" I said.

"Oh honey, the babies aren't usually in the plan." She was talking gently to me and moving the hair out of my face. "How far along are you? Are you sure you're pregnant?"

"Oh I'm sure. I'm 17 weeks and it's a girl." I was crying now.

"Jenny," she was laughing, "this is great news! A sister for Benjy, how great! Babies are not ever bad news." She was hugging me.

Mom was always great at times like this. Just when you thought all hope was lost, she'd come in and wrap her arms around you like a big warm blanket and talk you down from hysteria.

"I'm sorry Mom I know you have your own issues to deal with tonight." I said wiping my face and trying to pull myself together.

"Yes I do, but you're my issue too honey, you're my daughter too. So what are you going to do? Are you going to get married? I think 2 babies deserve a Mom and a Dad who are married don't you?" she said.

I couldn't possibly say no and break her heart, not now. This wasn't the way I wanted it, but she was right about one thing: babies are never bad news and maybe Ben would finally grow up now with this second one. He had been working a lot and he had been sober the last few weeks, I knew he was trying. It wasn't really about me anymore, now. It was about the babies, she made that clear.

"Yes, Mom. I'll get married. It's the right thing to do, and I know it's what Ben's been wanting. Can we not tell Dad tonight? I don't have the energy" I requested.

That's how I ended up married. No one was there, there was no celebration. Ben's parents even refused to come. Only my parents, Molly, Jamie and Khloe were there with us. We did it at the Town Hall.

Beth had disappeared after she was caught in the car that day. She would call sometimes, but I couldn't ever get her on the phone long enough to tell her. I only got random calls from her now; "I love you" she'd say and then hang up. I'd cry and cry every time. I couldn't trace the calls and I couldn't call the numbers back. It was all very secretive. I begged Ben to find out what he could and he did seem to want to help. All he could find out was that she had a new boyfriend and they were involved somehow with getting "things" back and forth from Mexico or South America somewhere. It was all very secretive.

Mom and Dad had tried to call the police and report her missing, but they said she would be classified as a runaway since she was over 18 and there wasn't much they could do. It was terrible. It was the first of many months of wondering where she was and if she was ok; of searching for her face in a crowd, but never finding it; of bracing ourselves for the local news, hoping not to hear her name in any fashion; cringing when the phone rings and preparing for the delivery of the worst outcome. It's no way to live, not for anyone. I can't count how many nights I looked up at the stars and wondered where she was, and why she wouldn't come home. I hoped she was ok, looking at the same stars, and knowing in her heart that we loved her.

I was sitting in my living room one cutting coupons one day with Molly when we heard a quiet tapping on my door. My 8 month pregnant belly made it hard to get up, but Molly didn't budge.

"Don't worry I'll get it" I said sarcastically to her.

"Not my fault you got yourself pregnant again" she laughed.

I opened the door and hardly recognized the girl in front of me. Beth stood there weighing all of 90 pounds. She could hardly even stand up straight. Her eye lids looked heavy and her mouth was droopy. Her face was covered in scabs.

"Beth!" I exclaimed wrapping my arms around her.

Molly came running over. She pulled me off Beth so she could hug her. We were so happy to see her, it had been so long. She had a boy with her, it was the new boyfriend. I had never met him. It wasn't J, like I was expecting, his name was Kyle. He stayed close to her like a guard

dog. She kept her eyes low, as if she wasn't allowed to look anyone in the eye. We pulled her inside and she followed.

"Are you pregnant?" she asked me

"Yes, you've been gone a while," I started to say.

Just then she saw Benjy walking out of his room.

"Is that Benjy? He's walking so good!" she ran to him and swooped him up.

I went over and hugged them both. I was so happy to have her back.

"Where have you been?" I asked.

"Shhhh" she signaled me.

Her boyfriend came over and introduced himself.

"We have to get going" he said pulling her away by her arm.

"NO, no, no, no please don't go" I was pleading. "We have so many questions. We've missed you so much we have so much to say, please…"

"Jenny I'll be back later. I promise. I'm staying just a few houses over now. I'm back in town for good." She held my face in her hands like she used to, only they weren't polished and shiny anymore, they were dry and dirty.

She kissed my cheek and left with him, guiding her toward the door, his hand on her back.

I was making dinner later that night when to my amazement she came back as she promised she would. This time she was alone, and she had cleaned up as best she could. Molly was still there. She was staying with me temporarily.

"Where did you go and why didn't you call more?" Molly was doing most of the asking as we ate dinner.

"It's better that you know less. I did what I had too for your own protection" she was saying between bites.

I could see scars on the back of her bony shoulder under her tank top, they looked fresh.

"What happened there?" I asked pointing to her shoulders.

"You wouldn't believe the craziness even if I did tell you but, long story short, I got thrown out of a moving car-at gunpoint" she said as if it were nothing.

"What?" we exclaimed

"Don't get excited. It's over, I'm fine, and I'm never doing that again," Beth reassured us as best she could but everything she was saying was so unsettling.

"Beth, before you left, what was happening in that car? Mom was hysterical when she called me and then you disappeared." I tried to ask as gently as I could but we needed to address the elephant in the room.

Beth stopped for a second, then put on her million megawatt smile and said "I'm done with that. I'm weaning myself down, just on some Percocet now, decreasing the dose on my own until I'm off for good."

At the time, no one knew about Perc 30's like we do now. I didn't know the power they would hold over her, making her want to scratch her face off when she couldn't have them, luring her to use anything as substitute for the high they gave her. They weren't a fix, they were a prison sentence.

Beth stuck around for the days to come. Her face healed over. She got a job at the mall and then down by the waterfront for the summer. She gained some weight back and assured us she would be ok. We believed her because we wanted too, but there were still some things that didn't quit add up. Overall, she seemed to be improving, and the last thing any of us wanted was to push her away, so we went by the 'don't ask don't tell motto' for a few months.

Baby Gabby was born with Mom and Jamie by my side, just as Benjy had been. Dad was waiting in the waiting room with Molly and Beth when she entered the world. She was a healthy screaming hair ball and we loved and adored her.

Ben was back to his usual criminal shenanigans. Before we even left the hospital, he had stolen my wallet and crashed my car. I didn't even care. I wasn't going to let him steal Gabby's thunder. She deserved a homecoming and she was going to get it. I had Mom pick us up from the hospital and we went to her house for a welcome home party for Gabby.

Things seemed to flow on, as life does after that. I was out of work getting the babies settled for a few weeks and then went back to working over nights. I got as much time as I could in with the babies and Ben and I hardly saw each other enough to fight. I started to worry over Beth again. I noticed the phone calls that made her hush her voice and sneak out of the room, away from our watchful eyes and ears. She started to disappear for a couple days at a time again.

I confronted my parents about it, but they only saw what they wanted too, as parents often do. They didn't want to believe that their baby girl would get involved in such things as hard drugs and dealing them. They did what most parents did back then and excused the behavior, making up excuses for everything she did, living in denial with her.

I talked to my friends at work about her, my new friends that I confided in during the long sleepless nights we spent together.

"Don't you think it's strange that she's still driving in these fancy cars even though she supposedly broke up with that other boy?" I asked Maura as we sat doing our charting.

"Yes I do I think it's very strange" Maura answered.

"So you don't think I'm being paranoid to think there must be something going on? I feel like it's right under my nose but I can't pinpoint it," I went on.

"I think sometimes it's hard to see the truth in our kids because that makes us feel like failures as parents. You'll understand that feeling more as Benjy and Gabby get older. Siblings can sometimes see the truth more clearly. Just my opinion, but I think if it's bothering you, you should confront her" Maura said.

"Jeez, I'm so tired I can hardly keep my eyes open" I said.

"When was the last time you slept?" Maura asked

"A whole night? Probably last week" I laughed.

It really wasn't funny. Ben would purposely not come home now so that I couldn't sleep and I usually only got about 4 nights a week to recover from my night shifts. The exhaustion was wearing on me and usually by the end of the week I could hardly get off the couch. Khloe would help when she could so I could get a nap here and there, and a new friend from work was always encouraging me to use her so I could sleep. But they worked nights and had kids also. It seemed selfish to me for me to want to sleep when they were without it, too. I tried to save them for the truly desperate times, or when I needed a quick escape from Ben during one of his fits. They got me by for a long time.

I had been saving for years, since my initial plan to move away from Ben and it seemed like all the hard work and sacrificing might finally pay off. I had put in a bid on a house. A 'fixer upper' we called it. Ben had been doing carpentry his whole life here and there, and seemed confident that he could do most of the work himself. I wanted so badly to give Benjy and Gabby a place to put down roots. Benjy had already moved 5 times in his 2 1/2 years alive and I didn't want to continue that pattern. The house was in a nice family neighborhood and only a few miles from my parents.

I was still at work one morning after working the night shift when the charge nurse told me my mom was on the phone. Mom was my realtor and I was expecting to find out if the family had accepted my offer on the house or not. I answered the phone, knowing our future hung in the outcome of what she had to tell me.

I answered the phone. "Good morning Mom! Did we get the house?"

"What?" Mom asked.

"The house…. Isn't that why you're calling?" I asked.

"Oh, yes, yes! You did get the house congratulations" Mom said.

I could tell by her tone that she wasn't happy.

"Mom what's wrong?" I asked.

"It's your sister… Beth…. She's down in CCU" Mom just about got the words out and the phone fell out of my hands.

I ran down the two flights of stairs and down the hallway to critical care. I swiped myself in and asked the nurse at the desk which room was my sisters. She pointed to the room across from the nurse's station and I slowly approached the glass doors. There was my little sister, freshly extubated, the nurses charting at her bedside carefully monitoring her vitals. I couldn't hold back the pain that poured down my face, my heart started to crumble into a thousand pieces as I felt all my hopes and dreams for her fade away with every beep of the monitor.

"What happened?" I asked the nurse.

"Are you family?" she asked me.

"Yes I'm her sister" I answered.

The nurse leaned over Beth and whispered something to her. I saw Beth mouth the words 'yes' and the nurse took me into the corner and started to tell me what happened.

"She came in last night. Someone left her on the curb outside the E.R. Luckily, they called and told the desk she was out there or who knows if she would've even made it." The nurse let out a long sigh "So young and so beautiful, such a shame. She was barely breathing when they got her inside. Her heart rate was dangerously low. She was intubated for a time and given fluids. Doctor said it seemed like she hadn't eaten or drank anything in days. She has a sore on her hip, a shallow one but still, looks like she's been through something terrible." The nurse rubbed my arm as she told me the horrible truths. "She tested positive for just about everything-opiates, cocaine, barbiturates, everything. She needs some serious help. She has blood clots too, in both arms, and more than one infection in her blood. She's septic. She'll be done detoxing soon. It's going to be a while. Hopefully this will be her wake up call."

I looked at my sister laying there, a shell of the girl she used to be, and I wondered how many secrets she had. What awful things she had been through. How she pulled it all together for the times that she saw us, and how we never figured it out.

We took shifts sitting there over the next couple days, waiting for her to come out of her delirium. Encephalopathy isn't pretty. Jamie and I turned her religiously, making sure we kept pressure off her hips. We swabbed her mouth and changed her socks. We went along with whatever nonsensical words she was talking, listening for clues that could tell us what was happening with her.

This is what addiction does.

One evening, I was sitting beside her eating chowder and watching the yearly showing of The Wizard of Oz on her TV. It was almost Thanksgiving and we were hopeful for her return home to us before the holidays. Judy Garland was on singing 'Somewhere over the Rainbow' when Beth suddenly came too, sitting straight up and singing as if she had been awake the whole time. It made perfect sense, it was her song. She sang it at karaoke more times than I could count. She loved that song.

She looked around in a confused panic. I stood up and tried to calm her down and stop her from moving too much. She was still connecting to IV lines and monitoring devices.

"It's ok, its ok" I was telling her as the nurses ran in the room.

"It's ok" I told them. "She's just waking up."

I went home that night hopeful that she would get through this, that this would be the last time. Jamie had arranged for her to be transferred up to a city hospital in the hopes that they would have farther reaching capability for getting her into a sober living program. We were naïve then. We thought all she had to do was ask for help and it would be there waiting for her. We were totally unaware that there really wasn't any help to be had, and what was available was only a Band-Aid for the real problems. We didn't know that she required an intense relearning of life, but would only get 3 days of detox. We had no idea that we were about to embark on a journey of heartaches and disappointments that would test our faith time and time again. A journey that would leave us wounded and weakened, and wondering where to turn for help.

Beth was transferred up to the city just as we had planned. I spent my days and nights packing for the move to the new house, working and driving back and forth to Boston to see Beth and be as involved in her care as possible. See was weepy most of the time and apologetic. She made promises that she would get help and be better. She signed a health care proxy naming me and the rest of the family as her persons to notify and release information to in case of emergency. I promised her I'd stand by her, that I would help her no matter what. She promised me that she would always tell me the truth. She cried and told me how she had been kept locked in a room for days, maybe even weeks, she wasn't sure. She was drugged often and used for payment for whichever man was in need at the time. She was scared to leave the hospital, scared to find out things she had forgotten, scared to find out someone was looking for her. She hadn't even been conscious for most of the time she was locked up. I told her that was a blessing. I cried with her. I held her. I washed her back and her hair. I braided it for her so it wouldn't get tangled, just like when we were little. She started to come back around. She started to be able to get through a sentence without crying, or apologizing. Mom and Dad visited every day. They cried a lot. It was hard for them, too. Aunty Rose and Uncle Rob drove up often. They had been at her side constantly while she was in CCU, praying at her bedside for a full recovery. She had a good support system. We were hopeful that would be enough to pull her out of the pit of hell she was in. We had no idea that this was only a very shallow pit, and there were many bigger pits still to come.

Molly wanted to see Beth finally. She hadn't been able to bear seeing her while she was in CCU, and she hadn't been up to see her yet in the city. The city hospitals brought back so many awful childhood memories for Molly and she wanted to avoid them as much as possible. She longed to hug Beth though, to hear her voice and look in her eyes.

I had a minivan and we decided to take the trip together. Ben and I, Molly and J.P. all piled in to the van with Benjy and Gabby in the back in their car seats. Beth had been asking to see the kids and I thought it might be refreshing for her to see some new faces. I didn't know my way around the city too good, but Ben did so I felt comfortable driving up in the dark with him, even though I usually made my trips during the daylight. He told me where to turn and we eventually made our way into the parking garage by the hospital. I pulled in and we all piled out of the van. We were almost inside the hospital when Ben said he forgot his phone and needed the keys to go to back to the car. I tried to convince him that we would be quick and he didn't need his phone but he wasn't going to listen. He went to the car and we all headed upstairs.

We sat with Beth for a couple hours. She stayed in bed the whole time. She told us how she had been working with physical therapy and had almost all of her strength back. She was close to being off the blood thinners and was hoping to be home by Christmas. She said she had detoxed and was confident that she could fight the urge to use any drugs once she got home. We thought she had escaped her demons.

I was getting nervous that Ben had taken off. He was a bad alcoholic and I knew every day was a battle for him not to drink. I had brought him to numerous counselors and A.A. meetings, but he didn't seem to see the problem the way I did. He still hadn't returned from 'getting his phone' when we were ready to go and let Beth rest. He had the keys so we couldn't get far without him. I was quietly praying through my anxiety that he would be sleeping in the car when we got to the garage.

The others filed out of the room and headed toward the elevator when Beth called me over to her.

"What's the matter?" I asked

"I have to go to the bathroom and I can't get up alone. Will you help me? I hate to ask but if I call the nurse they make me use a bed pan and it's so gross and messy." She looked down in embarrassment as she asked.

I went out and asked Molly to head down toward the car with the others. I promised I would follow soon and she agreed.

I went back in the room and sat Beth on the side of the bed. She put her arm around my shoulder and I tried to get her up but she was weaker than I thought. I looked at her to say maybe this was a bad idea and I could see the shame in her eyes. I knew what it was like to feel shame, and my heart burned for her to have to feel that way.

"Don't worry Beth I'll get you to the toilet" I said.

I bent down in front of her and put her arms around my neck. I carried her that way, on my back, over to the toilet. I stripped her bed and helped her bath and shave. She cried and I cried. I brushed her hair and fixed it for her, two long braids as usual. I put her back to bed and got her a drink, gave her a call bell, and kissed her on the forehead.

"I love you Beth. Please don't ever leave me" I said.

"I won't Jenny, I promise I won't" she said.

I turned to leave and she called after me "Jenny?"

"Yeah" I said turning to face her.

"Thanks for still loving me" she was crying.

"Beth, I love you more than ever. I'll see you tomorrow" I said as I walked out the door. And as I left, I heard Beth weakly singing a song we used to all sing to each other when we were younger and rebelling together. It was 'I'll Stand by You' by The Pretenders.

I walked back out to the garage. For a minute I had forgotten that I didn't even have my keys. Molly, J.P. and the kids were all sitting outside of the car. Molly was singing silly songs to them. Just as I approached the van, Ben came out of nowhere.

"Where have you been?" I asked.

"You don't want to know" he said. He was right, I didn't.

We got in the car and Ben sat in the passenger seat. He started directing me which way to go. I thought maybe this wouldn't be so bad.

We had been driving about ½ hour when I realized that we were driving in circles.

"Do you really know where you are? Or are you just yelling out right-left-right?" I asked

"I know where we are. Don't worry," he said with his eyes closed. "Go right."

"You're eyes are closed you don't even know where we are?" I said.

That was the beginning of a night that went down in the books as one of the worst ever. Ben lost all control. He had gotten drunk beyond belief while we were visiting Beth. He didn't care about how we may be feeling after our visit with her, and he didn't care that it was late and we were tired in a city that wasn't too familiar to any of us. He only cared about himself, feeding his demons, making his points. One thing was for sure, he didn't care at all that his two kids were sitting in the back seat witnessing the whole mess. His addiction was completely taking over.

I finally stopped at a gas station to ask for directions and fuel up when I thought he had fallen back asleep. I was inside getting directions from the poor clerk when Ben stormed in accusing me of trying to get him to take me to bed for money.

"Ben, stop it. I'm just getting directions so we can get home. Just go back out to the car and go back to sleep, please" I was pleading.

He didn't even seem to hear me, and he was yelling and screaming at me and the clerk. Molly heard what was happening from outside in the car and came storming in to my rescue. She blew past him and grabbed my arm, pulling me toward the door.

"Don't you ever yell at my sister that way" she was scolding him.

"I'm so sorry" I said to the clerk as we left.

We all got into the car. At least I had the first few directions to get us back to the highway. Ben was still ranting hysterically from the passenger seat and Molly wasn't helping, at this point she was only enraging him more. J.P. was crying in the back.

"J.P. stop crying," I snapped. "Everyone stop! I can't hear myself think."

"Maybe I should stop. Maybe I should just stop living too," Ben said.

"Yeah, maybe" I said calling his bluff in a desperate attempt to get some peace and quiet.

He opened the door and jumped out of the car.

"Oh my God, the door" I screamed.

Molly jumped in to the front seat and grabbed the door, pulling it shut.

"Where did he go? Can you see him?" Molly asked.

"No, I can't can you? J.P. can you see him?" I was asking.

"No" J.P. said "It's like he vanished! You need to go back."

"Yeah, Jenny you better go back and make sure he's ok." Molly agreed

"Are you kidding? I'm not going back there. I'm going home! I'm so done with his crap. Who jumps out of cars?" I said.

Molly starting laughing and it must've been contagious because before I knew it, we were all laughing.

"Does anyone know where we are?" I asked when the laughing subsided.

"Jenny, we better stop and ask. It's 1:30am. We got to find our way home. Besides I'm starving" Molly said.

I agreed and we stopped for directions and burgers at a McDonalds. We were in New Hampshire. After about 3 hours we were finally pulling into my driveway when my phone rang.

"Hello?" I answered.

"Hello, Is this Jennifer?" the man's voice asked.

"Yes" I replied.

"This is Sergeant Joseph with the Newton Police Department. We need you to come and pick up your husband" he said.

"Is he under arrest?" I asked.

"No he is just highly intoxicated and was making suicidal comments. He's contracted for safety and by the time you get here he should be fairly sober" he answered.

"Oh, I don't suppose he can stay there the night?" I asked hopefully.

"Ma'am, this isn't a hotel. He's your husband, you responsibility. Come get him," and he hung up.

I got back in the car. I hated my life at that moment. I had a very clear understanding of what addiction was doing to me and my life, and I wasn't even the addict.

Soon after that, Beth was discharged and our trips to the city once again stopped. She was sent home on a tapering dose of methadone. We were hopeful that she was going to make a full recovery and live a normal life. Certainly, that must've been 'rock bottom' we all thought. We were wrong.

When she got home I showed her my new house, and she came over often to visit. We filled out job applications and soon she was back to working and as usual, shopping. Spring rolled around and I brought the kids over to the pond to play as much as I could. Things were very bad at home and I liked to get the kids out of the house and away from the fighting as much as possible. I had just put Benjy down for a nap one afternoon at my parent's house when Mom came and got me.

"Someone's here for you" she said smiling.

"Who?" I asked

"You'll see" she said.

I walked downstairs from the loft and saw Julia sitting there holding Gabby.

"I can't believe you have a daughter" she said.

"Julia! Where did you come from? I haven't seen you in so long! Where have you been? " I asked running over to hug her.

"I know. I'm sorry. I just had to get my life on track, you know, like step away for a minute. Everything's fine, I just wanted to see you. I heard about the babies, and I heard about Beth. Is she o.k.? Are you o.k.?" She was teary.

"Yes we are all fine. Beth's here. How did you hear about her?" I was curious.

"I got a job at Oak Point Treatment Center. I do the billing. Her name came across my screen when I was looking through the methadone bills," she explained.

"Yes, it's been a tough ride, but we are hopeful. She seems to be doing well," I said.

Just like that Julia was back in my life, as if she had never been gone. A hole that I hadn't realized that I had formed was filled, and I felt more complete than I had in a long time.

It was only a few months before Beth went missing again. We knew we had to find her, and quickly, if we were going to avoid what happened last time reoccurring. We asked everyone we knew. I called the local hospitals and police stations everyday making sure she hadn't been picked up, but no one had seen her. Julia even had pulled some strings at work and had a bed ready and waiting for her to come in to detox, but it was no use, we couldn't find her. Just when we thought our hearts could finally heal, they broke again. We were back to jumping every time the phone rang, and searching for her name in the news and papers.

Ben had been sober since the Newton incident and was working regularly again. Jamie was over one day visiting when Ben showed up at home early.

"Jenny, Jenny" he was calling from the yard running into the house.

I jumped up thinking something must be wrong.

"What? What's wrong?" I answered with Jamie close behind.

"I found Beth. I mean I know where she is. She's with that bum J again in a hotel downtown" he explained.

"What? How did you find her?" I asked

"I saw a car that looked like the one he used to drive parked there. I paid a homeless guy $20 to tell me if he recognized her picture. He told me he's seen her around there and that she hasn't come out in the last couple days, not that he's seen. So I went in and asked if someone checked in under either of their names and they said yes. That's as far as I got before I came home to get you" he said he was out of breathe and trembling with nerves.

"We have to go get her" Jamie said.

"How are we going to get her out?" I asked.

Jamie was already on the phone calling Molly.

"We are going to pick her up and carry her if we have to" Jamie said. "Molly? It's Jamie. Hi, I'm at Jenny's can you come here? We found Beth!"

I could hear Molly's excitement through the phone.

"No just come here we need you to stay with the kids. Bring your boyfriend, too. Hurry" Jamie said and she hung up.

Within minutes they were running through the front door.

"Where is she?" Molly asked.

"The Blue Water Inn with J" I said.

"We are going to get her out" Jamie said.

"OK let's do this" Molly's boyfriend was on board.

Jamie and I put on some baseball caps and headed out the door.

"Molly, call Julia and tell her we are coming with Beth. She's at work" I said as we ran out the door into the car.

"On it" Molly said.

We pulled up to the back side of the hotel where we didn't think there were any cameras. I felt like we were in a movie, like this couldn't be real life. We knew what we had to do, and we were going to do it. I said a prayer that everything would go smooth and we went inside.

We stopped at the front desk.

"Hi, can you tell me which room Bethany Rogers is in?" Jamie asked.

The girl at the desk easily gave up the information. We walked up to room 301 and knocked.

"Housekeeping" Molly's boyfriend said.

Only he was standing in view from the door, the rest of us were over to the side so J wouldn't see us right away. He cracked the door and started to say 'no thanks' when Ben pushed through the door along with Molly's boyfriend. They grabbed him and pushed him down on the floor in the bathroom. They closed the door so Jamie and I wouldn't see what went down in there.

Jamie and I scooted in and closed the front door behind us. The room was very dark and filthy. There were flies circling around boxes of half eaten, days old food. It smelled. There were numerous self-made tourniquets all over the room along with splatters of blood on everything.

"Don't touch anything" Jamie said.

We heard a whimper coming from the bed and we went over to find a barely recognizable Beth naked curled up in a ball. She had lost whatever weight she had regained and scabs were back on her face and hands.

"Jenny, Jamie, help" she could barely get the words out.

I frantically searched for her underwear and a t shirt. I found some and threw them to Jamie. Jamie got her dressed. I grabbed her purse and anything that had her name on it. I didn't want her to be traced back as having ever been in the room. There were drugs everywhere.

"Leave them we don't have time" Jamie said.

I found a pair of flip flops and put them on Beth. I had her purse and her wallet. I saw her journal and grabbed that too.

"Come on. Grab an arm, let's go before the cops show up," Jamie said.

I followed her direction and we scurried out, each of us with one of Beth's arms around our neck, her feet dragging on the floor as we made our way out to the car. We put our baby sister in the back just in time for the guys to come out and jump in the car. We were out of there.

We drove to Oak Point where the doctor met us outside and took Beth. We all sat in silence on the way home, not really believing what we had just been a part of. When you love someone you'll do whatever it takes to make them well, sacrificing and risking your own well-being and putting them before yourself. That's what we did that day, and we wouldn't have it any other way.

We went back to Mom and Dad's and breathed a sigh of relief, at least knowing now where Beth was and that she was safe. Jamie and I went through her things carefully, so we didn't stick ourselves accidentally. We found pills and powders, we flushed them all. We found bloody tourniquets, we threw them out. We sorted her clothes that I had grabbed. Mom threw them in the laundry and started making her up a bag to bring to Oak Point. We found ways to feel helpful in a helpless situation. I opened her journals and read what she had been up to. I read the pages and pages of places she had called, reaching out for help, trying desperately to get in someplace to detox. Each entry was neatly dated so she could remember when she called and when she was supposed to call back. The words 'no bed' and 'call back tomorrow' written beside each entry sent shivers down my back. Beth had been reaching out for help. She had been calling day after day trying to get in somewhere and she couldn't. It was heartbreaking. It was even more heartbreaking that she didn't feel she could reach out to us. I found some poems she had written and I put them neatly aside. They were beautiful and I knew she would want them back someday. It was her pain, in her words, and she somehow made it relatable and poetic.

### Red Tail Hawk

'In my dream I'm a red tail hawk
soaring unreachable heights.
No one can touch me
so far above the city lights.
I feel so much freedom,
have no worries or pain,
nothing can harm me,
no snow, sleet or rain.
I see so much beauty,
there's so much to admire;
if something gets in my way,
I just float up a little higher.
I am a perfect creature,
feathers cream, mahogany and gold,
not self conscious at all,
I am fearless, proud and bold.
I cruise past the stars and up to Heaven,
stare in amazement at the colors and lights.
I know I'll see this place again,
when I take my final flight'—A. Beth Randall

I searched more and read on through her scribbling with doodles in the footnotes

'I began an intense love affair
With this enchanting toxic stranger
I disregarded the warnings

> And gladly welcomed the danger
> That evil monkey on my back
> Had a tight hold on my reins
> Driving me to do unspeakable things
> Just to put more poison in my veins'—A. Beth Randall

'Oh Beth what have you done?' we thought. We mourned her youth for her. We planned for her. We discussed how she would get through it all. We had no idea the torture she was enduring. We had no concept of the consequences of her choices, and neither did she. Of course she didn't, or she never would've gone down that path. No one chooses to be a drug addict. That isn't how it happens.

Beth called whenever she was allowed to use a phone and within a week she was transferred out to another facility, and then a sober house.

She told us how much she wanted to just come home, but of course we had heard that all before.

"I think you better stay their Beth, just a little bit longer. I think you should try to stay sober long as you can before you come home." Mom was on the phone with her when I walked in the front door.

"Beth, please don't cry, I know you hate it there-but- no, I just. Please, Beth please I don't know what to do! I don't want you to die don't you understand?!" Mom was so upset.

We were all upset every day. We waited for the phone calls, we gathered for the visits in the dirty run down disgraces they called sober housing. We packed her bags to send. We checked our mail and we sent mail. We were all becoming desensitized to the severity of the problem. We met other families going through the same things as we were, we watched documentaries, looked up laws, fought with the health insurance reps on the phone. We did everything we could to stay involved, to stay useful, to distract ourselves from the severity of the problem.

We went for a visit one Saturday afternoon. I had Benjy and Gabby with me. I couldn't wait to see Beth. We walked up the steps to the big old Victorian that had been converted into the sober house. A heavy woman with a cigarette opened the door.

"Yeah" she said.

I couldn't help but stare at her gut hanging out over her pants.

"Um, we are here for a visit with Bethany Rogers?" I said sounding unsure of myself.

She opened the door more and pointed to a small room to the left. "Over there."

We walked in and found ourselves a spot to sit on a worn out sofa. Mom and Dad filed in behind me and looked around awkwardly.

We heard a commotion coming down the hall and recognized Beth's voice immediately.

"Hey! I'm so glad you guys came! And you brought the kids! I'm so happy" she bent down to kiss them each and sat on the floor.

"Oh Beth, here, sit by me, there's room" I said moving over.

"Oh, Jenny thanks but I prefer the floor in this place. Someone died there yesterday right where you're sitting. I'm pretty sure they peed themselves too." She mouthed the words 'died' out of consideration for the kids.

I shot up and grabbed the kids, putting them both on the floor with me.

"Don't touch anything" I instructed them.

"Well, I'd offer you a drink or a snack, but I don't have anything" Beth said with her eyes low.

"That's ok, we brought things, and things for you" Mom chimed in, happy to add something positive to the conversation.

She reached behind her and dragged a cooler in front of her.

"Here, we have sodas, lunch meat, I packed you some of Dad's spaghetti dinner, some pasta, cereal..." she stopped when she saw Beth crying

"Please don't cry" Mom said to Beth.

"Momma, please, please take me away from here. I'm so sad here. People are mean, they steal everything. Soon as you leave they're going to steal all that stuff from me, and I'm so hungry! I'm so so hungry!" Beth was pleading with Mom.

"Mama, I have to go potty." Benjy was pulling on my shirt.

"Beth where can I take him?" I asked Beth.

"Down the hall, to the right. But you have to get a key from Miranda. They keep the bathrooms locked. I can't even go to the bathroom in private" she said

"Miranda?" I asked.

"Yes the butch one who must've let you in?" Beth responded.

"She works here?" I was shocked; I assumed she was an addict too, by her appearance.

"Oh yeah, she's a real gem too. She'll probably be the first one to rob me blind soon as you guys leave," Beth said.

"Jenny I'll come with you" Mom said.

She got up and followed me down the hall with Benjy. We got the key and opened the bathroom door. It was a disgrace. There was urine and feces on the floor, and blood splattered on the wall.

"Benjy are you sure you can't wait?" I asked him.

"Pee-pee" he said pointing to the toilet.

"OK I'm going to have to hold you" I said holding him over the toilet, being sure to keep him from touching any surfaces.

"Mom, are you ok?" I asked

"I don't see how she can get better in a place like this" Mom said, and I agreed.

The place was disgraceful. I wouldn't leave a dog there. Mom and Dad agreed if she could stick it out to pass her next drug test, just 2 days away, then they would take her home. Beth was home by Monday night.

Mom and Dad tried to set some ground rules when she got home. They like all of us had been trying hard not to "enable" and to set "boundaries", all things we had learned about in our visits and support groups. Beth knew she couldn't be taking off for multiple nights at a time anymore, she had to check in and tell someone where she was and who she was with, she had to keep her appointments at the methadone clinic, find a job, etc.; nothing too extraordinary or unreasonable. For a few months it seemed to be working out, and we all settled back in to our usual routines. Unfortunately for me, my usual routine included covering for Ben's heavy drinking again and hiding the abuse he was forcing me to endure. I had put it on the back burner while Beth was sick, trying to focus all my attention on her and protect Mom and Dad from any extra stress, but I knew I couldn't hide it much longer.

Molly covered for me. I always called her or J.P. when I was stuck. Mom was a regular go-to as well. I had been going to the police regularly for help, but my answer was always the same-'if you want to leave you can, but we can't make him let you take the kids'. I would do my best to convince them that it was unsafe for the kids to be left alone with him, but it was only my word against his, and he was innocent until proven guilty. His family was powerful, and they would never let me 'disgrace' their blessed family reputation. The police advised me to have him removed from the home whenever he was escalating, and to start making a record of the frequency and severity of the situation. I had him removed from the home 11 times in 6 weeks for 'violent threats' and 'excessive intoxication'. Each time, I would have to pick up the pieces and go about my business, bringing the kids somewhere safe so I could go to work and continue to provide. I had to act like it didn't bother me, even though I was a hollow broken shell of the person I used to be. I knew I couldn't let the truth show, not to my family, my co-workers, not even my sisters. They wouldn't understand. Mostly, I had to hide it from the kids. As long as mommy was o.k., they were o.k. in their minds, and that was how I wanted it to stay.

One evening, he locked me in the bathroom with him for 4 hours while he interrogated me on my whereabouts the prior evening. No matter how many times I told him I was at work he wouldn't believe me. He was high and drunk. Luckily, the kids were at my parents for the night. I was scheduled to work the 11p-7a shifts and I didn't want them to be home alone with him all night. I begged for him to release me from our tiniest bathroom, but he demanded an explanation before he would let me go. There was no window in the room and it was so hot. The sweat was beading on my forehead and every time I tried to get a drink from the faucet he would punch me in the stomach, saying the pain would ease the thirst. I was too dehydrated to even make tears. I became too exhausted to argue with him, counting the condensation of my breath as precious fluid being lost from my body; I decided to just sit in silence and wait for him to sober up. I hoped that it would be before my scheduled shift. I didn't want to be marked as a no show at work. My work ethic was one of the only things he hadn't been allowed to tarnish. I curled up on the tile floor and put my nose as close as I could to the small crack under the door, trying to catch a tiny breath of fresh air whenever the slightest breeze went by.

Finally after 4 hours, at ten p.m. he must've sobered up enough to realize what was happening. He nudged me with his foot to get my attention. I had a small, ceramic cross statue on the back of the toilet with the 'Our Father' written on it. It was a gift from Jamie on my last birthday. Ben picked it up and hit himself in the head with it, causing a crimson wave to run down his face.

"If you tell anyone about this, I'll say you did this to me, and you'll get arrested too."

That was all he said before he threw the cross to the ground, shattering it to pieces, and went to the couch to pass out. I went to the kitchen for water and stuck my head outside in the cold night air, filling my lungs with fresh oxygen and tasting the freedom on the breeze.

I remember getting dressed and then staring over him, sound asleep, before I left to go work for the night. This would be night 3 with no sleep for me. I looked at him with rage. Why was he getting to sleep? Why wasn't I getting to sleep? I shook it off and went to work. I could always find people who had it worse than me at work. My job kept me humble, and sane.

I just about made it through the night, thanks to a few 10 minute bathroom breaks in which I power napped, and made it to my parents to get the kids. I pulled in the driveway and saw them playing in the hose water outside while Molly and Beth were washing the cars. Mom was working in her garden and putting worms she found in a bucket for the kids to take fishing.

"Benjy look how big this one is" Mom said excitedly holding up a worm for Benjy to see.

Benjy went running over for a closer look with Gabby following close behind, squealing with excitement. I was so glad they had this place and these people in their lives. What would we do without them? I was daydreaming about when Mom used to find us worms when we were little, before Ben's tormenting and Beth's troubles took over. I was daydreaming when Molly sprayed me with the hose.

"Hey!" I snapped

"Jeez what's with you? I'm just playing around" Molly said.

"I'm sorry I'm just so tired and grouchy I guess. I haven't slept in days" I started to say when Mom called me over.

"Jen, come here" she called.

I walked over and sat beside her on the brick walkway she had recently built. The bricks were warm from the sun. I could hardly hold my eyes open.

"Benjy said you cry at night. He told us that last night" she said.

"Great" I said.

"I know you have tried to get away, but I think time is running out for you to get out of this ok, or get the kids out ok," she went on.

"I know" I said. "I just don't know what to do, Mom, I can't leave them there with him. I can't risk that it's too dangerous. What if he takes off with them, or worse? He says if I leave he'll kill us, and you know what? I believe him."

"I know. I just want you to be focused. You know Dad and I will help however we can. I think you should at least stay here a couple days with the kids. Get some rest. Be sharp minded, ok?" Mom said.

She was talking in that 'mother tone'. The one when moms are wording what they're saying as a question, but making it clear that they aren't really asking you something-they're telling you something.

Still, they were the best words I had heard in a long time. I went home that afternoon once the neighbors told me Ben had left and quickly packed a couple bags. I left a note saying we were staying at my parents for a few days to help my mom with a gardening project. He wouldn't care about a few days down the road. It would just give him an excuse to go on a bender.

The few days turned in to a few months and they were the most peace I had from Ben in years. He would sober up just long enough to take the kids here and there and get his fill. I got to spend that spring enjoying peace and sleep and water whenever I needed it. No one deprived me of basic life essentials. The kids got to spend their spring the same way I did growing up, carefree and joyous in the clear fresh water of the pond, with Molly and Beth smiling over them. It was a great time.

Beth had been doing well for months. She was tapering down her doses at the methadone clinic again and we almost felt like the burden might be lifted. But, her demon was only hibernating, not dead as we desired.

I started noticing her getting up in the middle of the night. She was sleepless again. She would go on the computer, take warm baths, read huge novels, anything to get that sleepy feeling back, but rest eluded her. She was changing again, too. Her smile was fading and her skin started turning back to that greyish hue. I grew nervous, we all did. Little by little, the dark undertone in the house began gaining strength again, sucking out the peace that we had fought so hard for. We had let our guard down, we had made a mistake.

There was a girl that I once knew
deep brown eyes and raven hair.
Her soul was bared with your first stare,
no secrets seemed to live in there.
This girl came from the place I did,
we grew as children do.
We laughed until the sun sank deep
beyond the horizons hue.
This girl grew tall and strong and brave.
She tamed the wild lands.
Soon she developed secretive smiles,
and grown up weathered hands.
Her eyes were full of secrets deep,
her smile didn't last as long,
it faded faster every time
despite her favorite song.
This girl who once would dance and sing
to every melody there was,
became a shell of dreams once had
A shell of distant loves---K.A. Morini

I tried to confront her, again, one afternoon with Molly. It didn't go over well.

"Beth, come here" I called while Molly and I sat in the spare loft I had been sleeping in.

"Why?" she called up the stairs.

"Just come up we want to talk to you," I said annoyed at having to explain myself.

"What?" she said when she made it to the landing.

"Is everything ok?" Molly asked

"Everything like what?" Beth asked

"Beth, you know what we are saying. We know you better than anyone. We can tell when you are having trouble. Just talk to us, we are here for you. We love you," I said.

"OK enough of this shit. I'm out of here. I knew you guys didn't trust me. I can't stay here right now," she started to say.

"Beth what the heck are you talking about? You're just making an excuse right now to run away. We aren't against you," Molly tried to convince her.

Beth stormed down the stairs, blowing by Benjy.

"Out of the way peck" she said as she went by, quoting 'Willow'.

Molly and I were speechless sitting on the bed. We heard the door slam and just like that she was gone, with Mom's car.

"Oh my God she took Mom's car" Molly said looking out the window.

"Maybe she just went to a clinic appointment or something" I said trying to justify her rushed behavior.

"She better get her ass back here before Mom and Dad get home" Molly said

"Where are they anyways?" I asked her

"They went to Home Depot or something I think" Molly said

Just then the phone rang. I expected it to be Beth from her cell. I didn't even check the caller ID before I answered it. To my disappointment, it was my husband; my very drunk husband.

"Where the hell you been?" he started

Molly came over and hung the phone up before I could respond.

"Screw him, Jenny. He knows where you are. Let him sleep it off. We've had enough drama today. Let's take the kids in the canoe" she said

She was right. Screw him. I was going to enjoy every moment I could with my kids. I was going to stay right there waiting for Beth to come home, too. I packed up the kids with some bottled waters and life jackets and off we went. Ben couldn't get us out there in the pond anyways. It was a great idea.

That was about the end of my peaceful getaway. Ben showed up at the house a couple hours later. Of course the children being so young and innocent were only excited to see him. They ran to him excitedly and he used the opportunity to let me know they were still his kids too. He had sobered up and wanted us all to go to the park. He told me it was time to 'come home with the kids', and I could tell by his tone that he didn't just mean tonight. It was ok. I knew in my heart that Beth would be rearing up again soon, and the family needed to have the focus be on her and her recovery, not my problems. This was my mess. I had made it and the only one who could clean it up was me. I needed to do what was best for everyone. Besides, maybe I could get him to go back in to counseling. That did always seem to help for a while.

We went to the park and pushed the kids on the swings. We fed the ducks and got ice cream on the waterfront. We looked like the all American family. It was an easy illusion to create. Sometimes, I even started to believe it myself. It would never last long though. It always came crashing down around me.

I got home to find Mom and Dad were pulling in my driveway as I was taking the kids out of the car.

"Hi guys," I said.

"Hi honey, we just wanted to check in on you, see how you were doing," Dad said glaring at Ben the whole time.

"I'm ok Dad. We just had a nice evening on the waterfront. I was just about to do baths but I can make coffee if you want to come in" I said, smiling at Dad as if to ask him not to make a scene.

"That's ok we just had coffee at prayer meeting," Mom said.

Mom and Dad were faithful to their Sunday morning and Wednesday night church services. I think it's what carried them through the difficult times.

"We will be home if you need us, call us. Have you heard from Beth?" Dad asked

"I'm sorry to say I haven't. Her counselor didn't call me though to say she missed her appointment today though, so that's a good sign. Maybe she'll be home when you get there?" I was hopeful, but doubtful too.

"Ok, tell us if you hear anything and we will do the same. Benjy, Gabby come give us hugs before we go," Dad said.

Benjy and Gabby went running to Mom and Dad for big loving hugs. They had grown so close, especially over the last couple months at their house. Family is the greatest blessing.

"We will let you get settled" Dad said coming in for a hug" I love you. I mean it, call me."

I gave them both a hug and waved good bye as they drove off. We all knew I wouldn't call them, no matter how bad Ben got. I would never jeopardize my Mom or Dad's safety for my own. I only called them if I needed emergency help with the kids, and I did that often. They came through every time.

That night was quiet. Ben was on his best behavior for the next few nights, trying to prove he could be a good husband and father. He agreed to counseling. He admitted he was an alcoholic. I was hopeful again for a time. I walked on egg shells, trying not to 'rock the boat'.

I talked with Jamie and Molly every day, each of us sharing whatever tidbits we might have regarding Beth and where she could be. I taught Benjy his letters and numbers and tried to get Gabby used to me putting little braids in her hair. I taught them how to swim in Jamie's pool and at the pond, Gabby wearing swimmies, of course. We went to Khloe's all the time and played in the yard and roasted marshmallows at night. We went to the beach with Julia and built sandcastles. I went on my runs to burn off my aggressions, once again scanning all the faces I passed, looking for my sister. I went to work and there too, scanned the patient's faces and names, hoping for someone who might know where my sister is. But I never saw anyone from her circle. They were gone again from sight of anyone who might know their secrets. They all just disappeared.

Weeks had passed when the unthinkable happened. I was at work one morning, finishing up my shift when I got a phone call. It was the charge nurse from the emergency department.

"Jenny? Hi, listen, I think you better come down here" she was saying
I could tell from her tone she was trying to be kind.

"What's wrong?" I asked

I don't know why but at the time, Beth did not pop in to my head. It didn't occur to me that she was the reason for the call.

"Well….we got a call from EMS…….there was a 911 call they responded too…… there was a body lying in the woods……"

For a second I couldn't breathe. It was as if I just had no breath to breathe. Then, just as fast my adrenaline was surging and I was flying down the stairs to the ED.

She was arriving on the stretcher just as I was walking in. The charge nurse came to meet me. It was shocking. She looked like a wild animal. She was filthy, and her hair was in a rats nest on top of her head. She was strapped down to the stretcher so her thrashing about wouldn't cause her to fall. She was gritting her teeth and drooling and growling at people.

The sight took my breath away again.

"Oh my God" I cried covering my face. "What happened to her?"

"They reversed her high with Narcan and she's been like this ever since. It looks like she's been through some awful trauma, like she's afraid. We are going to have to sedate her to examine her. I know you're her proxy. Do you know anything that can help us?" the charge nurse asked.

"I don't know. She had gone to treatment and we thought she was doing better. She took off the other day. We hadn't seen her since" I was trying to get the words out before I threw up.

"Jen, you have to tell me- treatment for what? What was she in treatment for?" the nurse was asking ever so gently.

"Heroin" I said. "She's been in treatment for heroin addiction."

She gave me a hug. She walked to the room and pulled the curtain. I could hear my beautiful, smart, funny sister who was going to grow up to be a star, cussing out every person back there that was only trying to help her. I could hear the nurses and paramedics calling her a junkie. I could hear it all, and so could she.

The words kept ringing in my head "heroin, my sister is a heroin addict'. It had just finally become real. Up until now, I had been living in denial.

"Honey, can I make a recommendation?" the nurse came over and said

"Uh, yeah, sure" I said.

"Get your sister some help. Section her somewhere" she said gently rubbing my arm

"Section?" I asked

"Yes, it forces her to go in somewhere against her will, and it makes it so she can't leave on her own," the nurse explained.

"How do I….?" I had started to ask when I heard my mother's hysterical voice coming through the door.

The nurse turned to leave as my mother saw me and came running over. She looked like she had just come straight from the shower.

"Where is she? Where is she?" was all Mom could keep saying.

I had to pull it together quick for her.

"She's alive, Mom. She's here. She's safe now," I said trying to calm her down.

A tech brought over a chair for my mom to sit and we tried to move out of the way. Finally a psychiatrist came over and brought us out to the family room.

I looked at the psychiatrist in his nice suit and tie and wondered what kind of perfect life he went home to every night. I remember feeling angry at him for no reason at all. He hadn't done anything to us. He was trying to help us. But, I wanted someone to be mad at. I wanted someone to blame for this mess, and he was there. I wondered how he could possible relate to all the things we had been through, the pain that we felt. I wondered what advice he could possible give us to make it any better. What help could he, with his perfect suit and tie and shiny shoes, have to extend to us? Luckily, I'm good at keeping my thoughts to myself.

"I'm glad you're both here since you're both listed on her proxy sheet" he said showing us through the door and offering us each tissues.

"I'd like to just go over a little of Beth's background with you if that's ok. First of all, how long as she been a heroin addict?" he asked

Mom jumped right in to Beth's defense "Oh, she's not an addict. She did a little experimenting a while back, but she was almost all better."

"Mom" I tried to stop her.

"She's not an addict," Mom insisted.

The psychiatrist leaned in and took Mom's hand "Ma'am, I know this is incredibly difficult for you, but heroin is not something that even the strongest person can just experiment with. It's incredibly addicting."

I was glad that I hadn't been rude to this nice man.

Mom pulled her hand away "Well, what would you call it if not an addict?"

"Actually, I'd say she IS an addict. Judging by the amount of track marks she has and the fact that she has hepatitis C, I'd say she's a pretty significant addict with a pretty significant problem," he said.

"Hepatitis?" I asked

How could we be so stupid? How could we miss all of this? Of course, that's why she was hiding her razors and her drinks, so we wouldn't share off of them. That's why she said she was so bloated and tired all the time. How did we not see? We saw what we wanted to see, that's why. We loved her too much to see her becoming this monster; we were blinded by our love.

'4 Love is patient, love is kind. It does not envy,
It does not boast, it is not proud
5 It does not dishonor others,
It is not self seeking, it is not easily angered, it
Keeps no record of wrongs
6 Love does not delight in evil
But rejoices in truth
7 It always protects, always trusts,
always hopes, always preserves—1 Corinthians 13:4-7 (NIV)

"I'm sorry, did you not know about the hepatitis?" he asked and took a deep breath "I think you need to know the severity of what Beth is dealing with. She is involved in a very dangerous lifestyle, especially for a young woman."

"I think we need a few minutes," I said to the doctor.

He understood and left us alone. We cried. We cried for the life that Beth should've had, and for the battle she would now have to fight to have any life at all. Then, we stopped crying and made a decision that we weren't going to give up on her. Mom said a little prayer and we waved the psychiatrist back in.

"Tell me how I section her" Mom said

The psychiatrist explained the procedure to Mom and she agreed that it was for the best, really the only option we had to ever get her help. The social worker met with us, too. She explained that she would have to do a bed search, which could take days, and that she would have to be medically cleared before she could go to any facility. She told us that we wouldn't be able to see or talk to her until she was done detoxing and that Beth would probably be very angry with us for sending her against her will. We understood. Mom signed the papers.

We kissed Beth while she was sleeping and left her a note so she would know we had been there. Mom told me to go home and get some sleep. She had some errands to run. The police had called and told her that they found her car, undamaged in a parking lot a few towns over. We figured we had some time anyways before the bed search turned up anything or Beth was cleared.

I went home and jumped in the shower. Molly was there with the kids, Mom had dropped her on her way to the hospital so Ben could go to work. I filled Molly in on what we had learned. Molly didn't cry. Molly was emotionally thicker than me.

"I can't believe it," was all she kept saying.

"I know, me either," I said.

"Did you call Jamie yet?" Molly asked.

"Mom was going to after she picked up her car" I said.

"Do you want to sleep a little and maybe then we can go see her, bring her a coffee and stuff?" Molly asked.

"Sounds perfect to me" I said.

I awoke from my sleep about 5 hours later, feeling optimistic that Beth wasn't a lost cause. I desperately wanted to go see her and try to piece together what had happened to her since we last saw her. I mostly wanted to tell her how much I loved her. I wanted to tell her that 1,000 times. I wanted to tell her that she didn't deserve this life was living and that she still had so much to live for.

We walked in to the emergency room where she had been and found someone else in her stretcher.

We assumed she had been assigned a bed upstairs. We went over to the receptionist and gave her Beth's name and asked her to look her up.

"Oh, she was transferred" the receptionist said from behind the glass.

"What? To where?" I asked.

"She got a bed at Worcester Salvation Army Rehabilitation program. I remember now, she wasn't happy" the woman said "are you her family?"

"Yes," I said.

"She wanted me to give you this, it's all her stuff" she came around the partition and handed me a garbage bag full of Beth's belongings.

"Thanks" I said taking the bag "So what do we do now?"

"You're done here, honey, just got to wait for her to contact you. She will, don't worry" and she shut the glass.

To others, 'just go home and wait' seems like such a simple task. The problem is when you're dealing with addiction you spend so much time waiting, but you never really even know what you're waiting for. You wait for meetings. You wait for a phone call. You wait for doctor's appointments and court dates. You wait for your loved ones to return home, or to call or to send a letter. You wait for detoxification, sobriety, and recovery. You wait for healing. You wait for peace. You wait for life to start again. You wait, and wait, and wait, and wait.......

The first phone call we got actually came from Julia. Beth had gone to Oak Point. She had secured her a bed, knowing it would take forever to find her one using any other method. She accepted her soon as she got our phone call. She was in detox and Julia was pretty certain that she would be moving to the Worcester Center in the next couple of days. She said the program out there was pretty good and Beth might do well there. It was a Christian based recovery program. The people there had to stay busy with meetings, working in the stores and factories and pass their drug tests. The workers were dedicated and mostly had been recovered themselves for a decent amount of time. She was hopeful and so were we. She explained that Beth's bed in Worcester had been given to another person who was already detoxed, so when she saw the opportunity to move her to Oak Point she did. She figured it would be good to have a set of eyes on her while she was detoxing and we agreed. We were thankful for Julia's help and support. She was a part of our family, too.

We weren't allowed to talk to Beth the next couple of days; you never are during the detox phase. We had some peace of mind because this time she was sectioned. We knew she couldn't leave even if she wanted too. I hadn't told my parents, but I had found out that Beth had been in a couple other facilities voluntarily, only to leave as soon as the detoxing got too bad. There was no need to tell them now. I was sure they knew things they didn't tell me, too. We all did what we had too to keep each other as positive as possible, always trying to move in a forward motion for Beth and for each other.

> 'God grant me the serenity
> to accept the things I cannot change;
> courage to change the things I can;
> and wisdom to know the difference'—serenity prayer

I got a call from Beth's counselor, Josh, a few days later. He wanted to make sure it was ok if Beth got on the phone for a talk. She was afraid I was angry with her and wouldn't take the call if she called me herself.

"I'd love to talk to her. Please put her on" I urged the counselor

"Jenny?" she said

"Hi Buzz! How's it going in there?" I tried to sound as positive as possible

"It's actually not that bad here, I've been in worse. I miss you guys though. There's no place like home" she said and she started to cry

"I know Beth just please, please, you have to stay focused and get well so you can come home to stay. You know that" I pleaded with her

"I know. It's just so hard. The detox was really bad this time. I have broken blood vessels all over my face from throwing up so hard and my stomach muscles are so sore. I never sleep either. The sounds in those places at night are terrifying" she was crying "I'm sorry I'm not trying to make you feel sorry for me. I just want you to understand."

"I want to understand Beth. I really do. I don't know why this keeps happening. I just want you to stop. We all need the old Beth back. You need her back" I said

This conversation happened more times than I could count. The begging and pleading for a change in behavior. Trying to reason with the addict and convince them that the old them needs to come back is so common, yet, such an unreasonable request. The old them are gone. Even without the drugs, the experiences have changed them.

"I don't even know if she's still around, Jenny….the things I've done…I'm so ashamed of myself. I've turned into a monster," she sounded so distraught.

"Beth, stop it right now! You are not a monster. This isn't over! You have a lot to live for still! You can beat this is I know you can" I tried to convince her.

"Jenny the things I've done and seen, you have no idea, you couldn't imagine" she went on.

"I don't care about any of that Beth. None of us do. We just want you back. That's all we care about. It's not our place to judge you. It's our job to love and protect you" I said

"I got to go, Jenny. We only get a couple minutes on the phone. Please don't give up on me. Tell Mom and Dad I love them and I'll try to call them soon. I sent you a poem in the mail. Send me one back ok?" she said

"Beth, I love you Boo Bear. I'll think of you tonight when I fall asleep. I'll send a letter too and send me your visitation schedule. Whatever you need, I'll send" I said as I started to cry uncontrollably

"Bye, Jenny. Don't cry. Please don't cry. I love you" and she hung up before I could say anything else.

I called Mom and told her that Beth had called and that she sounded good. I finished cleaning up in the kid's rooms and brought them over to Khloe's with me. I filled her in on what had been happening with Beth. I knew she would let me go on and on while listening intently. I knew she would make me feel better.

In life we have two families; the one we are born in to and the ones we choose. We choose our spouse, we choose our in-laws, and we choose our friends. I truly believe there is some reason for us having to have two families. God designed it so that we had to go outside of our birth families to reproduce, it biologically is necessary for healthy offspring. He didn't have to make us that way, but he did. I think it must be because we all have times in our lives when we need to be helped along, or carried in a physical sense. He wanted us to have lots of people around to do that for us. It wouldn't be enough to have just a small group of people around to laugh and cry with us, because at any given times they are carrying burdens of their own. And since families often cry together, we need to be able to escape to our friends to make us laugh, to hold us up and to convince us that everything is going to be ok.

Mom and Dad were becoming closer and closer to their chosen friends too. They mostly consisted of church people that they had known for years. They clung to them for support, love and guidance. They prayed with them for Beth, and for Ben, to get better. Mom and Martha had become closer again too. Martha's son, Michael, was also battling the demon of addiction and trying to free himself of the chains that enslaved him. Martha was going through the same thing Mom was. They clung to each other for hope and strength.

I had Julia and Khloe and my work girlfriends that got me through the hard days and the nights. They stepped in to help me with the kids when I knew my parents needed a break. They had coffee with me during the mornings that I couldn't be alone. The helped me research my rights as a mother and as a sister. They built me up, telling me that I could do it and I would be ok. They were my rocks, never wavering, never complaining.

Molly had her boyfriend and threw herself into her work to stay distracted. She had the hardest time with the whole thing. She couldn't even hear Beth's name without getting upset and was hardly able to pull it together enough for visits. She had started working as a preschool teacher and used the children as an escape from the reality she didn't want to face.

Jamie had Jacob, as she always had, and her best friend since childhood along with her church for support. She stayed in touch with us all and contributed whatever she could to help in Beth's recovery process.

It's during this time that maybe we should've tried to stay closer together, or maybe it worked out the way it was supposed to, I can't say either way is better or worse. Everyone deals with tragedy in different ways. Everyone has their own ways of coping and it essential that you do cope. Adaptation is a very unique thing. It makes us become who we are. It refines us. So, we all coped and adapted to this new life that we all had now. We all changed and gained strength however we could, and good thing we did. The battle was far from over. We were in the eye of the storm.

Days turned to weeks and I consistently checked the mail every day, afraid that if Ben got it he would throw away anything addressed to me, as he often did. I didn't want to miss Beth's letter or the poem she told me she sent. When I finally got it a few days after her phone call, I read it 3 times. It made me think of all the talent that was being wasted. I wondered how many people were throwing their life away instead of reaching their full potential. There was so much beauty in the world to see. After reading her poems, it was clear that there was so much beauty trapped behind Beth's veil of addiction, too. She wasn't a 'junkie' and she wasn't stupid either. She was incredibly intelligent. I wondered if she knew the magnitude of her beauty and her gifts. I looked at my 2 little children, happily playing on the floor with their trucks and dolls and wondered if their father knew how much he was throwing away from his addiction also. I wondered if they would ever know their father the way I used to know him when he coached kid's baseball teams and had dreams for his future. I wondered if they would ever see their Aunty as a carefree, strong, funny girl singing songs and riding her bike, without a care in the world. I wondered how I would protect them from the evil that was destroying our family. I wondered how I was going to make their future better so they could achieve their dreams. I wondered if I really had any control at all over any of. All I knew for sure was that my sister had a gift, and I was certain she wasn't the only one. It was a hard realization: addiction doesn't discriminate. In fact, it seems to take the most beautiful, talented, tender hearts and captures them in its trap of cold, hard, steel.

'If I could just live by their mottos
My life would be just fine
Let go, and let God
And one day at a time
I've got a devil on my left shoulder
And an angel on my right
I need to shake the devil off of me
And I'll try with all my might
But it's not going to be easy
Of this I am quite sure
For this disease that I am up against
Isn't known to have a cure
My love affair with this poison

Has made a prisoner of me
I've tried to run so many times
But it just won't set me free
My guilt haunts my dreams
My heart is filled with shame
I'm always looking for excuses
Instead of taking any blame
At first I loved the thrill
I was a fool for the euphoric charms
But I turned into a monster
Sticking needled in my arms
Friends and family always wondering
Will I ever be saved?
Never satisfied with my performance
Or the way that I behaved
I've missed so much time
Hope I can make it up to them now
But I'm unsure they even want me too
And unsure that I know how
If they say that life's a gift
Then mine is yet to be unwrapped
I have to search my soul for the real me
And try to bring her back
I want to stay clean this time
And I'll try so very hard
But it's hard to leave it all behind me
When I'm living with these scars
There's never enough sorrys I could say
No way to change the past
I'm chasing demons from my head
And praying I'll find peace at last---A. Beth Randall

I placed the poem in the box under my mattress where I kept all Beth's letters and got ready for work. I decided I needed to get my sister through this mess no matter what the cost. We had to do everything we could to show how much we loved and supported her. She was my family chosen for me, and I wasn't going to let any family there by choice take any energy intended for her away. I was going to tell Ben my plans after work and hoped that he would be supportive. Up until now, I had been supportive of him. I was always taking him back, going to therapy with him, getting him out of legal trouble, covering for him with work, family etc. It was exhausting and my energies were needed elsewhere; if not on Beth, then on the children. They were getting older and deserved my full attention, too.

I went downstairs and put on my make-up and straightened my hair. Ben still wasn't home. I was getting nervous so I called my parents as usual and had to bring them there for the evening. I had to go to work and he was nowhere to be found. This was so aggravating. He knew I had to work, he just didn't care. He couldn't face down the temptation to get high or drunk or whatever he desired that particular day. What bothered me the most was that he never seemed remorseful. He was never really sorry for what he had done. He was just sorry when he got caught. I feared for the night that I knew would be in store for me if he showed up at home tonight, in one his rages. He would be violent, paranoid and accusatory. On the other hand, I feared for what could happen if he didn't come home; drunk driving accidents, robbery, alcohol poisoning or worse.

I had been home one night when I was woken up by him making choking sounds. I jumped out of bed and followed the sound to the bathroom. I found him there on all fours, choking and gasping with white foam coming out of his mouth. Not knowing what else to do, I stuck my fingers down his throat and induced vomiting. He threw up some white and black goo with pills still whole in the mix. After that he was breathing ok and he just lay down on the floor. I turned him on his side and went back to bed. I had become completely desensitized to the whole situation. If I had known more about sectioning people back when his addiction was getting so out of control, I would've gone that route, but I didn't. I was so young and this life was becoming a nightmare. I wanted him to get help more than he actually wanted it for himself, or for us.

You can't make someone else get better. They have to want recovery. After 8 years together, I was starting to see that despite how much I was willing to invest or sacrifice, he didn't really want to give up that lifestyle. I was starting to realize that I was only enabling him. The kids were getting older, and I wouldn't be able to shield them from his destruction much longer. They were such sweet little kids. I couldn't stand by and let their childhood be destroyed. I had mentioned how I felt to Ben so many times recently. He would be good for a while. Then, he'd slip back into the same behaviors. I couldn't take it anymore. I didn't want to take it anymore.

I packed up the kids and headed to my parents. They didn't think anything of it. They were happy to go. I hoped he didn't show up there and try to take them home. I never felt secure when they were with him anymore. I was afraid they would wonder into the road or that he would fall asleep with candles lit. I went through every possible scenario in my head, always trying to stay one step ahead. Even worse, I was afraid my parents would try to keep him from taking them and then have to deal with his antics. Hopefully he would just stay away, at least until I got out of work.

My shift was fairly quick that night. I had worked 8 days in a row so I knew my assignment pretty well. I sat and talked with one of my favorite patients. I had been caring for her for 6 weeks as she tried to battle her newly diagnosed cancer that was ravaging her body. She was only 35 and had no idea that her life would be so seriously afflicted at such a young age. She told me to live every moment like it was my last, because it could be. She pushed this idea on me every day. She showed me pictures of her family as I picked up the hair off her pillow case and emptied her drainage bags. She knew her fate was sealed, but mine wasn't. I had still had a choice. I wish I could've made the other people in my life see that they still had a choice, too.

I went and got the kids who luckily were still at my parents. I carried them out to the car and brought them home. I brought them upstairs and tucked them in, one by one. I cleaned up the house and did a few loads of laundry. It was late and I was getting tired. I looked at some old photos of my family and me; photos of our trip to Florida with Julia in high school, of all our little puppies that we had over the years, of Beth and Delia at birthday parties. It was a good life so far. It could still be saved. This could all just be a bump in the road.

Ben still wasn't home, so I locked up and went to bed. I hid my car keys and my purse so he couldn't come home and steal them. I took my phone to bed in case someone needed me for something. I fell off in to that place between awake and asleep. The place where your heart and mind talk to each other and finally get to tell you things that you were too busy to hear them saying during your time awake.

I had a dream that I was in Florida, it seemed like I was on business. I was definitely older. There were palm trees everywhere and I didn't have the kids with me. I had on a nice business suit and sun glasses on. As I rode in the back of the cab, I looked out the window and saw someone I recognized but hadn't seen in a long time. Then, I saw that it was Ben.

"Hey, pull over I know him," I said excitedly.

The cab pulled over and let me out.

"Ben, Ben" I called after him down the sidewalk.

He stopped and turned around. He looked slightly dis-sheveled and not so thrilled to see me.

"Hi! It's me. Remember me?" I asked excitedly.

"Oh, hi, yeah, how are you?" he asked.

"I'm good. In town for business" I said still catching my breath from running after him.

"Oh," was all he said.

"So, you want to get some lunch?" I asked

"Oh, ah" he hesitated.

"C'mon, my treat. Show me somewhere nice," I said.

Then we were back in his tiny apartment, even smaller than the one he had when we were teenagers. I was looking around and noticed that he had pictures of the kids all over his dressers, only they weren't recent. They were very old. They were baby pictures.

Ben said he was going to take a shower. He didn't seem happy that I was there. I suddenly realized what was happening. We hadn't seen each other in years, and judging by the age of the pictures he had of the children, he hadn't seen the kids either. I was overwhelmed with sadness for us all. I wrote a note: 'good to see you' and left.

I woke up. I knew what was going to happen. I knew the end was coming. I just didn't know when.

I got up and checked on the kids. It was 6 am. They were sleeping peacefully. Ben still wasn't home. I felt my cell phone ringing in my pocket.

"Hello?" I answered nervously.

"Jenny? Are you ok? I just woke up with a sad feeling about you." Beth said.

"I'm ok. I just had a bad dream though. That's crazy that you could feel it huh?" I said.

"We're connected. We always have been. I have to go, though. I begged to use the phone so early. I said it was an emergency. I'll call you later if I can. We have a retreat soon so we have a lot of work to get done. I love you" Beth said

"I love you too" I said and we hung up.

I got a card in the mail later that day from Beth that she must've sent a couple days before. Beth always had a connection to me, as she had said earlier. When I opened the card, a quote fell out that she had put inside for me to hang on my fridge or wherever I desired. It was the quote from Peter Pan about waiting for someone in the place where you're not quite sleeping, but not awake, either. She underlined the last line 'That's where I'll be waiting'.

It sent shivers down my spine. I placed it on the mirror in my bathroom and put the card with the rest of her correspondence under my mattress. She had become so good at communicating through mail. She never missed a birthday or Holiday and loved when we would send her things too. She would often ask for DVDs and books. It was her connection to the outside world. It was her life. I treasured every letter she sent.

Dear Tweedle Beetle -

Hey... how are you? I hope everything is going good for you. How are          and          ??? I miss you and I miss them so much... more than you could imagine. I am doing alright considering the present circumstance. I have some good days and some really awful days when I get to thinking about what a piece of crap I am and some things that I've done. All I want to do is either lay in bed crying or want to call someone for a ride and get the hell out of this place, I'm having one of those days today and its really tough to stay here. Its just so overwhelming when I start thinking about everything: like my living situation, job situation, money situation, family situation, and court coming up in January. I'm really not writing this to try and get your sympathy or anything I just really need to let it out and I don't feel so comfortable talking to people here. No one can understand me like my sister and I love you so much and honestly appreciate you very much. I might not tell you enough or show you enough just how much I care, but I want you to know I'm sorry that I chose to live this life and put you and the family through this shit. I never meant for things to end up this way, I just wish I could rewind time and take back all those mistakes, I just want to live a normal fecking life!!! And its hard to stay positive when I realize that I've been through this before and it didn't make any difference. I wish I could be your friend and sister like you are to me. You deserve to have good people in your life because you are an incredible sister, mother, and friend. I'm going to stop now but I love and miss you too much. Hopefully I'll talk to you soon. Love you

P.S. If you could, can you please mail me some good pictures? And could someone please try to get my shit from ⟶ I WANT MY STUFF!

Ben didn't come home that afternoon. I had to be at work at 7pm. I got all ready and started to assume he wasn't coming. I called his cell-no answer. I texted- no response. I packed the kids up and got prepared to head over to my parents. I put their bag in my car and saw him driving toward the house. He was driving on the wrong side of the road.

I went quickly inside and started rounding up the kids. He came in hardly even able to stand. He went in the kitchen and turned the oven on.

"Where the hell you think you're going?" he mumbled to me.

"Ben are you ok?" I asked.

He grabbed Benjy and started playing with him. I started to panic. I couldn't leave without Benjy. How was I going to get him away? He told Benjy to go upstairs and get his blocks so they could play. Of course Benjy did, and Gabby followed.

"What you been doing all day! This place is a pit!" he was yelling at me already.

"Ben, why don't you take a rest? I got to go to work. We can talk later" I tried to keep it vague.

My efforts were for nothing. He had the fire in his eyes. He wanted a fight and he was going to get it. I knew that look very well.

He flew at me out of nowhere and grabbed me by the back of the head. He pushed me up against the wall so that I couldn't move.

"Don't tell me what to do!" he screamed in my ear.

He threw me on to the floor. I played dead. One kick to the stomach and he went into the bathroom. I lay there for a minute not sure what move to make. I looked up and saw Benjy on the stairs holding his blocks. I held my fingers up to my mouth to tell him to stay quiet. I mouthed for him to go back upstairs and stay with Gabby. He was such a good boy. He always did as he was told.

I walked quietly over to the bathroom door and put my ear against it. Ben was doing cocaine. I could hear him sniffing it. I knew my window of time to escape was small. I was tiptoeing up the stairs when the smoke alarm went off. I hadn't even noticed the smoke that was filling the air in the house. Ben must've left a pan in the oven when he turned it on.

"Crap" I said out loud and started running up the stairs.

I had already heard him coming up behind me when I turned the corner to the kid's room. He grabbed me from behind again. I motioned to Benjy to run downstairs with Gabby, and he did.

I fought myself out of Bens grip and flew down the stairs. The smoke was thick and I ran to the oven to shut it off. I didn't know how long I'd be there fighting and didn't feel like getting stuck in a fire, too. I saw Benjy holding Gabby in the corner of the living room. He was smart enough to stand close to the door. As I came around the corner, Ben clothes lined me and I was on my ass. He picked me up by my neck and slammed my head against the wall. He was yelling, but I couldn't hear what he was saying. My ears were still ringing from when he screamed in them earlier. I just focused on my kids. Everything else was a blur. They were my only concern. I saw Benjy sit on the floor and start to cry those big crocodile tears that little kids cry when they are really upset. Adrenaline must've kicked in because suddenly, I was able to fight myself free. In one swoop I had both of my kids in my arms and was running out the door to the car. I had left my keys in the ignition earlier when I put their bag out there. Thank God for small miracles. I literally threw them in the back seat when I heard Benjy scream out "MOM". I didn't even have time to turn around before Ben had me in a choke hold from behind. I couldn't breathe. He was dragging me back wards as I reached behind me frantically trying to find his eyeball or ear, anything I could grab at to set myself free.

"I told you if you tried to take them from me I'd kill you," he whispered in my ear.

He dragged me all the way back inside the house. He threw me on the ground. I gasped for air and tried to get up. He was on the ground too. He had my leg and was wrapping himself around it. I knew instantly what he was doing; he was trying to break my leg. Without a second to spare I heard a voice in my head. I don't know where it came from but it demanded attention and I listened. It was yelling "roll! roll! roll!" and that's exactly what I did. I rolled as fast as I could, freeing myself from his grip. I was almost to the door when I felt a hard pain on my shoulder. It spun me around and I was facing Ben.

"Ben, Ben please" I was holding his face in mine, trying to get through to him, but he didn't even see me.

His eyes looked right through me.

"Ben please don't do this, please" I was begging.

He put his hands around my neck and began to squeeze. I tried to loosen his hands, but that only made him squeeze harder. My feet were barely touching the floor.

At first I could hear my heart pounding in my chest, but that was slowly fading out. I started to hear voices in my head. Quiet, dull, happy voices. They were laughing. It was my sisters and my kids. It was the sound of their voices happily playing. It was my heavenly sound.

I came to on the floor. Molly was sitting there with me, my head in her lap with a cool cloth on my head. The police were there. Mom and Dad were there too with Benjy and Gabby.

Molly had walked in just as I was passing out. Ben lunged at her and let me fall to the floor. When she moved he tripped in his own drunken stumble and fell to the ground. He hit his head and knocked himself unconscious. Molly had called the police.

"Don't move just yet," a paramedic was saying to me. "Ms., I told you not to move her head" she said to Molly.

"Her neck is fine," Molly said as if she were a doctor.

"We still need her to wear this collar. We will need to take you in to get checked out" the nice lady said to me.

I was in no condition to put up a fight. I wanted them to see the truth, the proof of the hell I was living in. I asked Mom to call work for me and tell them I wouldn't be coming.

I told the police my account of what happened and this time they listened. They went on a search for Ben immediately as I went on record to finally tell my story.

"You know you're doing the right thing, telling us the truth. But, since the children were present D.S.S. is going to have to investigate" the officer said gently.

"Are they going to take my kids?" I asked

"I don't know why they would. You did the right thing keeping all your records of reports you made. You protected them as best you could. I'm sure you'll be ok" the officer said.

The night went on and we stayed at Mom and Dad's until the police called the next day and said they finally found him wandering Main Street in the early morning hours. He had drugs and stolen pills on him. They arrested him on numerous counts and I breathed a sigh of relief knowing he was behind bars and we were finally safe, for now.

Ben's parents were not so happy to hear of what had happened. Evelyn called me repeatedly, demanding that I drop all charges. She threatened to make sure I lost the kids for good if I didn't. I wasn't going to listen though. I knew staying was a death sentence for me. Who would raise my kids then? The only chance I had was to get away from him. That's what I set out to do. My family stood behind me.

When Beth called the next day I told her what had happened and that I was finally done with him for good. She was supportive and told me over and over how much she wished she was home to be there to help us. I told her how proud I was of her for staying past her 30 day section. She was going on 90 days sober and was soon to be released to all of us.

I can remember going up to see her one afternoon with Mom. There are times in life when you become weary. This day Mom was weary. So much had happened to our family in the last couple of years. There weren't enough smiles to outnumber the tears.

"Jenny I'm really sorry," Mom said.

She looked straight ahead as she drove for what seemed like miles and miles of highway. The back of the car was full of trash bags, all containing things for Beth. Every week she would send us a list of things she need; laundry detergent, shampoo, socks, and maybe some clean pajamas for someone that had less than her. We had the windows open, and I could hear the windows hitting the trash bags in the back. We would give Beth this week's necessities and take away the old things in the trash bags. We were bag ladies.

"What do you mean Mom, what are you sorry for?" I asked, caught off guard by such candid emotion from Mom.

"I'm sorry for all the things I didn't do while you guys were growing up," Mom said.

"Mom, you don't have to say you're sorry. We had a good life, what do you mean?" I answered.

"I should have been there more. I don't mean just in person, I mean in every way. Emotionally, I wasn't always there. I could have done better," Mom said.

"Mom, everyone could look back and say they could have done better. What happened to us is not your fault. We all made our own decisions," I said.

"I should have guided you more. I already talked to Beth about this. I need you guys to forgive me. I love you more than anything, but I didn't show you that."

I didn't know what to say. I never planned for this conversation.

After a few moments, I said, "Mom, you didn't have to ask but the fact that you did ask makes me love you even more. I love you, and you are a great Mom, let's leave it at that."

The rest of the car ride was spent singing along to Johnnie Cash together. From then on out we let go of the past, and focused on building a better future with each other.

I went alone to visit her couple more times. Mom and Dad went up often, and Jamie and J.P. went too. We would take her out to lunch, shopping or a picnic try to keep her life, and ours, as normal as possible. She often told us about the friends she made in rehab. She told us of the people who she grew to care deeply about. The ones she felt guilty leaving behind. Addicts are often ruthlessly selfish while also being painfully sensitive. She had her moments being both, but for the most part she was painfully sensitive. Her heart hurt for those who had less than she did. She felt so sorry for the ones that had no families, no gifts at holidays and no mail on mail days. She saw them as humans, not just addicts. She forgave them and believed in them. Everyone needs someone like that in their life. Everyone needs a Beth to pick them up when they need it or jump into the deepest of darkness's with them so that they aren't alone. Beth started to talk about getting better for good. She wanted to get into a position where she could help people who needed helping. That was her piece of hope. She clung to that hope while she hung over the pit of hell. She held on for dear life.

Beth finished her program and came home a short time later. She went right into the loving, doting sister role. She knew I was trying to put on a brave face for her, even though I was really dying inside.

The decisions I had recently made regarding my own children's fate weighed heavily on my mind and in my heart. When Beth came home, she made it all about me. I tried to tell her during her first night back that I was o.k. I tried to convince her that I didn't need her worrying about me and that I was going to be o.k. She saw through me.

"Jenny, I know when you're upset. Its o.k. I'll come hang out with you and you can just relax. O.k.?" Beth gently coaxed me.

I started to feel the tears falling down my face behind my sunglasses. They weren't tears of sorrow. They were tears of joy. I had my sister home, and I could let my guard down finally. I was overjoyed.

We went back to my house and had a 3 day chocolate and movie marathon. I had never been so happy to have nowhere to go and nothing to do. No one came screaming through the front door, no one tormented me or told me how awful I was. My kids laughed and played. My sisters were all o.k.; everything was just as it should've been. It was a time for healing and rebirth. It was a great time.

As we lay in bed one afternoon watching 'Now and Then', I couldn't help but get emotional again.

"Beth, I'm so glad you are home. I've missed you so much. I get such loneliness when you are away. Things were so bad for so long. I just want things to finally be good now." I was saying.

"Jenny, you've been through so much. We both have. People like us, we have to stick together. Kindred spirits just like 'Anne of Greene Gables', remember?" she asked.

It was so typical of Beth's style to incorporate a movie.

"Yes of course I remember. I miss being a little kid sometimes, don't you?"

"I still am a kid," Beth laughed.

"Yeah, things were so simple then. Did I ever tell you about the time that Ben chased Khloe and me out of the courthouse? I tried to get a restraining order on him and someone must've tipped him off."

"He chased you out? Of a courthouse? A real one?"

"Not only did he chase us out, but he jumped on top of my car in the middle of the road and started jumping up and down while I was on the phone with the 911 operator!" I couldn't help but laugh at the ridiculousness that I was telling her.

"Were you scared?"

"Terrified! And embarrassed! Khloe said she'd never believe it happened if she didn't witness it firsthand!"

"He did do some crazy stuff, Jen."

"Sure did. Oh well, at least I survived. I just wish we could stay little forever, like how Benjy and Gabby are now, don't you?"

"Of course I do, but "nothing gold can stay", remember Jenny?"

195

"Yeah, I remember."

I put my head on her shoulder and started to cry.

"Aww, Jenny, please don't cry. You know I hate to see you upset," Beth said.

"Just promise me, please, promise me that you'll still be around when we are old and gray. Who else will lie in bed with me all day if you're gone? Remember we were all going to share a room at the nursing home?" I asked.

Beth laughed, "I promise, Jenny. We will get our dentures mixed up. We will be awesome."

I don't think I've ever been so happy to hear about having someone else's teeth in my mouth. I loved her so much, especially at that moment.

We had one of the greatest summers ever that year. We hung by the pool and had bonfires and beach days. Beth started working again at the candy shop down town. Things seemed like they were finally going right. Ben had been locked up for a while and we had custody orders in place keeping the kids in my care full time. Molly did well at her job and loved waking up each morning in the same house as Beth. J.P.'s girlfriend, Emma, had moved in with me to help out with the kids. We were one big happy family.

> 1 There is a time for everything and a season for every
> activity under heaven: 2 A time to be born and a time to die
> 3 A time to kill and a time to heal, a time to tear down and
> a time to build 4 A time to weep and a time to laugh, a time
> to mourn and a time to dance – Ecclesiastes 3 1-4 (NIV)

I had started dating again, too. It had been so long since I had been in a normal relationship. I didn't know what was acceptable and what wasn't. I took my time and eventually started seeing a nice guy I had known for a while at the hospital. He was newly separated and had two kids of his own. He was quiet, reliable and safe. I liked feeling safe. Things were looking up.

"Higher, mama, higher" Gabby was squealing as she jumped on Emma's bed.

"Gabby you aren't supposed to come in here, silly goosey. You better come out before Emma finds you and eats your little toes" I said tickling her and trying to get her out of Emma's room.

"Mama what's that?" she said

"What honey? I don't see anything" I said looking in the direction she was pointing.

"Orange" she kept repeating.

"Honey I don't see anything" I said. "C'mon now let's go outside and play with Benjy."

She jumped off the bed and followed me. A short time later I was putting laundry away when I got a feeling like I should double check what Gabby was pointing too. I went in Emma's room and looked on the bookcase, but I couldn't see anything. I got a chair to stand on and looked on the higher shelf. There it was. Now I knew why Gabby kept saying 'orange'. It was a syringe with an orange top.

I knew I had no proof that it belonged to Beth. If I confronted her, she would probably say it was Ben's or anyone else's really. I didn't want to make it seem like I didn't trust her either, even though, in my heart I knew it was hers. I decided I would just tell her that I found it and how scared it made me to find it in my house where my children were. I would let her take it from there. From now on, though, I would have to be on high alert.

Beth always seemed to be in such a good mood when I saw her, I hated to be the Debbie downer, but I knew I had to eventually tell her what I found. I decided to wait until after her birthday. It had been so long since we had a decent reason to peacefully celebrate, I didn't want to take that away from any of us.

I packed everything up and got the brownies and cookies together that I had made for her party. It was going to be a great night. Everyone was coming to celebrate. Jamie and Jacob, of course J.P., Grandma and Aunty Nellie were even coming down from Scituate. Mom had lost her older sister Janice to cancer when we were all in middle school, but Nellie was coming around more and more now. It was nice for Mom to have the support, especially since Delia was gone.

I decided to stop at the store for a couple last minute goodies for Beth. I wanted this birthday to be great. I brought the kids inside and let them each pick out a candy bar for Beth from them. I put my cards, candy and gifts on the counter and reached in my purse for my credit card to pay. It wasn't there. I fished around a few moments more and sorted through my wallet. There was a line forming behind me, and of course the kids got very restless at the hold up. I apologized to the clerk and searched for one more minute before I gave up.

"You take checks?" I asked and wrote a check to pay.

We pulled in to Mom and Dad's and the joy was palpable. I could see the fishing poles out front against the porch, ready and baited for who ever wanted to take them out. Through the open windows I could hear the Eagles melodic voices singing 'Take it Easy'. The house hadn't been this bustling with excitement in months. I looked on the porch and was happy to see that Aunty Rose and Uncle Rob was there, along with the neighbor, Ellie, who had watched us all grow up since we moved in to the tiny house. 'Yes' I thought to myself 'this is going to be a great night', and it was.

We enjoyed Beth's birthday celebration and felt good knowing that we gave her a good time. We talked about how relieved we were that she seemed to be doing well. We were blissfully ignorant to the warning signs once again.

I was standing in my bathroom getting ready to head to the park with the kids a few days later when my phone rang. It was Mom.

"Jenny?" she said in a muffled shaky tone.

"Mom what's wrong?" I asked already dreading the answer.

"There's something wrong with Beth. Can you come over right away?" she said.

"What do you mean 'something wrong'?" I asked concerned.

Why? Why did this have to keep happening? She had been doing so well!

I had already started running upstairs. I needed to see if Emma was still here to keep an eye on the kids. I was already on my way out the door when Mom answered me.

"She's walking around in a daze. She won't answer me and her speech is all messed up. She looks like a zombie! I don't know what to do! Please help me I'm here alone!" Mom was hysterical.

I was already half way to her house by the time we hung up. I kept catching myself holding my breath and had to remind myself to breathe.

I was dreading the ideas of what I might find when I got inside. I had already called Julia and told her, again, that I needed a bed.

"Where is she?" I said as I ran through the door.

Mom was crying so hard she couldn't even answer me. Her head was in her hands.

This is what addiction does.

"Mom! Where is she?!" I bent to her level and pulled her hands off her face.

Mom just pointed to the bathroom.

"Get ready Mom, I'm going to need you." I walked to the bathroom and knocked on the door

"Beth" I called "what are you doing?"

"Just showering Jenny" she slurred back.

"I need to come in let me in" I said.

"In a sec, I'm on the toilet" she answered.

Just then I heard the back bathroom door that connected to the spare room squeak open. I ran around through the dressing room and saw her sneak back in the bathroom with a lighter in her hand. My heart sank.

"Beth open the door I mean it," I was yelling and pounding on the door.

"Beth, please, open the door," Mom was pleading.

No response. Just silence.

"Mom I have to break through this door. You understand?" I asked Mom

She just nodded yes. I found Dad's old softball bat in the closet and used it to open the door. When I got through Beth screamed and hurled her body around her drugs like a snake coiling around its prey. She hissed at me, as if a warning to back off. I saw the spoon and the powder laid out on the counter and I ruined it all with one swipe of my arm.

"NOOOOO" she howled at the sight of her drugs being destroyed.

She lunged at me and landed a good punch to my head. Mom was standing there frozen at the sight of what she was witnessing. I could still see Beth's freshly cooked witches brew sitting by the sink.

"Mom, get the drugs! Get them quick!" I said holding Beth around her arms from behind,

She was thrashing against me and hurling profanities so vulgar they burned my ears. Mom did as I said and threw the drugs down the toilet.

"No, no, no," Beth was screaming.

I loosened my grip knowing the drugs were gone. She reached up to a glass framed photo on the wall. She smashed it into pieces on the ground and took a piece of glass. She slit her wrist right in front of me. The blood splattered across my shirt.

"Call the police, Mom, now!" I ordered.

Mom ran out of room as Molly and her boyfriend came running inside.

"Oh my God! What happened?" Molly said coming through the door.

I was making a tourniquet to wrap around Beth's wrist. She had collapsed in to a pile on the ground.

"Help me please! Help me," I ordered Molly's boyfriend. "I need to get her in my car."

We picked her up by her under arms and ankles and carried her out to the car. We had just put her in when the police pulled up.

Two officers got out and walked over to us.

"We got a call about a domestic. Can you tell us what is going on here?" the first officer said.

The second officer looked down and peered in at Beth nodding off in the back seat. He nodded to the other officer to look in the window, too.

"My sister is in a bad way, as you can see. We have a bed for her, but she will lose if we don't get her there quick. She was escalating and we did call you...we just don't want anyone to get hurt," I explained.

The officers looked at me, my sister's blood all over my shirt and they looked at each other.

"O.K. let's go. We will follow you down there," the second officer said and they turned and got in their cars.

We got down to Oak Point and brought Beth inside. The doctor wanted to talk to us about Beth's goals and setbacks and how to avoid them. The ugly truth was that Beth was well known not only to Oak Point, but also to Gosnold, Danvers, Salvation Army and a long list of other facilities some of which are no longer even open. She always wanted to get better, but she just couldn't seem to fully transition in a recovering addict. She could never totally shake that demon off her back. It always managed to have one claw dug into her. She would cry and beg for help and forgiveness. She hated who she had become. We had talked so much about her dreams for the future when she stayed at my house those 3 days the last time she got out of her program. She told me how she so badly wanted a home, children a career; all the things she always dreamed of. She wanted to grow old with us and watch our children accomplish their dreams. She wanted more than anything to make us proud, and to make a difference in the world. She wanted it all so bad that it only hurt when she couldn't have it. She had confessed to some awful acts and told us there were more that she could never bear to repeat. Even she didn't know why she was doing the things she did. One thing she did know was that she wouldn't wish the life she was living on her worst enemy. She felt that everyone would be better off without her.

Hey P wanted to write you and tell you how I feel... just so you know. This is not to sound mean at all, just honest, hard as it is. P guess P don't really know what to say or how to say anything so this is the best P can do. P really don't think you know how much P love you and how much your disease is killing me and everyone else who loves you and has had to watch yourself destruct. It's too much... Until recently P had thought all these years you really wanted to get better. P really believed that someday this would all be a painful memory and we would all have you back. P miss you and P feel like P have totally lost you. P never thought you would do things you have recently done and it hurts me. P want you to get better but P don't think you do. If P could switch places w/you P would. If P could quit the drugs for you P would. We both know P can't. If there is some underlying reason why you do this now is the time to tell me. Otherwise P want you to know P will always love you. P will always think of you every day... wonder where you are and if your ok... if your happy. P will wait for you every day to come back to me truly clean. P know you can do it— Please do it. P can't watch you like this one more day, none of us can. We love you too much and it's hurts too bad. P hope you understand. I love you.

Love,

Remember you promised we'd get our dentists mixed up

That's the things about addiction. It isn't just addiction. It grows into so much more. It leads to abuse, poverty, ignorance, shame, depression, anxiety, PTSD, crime, and so much more. It doesn't just affect the addict either. It affects the parents, siblings, spouse's friends, family and the children around the addict. It's huge problem and when left unresolved, it spreads throughout the entire community like a virus. Like a plague.

Beth had become lost in her addiction it was hard for her to find her way out of the darkness anymore. It was as if there was no light at the end of the tunnel. Addicts need to know how to feel good, so that they know that they don't want to feel bad. That isn't the kind of treatment available though. Instead, they have one numb baseline all the time. They start to live a flat, monotone existence. Beth was on Seroquel, Ativan, Ambien, Methadone, Suboxone, Neurontin and many other medications over the years. It was one pill for this, another for that; the answer to everything another pill. She never learned how to deal with the root of her problem or how to stop and take control of her life. She was just told 'here take this it will make you feel better'. She never got the rush of true happiness anymore because she was too numb from all the meds. Perhaps the worst feeling of all for her, was that none of this had to happen. She didn't have to live this life, but she didn't know how to live any other way.

I dropped Molly's boyfriend off and thanked him for his help. I apologized for Beth's behavior and asked him to not judge her too harshly. I left feeling defeated and sad. I thought we had moved past all of that, just another disappointment. I went back to Mom and Dad's and filled Mom in on what had happened. I went down to Beth's room to put away a few of her things and tidy up. I looked down and saw my credit card on her vanity table. It hurt. Up until now I had really wanted to believe that she had some control over herself, that she was capable of some kind of boundaries and limits on her behavior. I could see now that she wasn't. It was clear that how we dealt with her wasn't working and that we needed to make some drastic changes and quickly if she was ever going to survive this.

Mom and Dad, Jamie, Jacob,-myself and Molly all met to decide what we were going to do. Mom and Dad couldn't deal with having her home anymore. Every time she went in the bathroom they held their breath until she came out. Every phone call she got grew suspicion. They had started fighting with each other terribly over how to deal with her and the whole situation. It wasn't working out with her there anymore. I couldn't take her at my house and neither could Jamie, not since I had found the syringe in my home and I knew she stole from me. We both had small children and we couldn't subject them to a risk that high. She had already briefly lived with friends and that always turned out badly. We decided it was best for her to stay in someplace where she could learn life skills over again and how to cope with her state of mind. We didn't know that no such place existed. We banned together for strength and established our own boundaries. We weren't turning our back on her, we would never do that. We weren't pulling our love away from her either. We were taking away the option of her coming home though. She still had choices but that wasn't one of them. It was best for her, we thought, to not be around the familiar temptations. We made the best decision that we were equipped to make. It wasn't easy, but it was necessary. We had to protect each other. We had to stay strong for her or else she truly would have no one. We knew we couldn't stay strong like this. We were getting the life sucked out of us.

Before Beth had even had a chance to call, I got disturbing news in the mail. Ben's parents wanted custody. It was the first of many summons's that I would get from them trying to maintain control over the family that he threw away. I put all the energy I had into securing safe plans and homes for my kids. I protected them from the monster that their father had turned into. I tried to give them the life they deserved and would've had, if addiction hadn't torn through our life like a hurricane. I didn't know much about the law at that time. Jamie had lent me money for a lawyer during the initial divorce, but I hardly had money to keep food on the table, never mind another lawyer. Ben's family completely cut me and the kids off financially. The divorce had dragged on for months, and was only cut short when Ben's dad suffered a heart attack. Of course, Evelyn blamed me for that too, but at least it finally made her subside her efforts to keep me married to her son. Finally, she had other things to focus on and I could move on with my life; at least, for that moment.

I had spent countless hours on-line, getting free consultations, talking with the woman's shelter and seeing the free lawyers at the court house. I equipped myself with the knowledge I needed for my kids. It was a time consuming and painful process; the consequence of bad choices that were still causing a rippling effect through my life. I was determined to break the cycle. I agreed to let him see them in a supervised setting only, a deal the judge agreed was more than he deserved. Ben refused that deal though. He wanted time with the kids alone. I saw red when he would demand this. No way. I knew I'd never see them again, and if I did, they wouldn't be the same kids I sent off to him. He would ruin them. I would die before I let that happen.

Sitting in the court is such a shameful experience. I watched as all the other woman would get up and plead their case, begging for restraining orders or to not have to testify against the one who hurt them. Most women were younger with small children, their purses full of little toys and diapers, a sippy cup in case they needed it. But, some woman were older, successful looking, and well-polished. I looked at them with sadness. What hope did they have? I was thankful for the new life I was sure I could still give to myself and my children. I kept the faith and pushed on, all the while my sister in my heart and mind. I wanted so badly for this to be a battle they never had to know. Unfortunately, addiction and abuse are like husband and wife. Where one goes, the other usually follows in a horrible cycle that goes round and round until you become insane.

'Insanity: doing the same thing
over and over again and expecting
different results'---Albert Einstein

Time went quickly. Ben ended up in jail for violating the restraining orders I had in place against him which only helped my case. I breathed easier when he was locked up. It was like a vacation.

Beth was doing well from what we could see. She had stayed in her program and was back to working and attending her meetings. She didn't call anymore with the crying and begging to come home. She had accepted that she needed to be sober for a while before she could come back around. She needed to be stronger on her own. At least, that was the best we could figure for her. She would come home on the weekends and visit. She came home for every single holiday and celebration. She never missed a good family time. We got so excited when she came home. It was like having the princess in town, although the bathroom was still a concern. Every time she went in we noticed, and every time she came out alive we thanked God.

Her life had started to take on new troubles and concerns as she got older. She would need help with paying for things, she got robbed a lot, or her money would mysteriously disappear. These things were easy fixes for us, but a sign still of underlying problems for her.

It was about 1-1/2 years later that I was planning my wedding. Mom had gone wedding dress shopping with me, Molly, Julia and Julia's mom, and my soon-to-be in laws.

I put my dress on the counter and pulled out my credit card. Mom came over with a teary smile and put her hand on mine.

"No Jenny," she said "me and Dad want to pay for this for you."

I was so thankful. Finally, things were starting to get easier again. We were back in the honeymoon cycle. Addiction was our unstable relationship. We were all in a relationship with addiction. I knew it, but at that time, I didn't care. We were desperate for a good time. It was so needed. We needed to laugh and smile. We needed something "normal".

We spent months preparing for the wedding. The girls and I made centerpieces, invitations, and favors. We even made our own bouquets. It was a beautiful and needed distraction. We worked during the day and toiled away together at night. A process we would repeat later when Molly had her baby and then when Julia got married. My kitchen became the hub of wedding beauty and excitement. We were together. Happiness.

Happiness
A giggle from a child
Laughter with a friend
A smile from a stranger
Staying warm by a fire
Sand between your toes
Snowflakes on your tongue
Sunny days.......
...Being with you
---A. Beth Randall

The wedding went off without a hitch. I couldn't have been happier then when I looked out and saw my family proudly watching as I took my vows. Molly, Julia and Khloe stood beside me. Jamie watched from the seats with all her babies as the warm summer air kissed our shoulders and cheeks. Beth gave the most beautiful speech and of course brought everyone to happy tears, filling our hearts with love with her words as only she could do. We danced the night away and laughed until our faces hurt.

[illegible]: Welcome to the family, officially!! (You're in for it now! :) )
I know you'll take very good care of my favorite sister/best friend.
I love you!

Congratulations
to you both,
And may you always stay
As happy
and as much in love
As on your wedding day!

I am so happy for you guys, I love you both!!
I hope this day is everything that you've been dreaming and more! You both deserve the ultimate happiness! Love Always,
XOXO

When it came time to dance with Dad, I cried the whole time. I couldn't help but look back on all that had happened in our life and all that we had been through. I saw Mom watching with Gabby on her lap. Jamie was sitting with Jacob, her head on his shoulder. Molly and Beth were laughing in their seats. My new husband was sitting with Benjy and his boys. Everyone was there. It was the way I had always hoped my life would be. It was proof that dreams do come true.

Life had settled down and I was no longer denied necessities of survival like sleep and safety. The kids were thriving and happy. Benjy was doing well in school and Gabby was about to start kindergarten. Beth had been doing so well in her program that Mom and Dad decided to let her try to come home again. She didn't come alone. She had met a boy in her program and he needed someone to 'give him a chance'. His name was Eddy.

"Hi I'm Jenny" I said extending my hand for a hand shake.

I had just got to Mom and Dad's and was surprised to learn Beth had brought home a friend. Something about this kid made the hairs on the back of neck stand up. I tried not to be judgmental about the gang signs tattooed on his neck. It was the look in his eye. I had seen that look before. It was the same look Ben had in his eyes toward the end. It made me very nervous.

"So what's up with your friend?" I asked folding clothes with Beth

"He's a nice kid. Give him a chance, o.k.? He made some bad choices, but that doesn't mean he's all bad right?" Beth said

I got it. She felt that if she didn't give him a chance, she didn't deserve one either.

"I will Beth. Just promise me, please, that you will take care of yourself. You've been doing so good. I'm so proud of you." I gave her a big hug and started to cry.

"You know I hate when you cry Jenny" Beth said. "Please don't cry."

"I'm just so happy to have you back" I said wiping my face.

"I'm here to stay. So you better watch it" she said laughing.

She walked out of the room and went outside. Dad was cooking on the grill and Eddy was beside him talking and laughing. Something just didn't seem right. This kid was just too comfortable here. He was too easy to get along with. My gut told me he felt entitled to my family, and this little home on the pond. I was going to keep my eye on him, I decided.

Once again, time moved on and as usual, things started settling into their own routines. Beth was working 3 jobs. While we were glad to see her back to her old ways of setting goals and wanting to move forward in life, of course we worried more when we saw her less. Less time at home mean less time for us to keep our eyes on her. Eddy seemed nice enough although I still didn't like his overly charming attitude and his nonexistent explanation for how he came to be here with no friends or family willing to help him.

"It's not normal, Mom" I said during a conversation we had while jogging together one day "if he's such a nice guy then how come no one in his family is willing to take him in? Where are his friends?"

"Maybe he doesn't have any family around here and not everyone is blessed with good friends, Jenny," Mom replied.

"I have a feeling he's burned a lot of bridges, Mom. I worry about you guys here with him alone at night" I explained.

"People have helped Beth along the way. When we couldn't take it anymore and needed a break she has found kind hearted people who were willing to give her a chance. We need to pay it forward. It's the right thing to do. He was good to Beth while they were in treatment," Mom went on.

"Mom, the boys and girls are usually separated so I don't even understand what that means. Did he steal her cigarettes or something?" I said sarcastically

"You're being kind of harsh," Mom snapped.

I knew I sounded judgmental, but I couldn't help it. There was something about this kid that creeped me out. I worried he'd tie my family up and rob them or burn the house down while they slept. I had a very strong suspicion that Eddy knew I was on to him, too. I could tell Mom was getting annoyed at my question so I decided to let it go.

We got back to the house and Molly had returned back from the store with the kids. I looked in the kitchen and saw Eddy's jacket hanging over the chair. Molly was in her room changing her clothes.

"Molly, where are the kids?" I asked slightly panicked.

"They're over the pond with Eddy. We are going for a walk."

She didn't even finish her sentence before I was out the door. He might have everyone else fooled with his church on Sunday mornings and willingness to help with chores and dinner, but I saw right through him. I ran over to the pond and saw him swinging my precious baby girl around by her arms. She was laughing and he was calling her by a pet name. I pretty much ripped her from his arms and grabbed Benjy by the coat.

"We have to go," I said sternly.

"Hey, relax we were just playing," he said with a devilish grin on his face.

I turned to look at him and couldn't help but notice that his eyes were black. I couldn't even see were the pupil began or ended.

"Let's be honest, Eddy. Why are you here? Don't answer me," I said holding my hand up. "I wouldn't believe a word you say anyways. I know your type. Stay away from my kids and God help you if you hurt my sister you, hear me?"

I went back to the house, gathered my things and put the kids in the car to leave. On the drive home I started to second guess myself. Had I become paranoid? Was I being judgmental? I decided to just sit on it for a while and let it play out from a distance. I couldn't control what happened at my parent's house, but I could control my kid's influences, and he wasn't going to be one of them.

As I was pulling in my driveway, my cell phone rang. It was Mom.

"Jenny, you left before I could ask you if the kids could sleep over this weekend. Dad and I wanted to take them to the movies," Mom said.

I took a deep breath.

"Mom, this is going to be really hard to say but, I don't think so. I just don't want the kids there when Eddy's there. I'm telling you I know there's something wrong with him. You can go out with the kids, but you'll have to drop them off after, ok?" I asked cautiously.

Silence on the other end of the line.

"Mom?" I asked.

"Jenny, I'm glad you're doing that. As a Mom we have to trust our instincts. I'm proud of you. You have to do what's best for the kids, always. We will drop them off after the movie Friday night," Mom said.

I was so relieved that she understood. I waited for a call from Beth about my little outburst, but I never got one.

I told my husband about what had happened later that night.

"Beth won't call because she knows you are right unfortunately, Jenny," he said. "Just give it time. It will play out one way or another."

Eddy dug his heels in a cemented himself as a part of the family. Months passed and he was still around. I couldn't help but feel left out as everyone else seemed to get along so well with him. Maybe it was me after all I started to think. I caught him looking over his shoulder at me time to time, as if to let it be known to me that he was still in my family.

'I see you' I said to myself 'don't you worry. I'm watching every move you make'.

My fears were confirmed a few weeks later when Beth came over for a visit. She was quiet and withdrawn.

"Jenny? Can we talk for a minute?"

"Yeah, what is it?"

"There's something about Eddy you need to know."

"Tell me Beth. What is it?"

"Jenny, he's crazy. He's like two different people. Last night we were out back by the pond and he didn't like the way I told a story. He banged my head off the ice in the pond until the ice broke! The water was so cold and he kept holding my head under the water…." She was sobbing

"Beth, nooo" was all I could say.

"I don't know what to do. Sometimes I feel like he could change and when he's nice he's really nice. But, Jenny, when he's bad, he's really bad. I'm afraid of him. I'm afraid of what he'll do if I try to end it and I'm afraid of what he'll do if I don't. I'm trapped. If I go to the police he's going to do whatever he can to get me in trouble too. I'm still on probation! I can't go to jail, I just can't."

"Well, you have to end it. We just need a plan Beth and you have to try to not be alone with him. It's not safe. Does he have weapons?"

"Well there's a kitchen full of knives!"

I knew how she felt. It was familiar territory. The scope of addiction is so broad. It affects so many people in so many different ways. Abuse almost always goes hand in hand in one form or another.

"We have to tell Mom and Dad," I said.

"I know. Not tonight though. They have that party to go to and they've been looking forward to it. Tomorrow is Grandma's birthday party. Maybe the next day?" she asked

"We can't wait too long. Can you come over here the next couple nights so you aren't home alone with him? Make up something?" I suggested.

"That sounds good. Please don't tell anyone until I'm ready Jenny. Promise me. It will just go all wrong and I'll end up feeling bad. I'm so sick of messing everything up all the time. I ruin everything for everyone," she said.

"Beth, you do not. You can't think like that. We are so happy to have you home. We love you more than you will ever know," I hugged her and she left.

She came back that night. I could hear her on the phone with him, explaining herself. It's such an awful thing for a grown woman to have to explain herself. She didn't deserve this. I was so glad she had come to me and finally confessed the truth about this man. It wasn't a good enough plan though. He saw right through it.

Mom called the next day looking for Beth and Eddy. They were both gone and she couldn't reach them on their phones. My heart sank into my toes.

Six agonizing days passed. We heard nothing. Every call we made to their phones was unanswered. We Googled Eddy and discovered he was a fairly hardened criminal who had spent most of his life in and out of jails and rehabs. Beth had good reason to be afraid of him and so did we. I wondered what kind of lies he told her when they first met to win her over. He saw easy prey and he pounced. She was a prize to him. She was vulnerable and easy for him to control. It was probably too late by the time she saw his true colors. The meshing together had already started, and once that starts it's too hard to remember where that other person stops and you begin. It becomes almost impossible to separate their problems from yours, their hurt from yours and their happiness from yours. Your self-worth becomes defined by what they say it is. You lose yourself. It just happens. I never wanted it to happen to her. She had already been through enough.

On the night of the 6th day, I was in the kitchen making dinner when a number I didn't recognize came up on my caller id.

"Momma, your phone's ringing," Gabby said handing me my phone.

"Hello?"

I could barely make out a whisper on the other end.

"Hello? I can't hear you. Hello?" I was saying.

"Jenny," I heard Beth whisper, "Jenny it's me. I have to be quick and quiet can you hear me?"

"Beth! Are you ok? Where are you?" I said sitting at the table.

"I have the address. Write it down quick. He'll wake up any second. I'm in the bathroom," she whispered.

I could hear the fear in her voice as she gave me the address.

"He'll be getting high all night. Soon as he passes out or dies I'm gonna make a run for it. There's a train station nearby. I'll call you when I'm there. Will you buy me a ticket?" she asked.

"You know I will. I'll take my phone to bed. Beth please be careful..." I kept talking even though I knew she had hung up.

My hands were shaking as I dialed my parent's phone number.

"Momma, what's wrong? Was that Aunty Beth?" Gabby asked with Benjy looking on from the other room.

"Everything's o.k. my babies," I said trying to appear relaxed.

Dad answered the phone, "Roger's residence."

"Dad, it's me. Beth called. I know where she is. I'm scared for her" I filled him in on our conversation.

"Give me the address" Dad said.

I could hear the rage in his voice.

"Dad, promise me you'll be safe."

I already knew he would go and get her. That was his baby. He wasn't going to let her sit there another minute at that dirt-bags mercy.

I gave Dad the address and we hung up. I waited by the phone for a call to let me know what was happening. Beth was in Western Massachusetts. It would take Dad a few hours, even speeding, to reach her. I finally got a text I the middle of the night. It said "I'm with her. Long story. Talk tomorrow" I finally sank in to the first decent sleep I had gotten all week.

I got the kids on the bus in the morning and drove to my parents. I was anxious to see my sister and hug her. I pulled in the driveway, but there were no cars there. I grabbed my key from the car and went inside. No one was home. I picked up the phone and dialed Molly's cell. She didn't answer. I reread the text from last night and my heart started to pound. Dad wrote "I'm with her," not "I got her". What does that mean? Just as I got ready to call the police, Dad pulled in the driveway. I went running outside.

"Dad, what happened?" I started to say as he walked toward me.

"Jenny, try to be calm," he started to say as Beth got out of the car.

I took one look at her and had to turn away so she didn't see me cry. She had two black eyes and stitches on her nose. That bastard broke her nose.

I took a deep breath and walked over to my baby sister and wrapped her in a hug. As I let her go, I noticed the fresh tracks in her neck. Just when we thought it couldn't get worse, it somehow always did.

We went inside and Beth went to take a shower. When she was out of ear range, Dad told me what had happened.

"I got there just in time. As I pulled up there were ambulances, fire trucks, cops, everything. They were running all around. I tried to go inside but they wouldn't let me. I lost it. I thought she was gone for good. They told me what had happened when I explained why I was there. Someone had called 911. The reported a possible murder happening. They said a woman was screaming and they could hear her getting beaten. Thank God they called, Jenny. He had tried to get her high and when she declined he got angrier and angrier. He held her at knife point. She still resisted and started screaming for help. He started beating her and she fought back. He grabbed a 60lb chair and smashed it over her face. That's how her nose broke. When she went down, he shot her up. The E.M.T.'s gave her Narcan when they got there. They said a few more minutes, and she may not have made it. They arrested him. He's in jail. I had to stay with Beth at the hospital all night while she got checked out. She's going to have to detox again, Jenny," Dad could barely get the story out any louder than a whisper.

I could tell he was drained. I worried about him. I worried that he would have a heart attack if this kept up.

"Does Mom know?" I asked

"Yes. I called her last night and kept her updated. She went to Martha's. She couldn't sit here alone. You know Mike's not doing well either," Dad said.

"Yes I heard. Dad this is so terrible. What are we going to do?" I said

"Same thing we always do. We will keep trying. Pray for her. Get her help. Try to move past it. I'm beat. I need to lay down."

Dad kissed my forehead and went to bed.

Try to move past it. How does one do that? That is the question, isn't it? Jamie had offered to pay for Beth to go in to a Christian rehab called Teen Challenge. It had an exceptional success rate. Beth adamantly refused time and time again. It wasn't because it was a "Christian Program". She had been in the Salvation Army program and did well there. She was a Christian herself, that was something she was proud of and I had heard her defend her faith on a number of occasions. I did wonder why she wouldn't go, though. Maybe she didn't want to have Jamie paying for her recovery. Beth never really was one to ask for money. She liked to be independent, but she was humble enough to ask for help when she needed it. She had a good balance in that sense. She wasn't one to live off the system. I've thought that maybe she wouldn't go because she reached a point where she had been living as an addict for 1/3 of her life and was afraid that if she actually succeeded at becoming sober, she would fail in what living a sober life successfully meant to society. She had told me that she knew she's never hold an esteemed job because she could never pass a CORI check. She said no decent man would ever marry her. She had found out she couldn't have children throughout her many hospital stays. Maybe she felt she didn't deserve sobriety after some of the things she had done. Whatever the reason, it was as if she was becoming her own worst enemy. I started to see the light in her eyes that used to shine so bright, get a little dimmer.

Then, something happened that we are forever grateful for. She met a man named Elliot at her AA meeting. He breathed a little bit of hope into her again. Suddenly, Beth was coming back to life.

Elliot was an older gentleman. He had no kids, but he did have an ex-wife. He was kind and took Beth in as someone he truly cared about. She lived with him for a long time, a couple of years. They were good years for the most part. He looked after her as a big brother type figure. He made sure she took care of herself and knew where she was day to day. He helped her with her car when she had car trouble and gave her a warm safe place to live. She seemed to be thriving. Of course, set-backs still happened, but they seemed less severe when we weren't right in the midst of them. It seems selfish, but it was easier for us to know she was ok, and looked after, but not so close to home that the ashes from her fires burned us.

We would go to the beach in the summer. We could meet half way between us at Horseneck Beach. Beth loved the beach. We would spend the day running and teasing in the sun.

I remember one trip in particular. We were all there: myself and my family, my husband's family, Mom and Dad, Molly and her baby Dallas and her boyfriend, Beth and Elliot. The weather couldn't have been better. We had just come out of the ocean for a break from body surfing. Benjy and Gabby were hungry so we sat on the blanket for a sandwich break. The seagulls started ruthlessly circling over-head.

"Mom, the birds are going crazy," Benjy said pointing up at the sky.

"I know. Just sit down and eat they won't bother you," I told him, hoping that was true.

Beth came walking up from the water and grabbed her towel to dry off.

"Hey, Jenny, you ever see the movie "The Birds"? she asked with a sly grin.

"Very funny," I said. "Don't freak me out."

As if on cue, the birds moved in closer.

"Seriously? What the heck?" I started swatting at them.

Benjy stood up and started swinging his wiffle ball bat. Gabby was crying so I picked her up and brought her down to Mom at the water. The birds seemed to clear out a bit and we resumed our conversation. Beth reached into her cooler and took out her sub. She had just unwrapped it and was going in for a bite when out of nowhere a seagull swooped down and snatched it from her hands.

She sat there with her hands still in position and mouth wide open. I was rolling with laughter.

"Are you kidding me?" she was so angry.

"Oh my gosh, Beth that was the funniest thing I've ever seen," I was saying as she got up and chased that seagull all over the beach.

I think she would've still eaten that sandwich had she retrieved it. The whole family watched from the shore as she chased and ridiculed the bird. Benjy and Gabby were behind her 'helping' her cause. It was a typical Rogers outing.

She came back and sat beside me on my towel. I gave her half of Gabby's sub. She wouldn't have eaten it all anyways.

"Should we hide Molly's Coach purse and say a seagull made off with it?" I asked with my mouth full of sandwich.

"Yes, yes, we should," Beth answered.

The prank went off beautifully. It was even completed with Mom scolding us like little children to 'leave each other alone'. Each day together is a day to be grateful for, and we were. We were so grateful.

Benjy had started playing football in the 2nd grade. Beth loved to come and watch him play. For many seasons she was there in the stands cheering him on. There were many away games when she was the only company I had as I watched my boy growing into a man. Often times it was cold and raining or snowing, but she was a faithful fan.

She was just as faithful to Gabby. I had started having some bad dreams about Gabby when she was smaller. Beth had them too and we vowed to take extra care of our special little girl. Gabby and Beth shared a connection just like the rest of us girls. They had so many similarities, physical and non physical. They both had webbed toes and hair that was thicker one side of their head than the other. They both had a puffy face when they got up in the morning and loved to be the center of attention. When I held Gabby's hand, it felt like I was holding Beth's hand. The both had the same tough skin and wide fingers. Sometimes these similarities would scare me. I was afraid Gabby would go down the wrong path, just like Beth did so many times. I think that's why I had the nightmares. I was afraid. I told Beth she had to be around always to help me with the kids. She always promised she would be. She promised that no matter what, she would always be there looking after them.

HELLO MY SUNSHINE~

How are you? I'm doing real good, Mom+DAD came up here today and took me to lunch @ Applebees, they gave me the letter you sent w/them. Thank you for that. Whenever you write me letters you always make me smile at the things you say, and always have me in tears at other parts. Thats cuz you know my soul like no one else. Its crazy, our bond. That gave me the chills, what you said about your dream, because a few nights in a row, I wake myself up sobbing into my pillow, and I hadn't the slightest idea why, but I woke up thinking: "...". I don't know what it means. I wish I did. Just keep an extra eye on her for me okay?? So I had a great time on the womens retreat, I'll tell you all about it when you come up and visit me. Do you have any idea when that will be? I hope its soon. I miss you so much. I keep your picture (well, its of US) in my wallet and I show everyone, they all say you're beautiful.... and I say, thats my angel on earth. Miss you, I'll write again soon. Love, love, love you!
                                    I BOOBEAR

Mark and I had lost two pregnancies since we had gotten married. We were about to give up hope when finally, I was able to carry to term. We were all anxiously awaiting the baby boy's arrival into our family. I was at the hospital with Mark and Mom when things started progressing very quickly.

"Call Molly, Mom. If she's going to come she'd better hurry."

Beth had been in touch via phone and was kept up to the minute on progress as was Jamie. Jamie had seen Benjy and Gabby be born and this time, Molly was the one who wanted to see her nephew come into the world.

"Well, I will but for heaven's sake don't wait for her or that baby will never come out." Mom went into the hallway to call Molly as the doctor came in to check my progress.

The doctor pulled up a stool and told me to try to relax as he checked the baby.

Mom walked in "She's on her way."

"OK," said the doctor, "anytime you want to start pushing you are ready."

"Oh, I just need to wait 5 minutes for my sister. She'll kill me if I have this baby without her," I said panting.

"5 minutes. That's all. Then we are pushing," the doctor said with a smile.

I shook my head 'yes' as Mark paced the floor. The contractions were killing me and I wanted desperately to push, but I had promised Molly I would try to wait.

She made record time and came running through the door about 10 minutes later.

"OOOO Jenny I'm so excited! Thank you for waiting!" She gave me a hug and then hugged Mark and Mom.

The doctor had already come in and set up with the nurses. Mom got her camera ready and in just 15 minutes we had the newest member of our family. Harrison Mathewson was a healthy bouncing 9lb 10oz ball of pure happiness. Beth was on FaceTime immediately after the delivery sharing in the joy of the room.

"Jenny, he is just gorgeous. I love you guys so much." She was crying her happy tears.

Mark's boys were the first in the room as they had been waiting anxiously with the rest of the family in the waiting area. The baby that we had waited so long for and wanted so badly was finally here. The timing was perfect. Everything happens for a reason.

The next 8-9 months went on pretty well. We all enjoyed the excitement a new baby brings. I had never had the experience before of bringing a baby home into such a mentally healthy environment. It was wonderful. The family was thriving.

That first Christmas was beautiful. We were all together, celebrating life and the joys of the season. Spring came and brought with it our favorite time of the year-a time for outdoor activities and a fresh start. New beginnings happened all around us.

Beth had decided to move in with someone who she considered a friend that following summer. We hadn't known this girl to long, but she did promise to mentor Beth and keep her safe. She lived on the Cape and that meant Beth would be nearby. I remember Beth talking excitedly about having a fresh new start.

"I just think it's time Jenny. I need to open a new chapter in my life. If I don't move on I'll never grow," she explained on the phone.

"Sounds like it could be good for you. What about work though? How will you make a living?"

"There's a bunch of cafes and restaurants by the beach. I'm sure I could do great there in the summer. I actually already started applying at some places. I could probably waitress 4 shifts a week and make enough to get by. We are splitting the rent, so it's not much."

"Sounds good."

"I just need to get out of the city, especially for the summer. I need some fresh air and the ocean. I want to be inspired. I've been writing a lot lately, too. I'm hoping that goes somewhere."

"Did the police ever get back to you about your laptop?" I asked referring to her stolen laptop with all her writings in it.

"No. I'm not holding my breath either. They don't care about me. They can't even keep up with all the crime out here. Seriously, I need to get out of here. I'll never make it if I stay," she said.

I knew she was right. She had been out in Worcester too long. She needed a new start.

"I heard about that pregnant woman that was killed by her best friend. How tragic. It was on the news," I said.

"Jenny, that's what I mean! I knew them! I went to the baby shower. I had no idea she was capable of such things! Can you imagine? Seriously, I don't belong out here. I really think I'll be o.k. if I can get out," she said.

"Well, sounds like you have a good plan and a safe place to go. Is it going to work out with probation and the clinic?" I asked.

She wasn't really a free person anymore. She couldn't just move like the rest of us. She had to work it out with a number of agencies first.

"So far everything is working out. They are switching me to a clinic out there and my probation officer seems to think I'll be off probation shortly after I move so it'll just be a couple long trips to the city to check in and pass my tests and stuff. Jenny, I'd be so happy if it worked out," she said.

"I think it will. I can't wait to have you closer! More beach days and bike rides! Just like the old days!" I said.

It was the truth. I agreed that she needed to get away from that city. I wanted her closer to us all again. We all did.

Over the next few weeks she moved all of her stuff into the new cottage on the Cape. Everything she had was in those boxes. Everything she had accumulated, that hadn't been stolen, in her adult life was there. All of her writings, birthday cards, clothes, electronics, everything was packed away and ready to start fresh. She had done good. She had a lot to be proud of. Her collections were extensive and she knew every single thing she owned. Nothing was more loved than another thing. But the things she loved most were her journals. Her words that captivated her emotions as truly as she felt them were priceless to her. They were a piece of her.

When she finally moved in she had such optimism. She was like a child on the first day of school. She was hopeful, excited and a little nervous. We all were.

That first night she was quiet. We didn't hear much from her. I texted her the next day and she was withdrawn. She attributed it to nerves. She said she was fine, just a little homesick for her old surroundings. It was the second night that Mom and Dad got a call. She had been arrested during a raid in the house. She was in prison.

This was a devastating blow. The higher you are, the harder you fall. For the first time in so long, Beth had let her guard down. She allowed herself to get excited, and to feel something. Look what happened. It all came crashing down on top of her.

None of us knew what happened. Beth would call collect from Framingham State but I didn't have a credit card at the time to take her calls. Mom and Dad talked to her and she begged them over and over to get her out. She had been caught with drugs during the raid. She swore they weren't hers, but we just didn't know what to believe anymore. We knew we couldn't get her out. The only way for her to finish her probation and clear this all up was to stay in there and face everything once and for all. They offered her 6 weeks for everything and then she was free from it. We knew her calling every day only meant she wanted to use. We knew she would run, too. It had to end. The course had to be done.

She desperately wanted her stuff back. All her beloved possessions and all her writings were sitting down in the cottage still. We were quite surprised to find that the other girl in the cottage had escaped with no charges. We were suspicious. We called her daily, many times a day, for Beth's things. She would tell us we were harassing her, and that she was going to get restraining orders. Then we found out she was selling off her stuff. In my whole life, I've never had the feelings of anger that I had toward that woman. How could she do that? We called the police, but the process was going to be long and tedious. Still, we got the ball rolling.

Beth was broken after that. She served her time and got out. She was more depressed over losing her journals than I had ever seen her. She spent a few nights with someone she had met years before in meetings. This was someone she could trust and he was willing to take her in a few nights until we could make arrangements.

Mom and I had started doing a bible study on Angels a few months prior. We wanted to learn all that we could about surrounding ourselves with God's love and protection. It was deeply intensified when all of these changed started happening so quickly. We found ourselves in the midst of changes. We could feel it in the air, it was pulsating. We just prayed and prayed for Beth. We used all of our energies in begging for an end to her suffering. I remember Aunty Rose warning us at study one night to be careful.

"God works in mysterious ways. You may not understand why he does what he does. One thing is certain though, God will always prevail. Be careful what you wish for ladies and understand that we are opening up a gateway here. Prayers are always heard. Praying like this…you may stir something up. This may be war. Be ready for the outcome. Arm yourself with his love."

I had no idea at the time of how significant her words were.

Beth came home for her birthday weekend. She was 29. Mom Dad had a small party for her at the house. She was quiet but seemed happy to be home. She would go down to the hill in the back where Mom had started a new garden and just look out over the water. That was where we used to catch frogs and cast our fishing lines as children. That was where Benjy and Gabby learned to catch tadpoles, just as J.P. had years before. That was looking off to the place we used to run away to in the woods, where Grammy would come and find us. That was so much of our childhood and so much of our history. I don't know what she was thinking about as she sat there for so long. I have feeling though, that she was praying. She seemed oddly peaceful and happy when she came inside. She was affectionate and had a resonating joy about her. The way she was when she was little.

The next morning she came to church and purposely sang just loud enough so that her voice carried over the others. She loved to do that. She was making her presence know. She wanted to be heard desperately. She looked at me with her mischievous grin.

The next weekend she came back home. The church had a family night on Saturday which we all went to. Beth sat beside me and repeated the words of the actors in the movie we watched in a southern accent.

"Nothing sounds the same when you add an accent" she would always laugh "you can change the meanings simple as that"

She came over after church that night and helped us move Gabby into her new big girl room. She kept baby Harrison close on her hip and gave him a little cross to hang in his room.

"This will keep you safe," she said to him as she hung it on his wall.

We had dinner together and she went home. In the morning I sat beside her in church. I kept noticing that she was wiping her eyes and nose with tissue. She was weeping. I put my hand on her hand. She put her head on my shoulder. I patted her cheek. She wanted so badly to have a fresh start. She wanted to be free from the binds that held her.

She had her bible in her hand. It was the one that Aunty Rose and Uncle Rob gave her with her name engraved on the front. She got it the day she was reborn and baptized way back just after high school. She had never lost that. Everything else had been lost, but not that.

I showed her a passage from the book of revelation that I always liked.

> 'And God shall wipe away all tears
> from their eyes; and their shall
> be no more death, nor sorrow,
> nor crying, neither shall there be any
> more pain: for the former things
> are passed away'—Revelations 21:4 (KJV)

She read it and smiled a little smile.

"I know," was all she said.

She put her head back on my shoulder and I felt a tear roll down my arm.

'Please God. Please make this stop for her' I prayed.

After church we went over to Mom and Dad's house. I had a thousand things to do, but Beth had asked me to come for a visit.

When I got there, she was outside with Mom and Dad. They looked deep in conversation so I decided not to interrupt. I put Harrison in the bouncy seat and jumped on the treadmill.

"Hi," Beth came in all smiles. "Look what I have."

She held up a copy of 'Dirty Dancing.'

"Want to watch it while you work out?" she asked.

"Yes that would be good. Keep me company for a few while I finish?" I asked.

"You got it," she said putting the movie in.

She knew every word and played along as if she were a member of the original cast. She sat there the whole time I ran, just like she did when we were teenagers.

"What were you guys talking about out there?" I asked.

"I'm moving home," Beth said, "I can't wait. I just want to be here with you guys. It's really all I've ever wanted."

"That's so awesome Beth! When?" I asked.

"Next week," she said.

"Great and I'll take you out. I owe you a birthday gift. Let's finally go and get those matching 'Stay Gold' tattoos! My treat and we have to write that book we've always talked about, too," I said. "Oh I got to get going."

"That's o.k.; I have to go soon anyways. My ride will be here in a few. I'm going to shower before heading out. Molly said she'd braid my hair," she said giving me a big hug.

"Beth, I'm so glad you're coming home. Everything is finally going to be ok," I said holding her face.

"Yes, it is," she said walking away. "I'll call you this week, Boo."

"O.k." I said

I rounded up the kids and put them in the car. We went about our evening. I had to mow the lawn and drive Gabby to her friend's house. My cousin Abby and her kids came by for a visit and a night swim. I did some laundry and put the baby to bed. It was a pretty regular Sunday night. I was tired with a long week ahead so I decided to call it night around ten.

At 12:05am I was sitting up staring at my phone. It was lighting up with my parent's number.

Something inside me felt very wrong.

"Hello," I answered hesitantly.

"Jenny? It's Dad. It's Beth."

"No, Dad, no."

I began to shake uncontrollably. My body already knew what he was going to say before the words came out.

"I'm sorry honey. Beth's dead. I'm sorry."

"NO, Dad, please! Please! Where's Jamie? Where's Mom?"

I wanted my family so bad at that moment.

"Mom's here. Jamie doesn't know yet."

The next thing I knew Mark was standing in front of me.

"Jenny, what's wrong. What is it?" he was saying holding me by both my arms.

He had heard a wailing sound and came upstairs thinking it was the baby crying. When he saw that it wasn't the baby, he noticed me standing there hunched over. He didn't see that I had the phone in my hand. He just heard me saying "I can't breathe" over and over. I have no recollection of that moment or saying that. I just looked up and there he was.

"Should I call 911? Are you having a heart attack?" he was asking

He thought I was having a heart attack. In a way, I was.

"Beth's dead! She's dead!" I said hysterically.

"No, oh, no," he wrapped his arms around me.

"Dad, I'll be right there" I said and hung up.

In that moment my world as I knew it ended. It felt like the life got sucked out of me in a vacuum. So many hopes and so many dreams all vanished in an instant with 2 words: Beth's dead.

This is what addiction does.

I was hysterically pacing in my room. What do I do? What should I do? I had to call Jamie. I dialed her number 5 times before I got it right because I was trembling so badly. She answered right away.

"Hello?"

"Jamie? It's Jenny. It's Beth, she..." I started to say.

Jamie cut me off "No Jenny please don't say it!"

"She's gone. Oh my God, she's gone" the words came out like pain leaving the body.

"Oh no,no,no," was all Jamie could say.

"I'm going to Mom and Dad's. Can you come?" I asked.

"I'll be right there," she said.

I must've walked in 5 more circles before Mark guided me down the stairs, out the door, and into the car. My heart felt like it was being squeezed in a vice. 'If this is a dream, please wake up. Please, wake up' I kept saying to myself. But, I knew it wasn't a dream. It was a nightmare.

We pulled into the driveway at my parents. I got out and heard the peepers chirping as they always do that time of year. How could they be chirping? Didn't they hear what happened? Don't they know she was gone?

I walked in the door and found my Mom and Dad sitting at the table with Aunt Rose and Uncle Rob. Dad got up and helped me inside.

Aunty Rose got me some water. Mom was crying. Jamie pulled in a minute later and Dad started to tell us what had happened that night.

"Beth went home around 7. She seemed fine. Ryan (her ride) says she was in a good mood and happy to be moving back home. They got back to Worcester and she said she was going to shower. He went in the kitchen and started making some burgers. He called up assuming that she was in her room. She didn't answer, so he went up looking for her. He pushed her door open and could see that her stuff was still just as she left it when they first got home. He said he knew then. He opened the bathroom door and she was in there on the floor. He called 911 and did CPR until they got there but it was too late," Dad had to keep stopping to swallow so that he didn't burst into tears. "Around 11:50pm I heard a knock on the door. I got up and there were 2 police officers standing there. When I answered they took off their hats, and I knew. I knew something was wrong, I just didn't know which name they were going to say. They told me that Beth was gone. After they left the doctor from the hospital called. She said she did everything she could and that she worked on her very hard…for a very long….." he couldn't say anymore.

We just sat there, in grief, in the deepest hole of sorrow. I thought of my baby sister. I thought of all the beauty and wonder that she held and I knew the world would never be the same without her. We all sat there like a bunch of wounded soldiers that just lost the greatest battle in history. We fought so hard, for so long, and we still lost. That's how it felt in the beginning. I lost her to the bathroom. The one place in the whole world that I didn't want her to take her last breath in was a bathroom. Why did this have to happen?

### The Ones I Love

The Ones I Love have watched me leave.
The Ones I Love now have to grieve.
Their beautiful faces streaked with tears,
as they mourn my lost years.
The Ones I Love have had enough,
they're tired of watching me kill myself.
And in death there is only truth;

227

they read the pages of my mispent youth.
The Ones I Love have seen my soul,
they watched me slowly lose control.
The Ones I Love believed in me,
even as my addiction had me on my knees.
So many times they watched me fall,
but they never lost faith in spite of it all.
The Ones I love watched me hide,
because I felt so ugly inside.
I hope they realize that I always cared,
I never meant to make them so scared.
The Ones I Love had to set me free,
because all my misery wanted company,
it was almost as if they didn't want to see,
that there was no resemblance of the girl I used to be.
The Ones I Love will all eventually die,
but I went first and so they cry.
As they stare into my lifeless eyes,
I wish I could have said goodbye
.........to the Ones I Love.
-A.Beth Randall

"Where's Molly? And J.P.?" I asked

They were going to take this very, very, badly. We all knew it. What about Benjy and Gabby? I cringed at having to break the news to them. They loved their Aunty Beth with every ounce of their hearts. This was just the beginning of the worst days in our lives. We clung to each other, our friends and our faith for hope and understanding. We decided that we needed to have faith that Beth was only gone from us in the physical sense. We had to remember that she was in a better place.

It was the setting of a crossroad for us: would we let this tragedy tear us apart or were we going to take a deep breath and deal with this for what it really was-a moving on from one life to another. Once the initial shock wore off, it was easier to see how much we had to be grateful for. Beth had been with us all the very day that she passed. We all got to tell her how much we loved her. Mom and Dad had told her she could come home. The children all got one last weekend in with her. She was at church and, I really do believe, she made her peace with God. None of us were the ones to find her, as selfish as that sounds. I am grateful for not having that awful image of my sister in my head. I will always remember her as beautiful and full of life. There was so much to be grateful for. And though we were still hurting with the worst burning in our hearts imaginable, we decided to be at peace knowing that she was finally at peace. Her struggle was over. That's what she wanted. She wanted peace. Still, it's so hard to accept. It's so hard to lose someone in such a needless way. It's only human to grieve for them and we did. We grieved for her.

'Why did you have to go away?
I would've done anything to make you stay
Chased all your demons far away,
If only to have you one more day.
I miss the you'd always say
'It's ok don't cry today,'
And the way you'd make me feel o.k.
at the end of all my darkest days.
I miss your thick dark hair in my hands,
getting you ready for all your plans.
Weaving over and under every strand,
as we laughed and joked, your smile so grand.
Why did you have to leave me here?
You knew that was my greatest fear,
a future without my dearest dear,
now everything seems so unclear.
You promised you would always stay,
until we both were old and gray.
You said we would laugh about the day
of silly games we used to play.
Now you're gone and it burns in my soul,
your absence like a giant hole.
My heart feels hard and dark as coal,
from watching life's unfair role,

trap you in its ruthless frame
of fear, manipulation and shame.
Addiction plays the dirtiest game,
taking victims and making them lame.
I miss your smile and joyous eyes.
I miss your witty smart replies.
I miss your sarcastic sighs,
I miss your laughter and quoting cries.
I long to hug you sister dear,
I long to whisper in your ear,
'I'll always be waiting here,
for you to return and bring me there'.
So when the silver's in my hair,
and my time is drawing near,
it's your voice I wish to hear,
softly calling in my ear-
'Don't be afraid, just come with me
I'll take you where your soul will be,
at peace in heaven guaranteed,
there's love and joy endlessly.'
With my last breath off we'll go,
to where the eternal fountains flow.
Where his majesty so brightly glows,
for ever well with both our souls ---Katie Morini.

Losing someone so close to you opens your eyes to what is really important. You see people for who they really are. We were incredibly blessed to have the love and support of so many great friends and family, who held us up through that when we were too weak to do it alone. Friends poured their affections around us, building a wall of protection made of love. My cousin clung to us and did everything and anything we needed for the services. She saved us from the hard parts. She was our voice when we couldn't speak. We got to see Beth's true colors, too. So many people came forward that had loved her, and been affected by her in both life, and in now in death. She was loved. She still is. The posts on her Facebook wall were beautiful. People shared their stories and pictures. They didn't have too, but they did. We were showered with cards, letters and flowers from so many people who wanted to express their condolences. The support was overwhelming and so much appreciated.

I think so many of us wonder who will come to our funeral when we die. We wonder what it will be like. It's a natural thing to wonder. Beth wondered about hers, too. She had told us exactly how she wanted it. We do believe that she had a feeling from the time she was very young that she would go on before us in one way or another. She told us that she didn't want a sad procession of mourners. That wasn't her style. She wanted a celebration of her life that reflected who she was, what she came from and what she had always wanted to become. So that's what we did. Dad and Uncle Rob played songs on their guitars and sang for her. Jamie and I read a poem that she had written. Uncle Rob gave a sermon about what we can learn from her life and how we should want to make the world better now knowing what we know. He spoke of how she had gone to the other side of the metaphorical river, and when she wanted so desperately to come back, the bridge had crumbled and fallen away. We decorated the hall with all her meticulously kept photos and poems that had survived the multiple moves she had been forced to make throughout the life she had chosen. People came to show their love and respect for her. They filled the church and they lined the street. She would have been pleased to see that she did make a difference to so many, and she did matter. She still does.

Dear Beth,

I miss you. I would give anything to hug you. I want you to know that I'm not mad anymore at the way things turned out. I think you impacted people with your death as much as your life. That's saying a lot for how much you were loved. After you passed the sunsets were more beautiful than ever above the pond. Thank you for that. The kids miss you. We talk about you all the time. I still think I hear your voice sometimes calling my name. I should've known you would go on early. You always were brave, traveling all over. You loved to see new places. I bet the angels love you. I keep your picture on my dash board so that you come everywhere with us. I know you promised you would always look over the kids, I hope you are around us still. I wish things were different for you while you were here with us. You would be amazed to see all there is for addiction now. It's so different than when you suffered alone. You should know that you were never alone. There are so many people like you. I hope you know how much we loved you and still do. I think you know. I hope we can help others the way you did. Mom has made a beautiful garden for you. It's gorgeous. I can imagine you would love to sit out there with a book and read the day away. Since you've been gone, we notice the hawks around more and more. We notice everything more now, always looking for of signs of you. Sometimes at night I still talk to you, just because that's what we used to do for so long I guess. Visit in a dream if you can, I love when I get to see you. Until we meet again dear baby sister, let your soul shine. I miss you every day. I love you.

Stay Gold,
Jenny

# EPILOGUE

W E ARE LIVING IN the midst of a huge epidemic. We need to find a solution. I don't know what that solution is, but I do know that education on the pain and the struggle that comes with addiction is so very important. These addicts aren't bad people. They've just made some very bad choices. I loved my sister with all my heart. I know this wasn't the life, or death, that she wanted and she would've done anything to change it. So when you see someone struggling with addiction, please fight your instinct to judge them. Pray for them. See the person beyond the addiction. Give them a hug or even just a smile. You never know how much a simple act of kindness can change someone's whole life.

Things that people said to me in the days following her death changed everything for me. I remember being at such a loss over the fact that my sister had passed away in a bathroom. One of my dearest friends said to me "Jenny, she was never in that bathroom, she was in heaven before that door even closed." Those words changed everything for me. So please, let's find a solution and educate our young people about what it means to be human and humane. Let's educate them on how to make good choices. Let's make sure they have options and help when they need it. Let's find a way to make sure they never have an addiction to recover from. Let's not lose anymore beautifully created souls to addiction. Let's raise a generation who can feel emotions, all of them, and cope in a healthy way, the way we were designed to. Let's bring back order and respect and joy. Let's push through and move forward. Let's heal together.

*guys are safe + happy always. I think about you all the time! Wherever I am, just remember that I love you so much, always! See you at Christmas! Love, ___ ___*

Amanda Randall

## Amanda Beth Randall

*August 9, 1985 - August 17, 2014*